RUNNING FROM BONDAGE

Running from Bondage tells the compelling stories of enslaved women, who comprised one-third of all runaways, and the ways in which they fled or attempted to flee bondage during and after the Revolutionary War. Karen Cook Bell's enlightening and original contribution to the study of slave resistance in eighteenth-century America explores the individual and collective lives of these women and girls of diverse circumstances, while also providing details about what led them to escape. She demonstrates that there were in fact two wars being waged during the Revolutionary Era: a political revolution for independence from Great Britain and a social revolution for emancipation and equality in which Black women played an active role. *Running from Bondage* broadens and complicates how we study and teach this momentous event, one that emphasizes the chances taken by these "Black founding mothers" and the important contributions they made to the cause of liberty.

Karen Cook Bell is Associate Professor of History at Bowie State University. She is the author of *Claiming Freedom: Race, Kinship, and Land in Nineteenth-Century Georgia*, which won the Georgia Board of Regents Excellence in Research Award. She specializes in the studies of slavery, the Civil War and Reconstruction, and women's history.

RUNNING FROM BONDAGE

Enslaved Women and Their Remarkable Fight for Freedom in Revolutionary America

Karen Cook Bell

CAMBRIDGE
UNIVERSITY PRESS

University Printing House, Cambridge CB2 8BS, United Kingdom

One Liberty Plaza, 20th Floor, New York, NY 10006, USA

477 Williamstown Road, Port Melbourne, VIC 3207, Australia

314–321, 3rd Floor, Plot 3, Splendor Forum, Jasola District Centre,
New Delhi – 110025, India

79 Anson Road, #06–04/06, Singapore 079906

Cambridge University Press is part of the University of Cambridge.

It furthers the University's mission by disseminating knowledge in the pursuit of
education, learning, and research at the highest international levels of excellence.

www.cambridge.org
Information on this title: www.cambridge.org/9781108831543
DOI: 10.1017/9781108917551

First published 2021

Printed in the United Kingdom by TJ Books Limited, Padstow Cornwall

A catalogue record for this publication is available from the British Library.

ISBN 978-1-108-83154-3 Hardback

To the countless enslaved and free Black women whose stories have yet to be told.

Contents

Figures and Tables

FIGURES

TABLE

Introduction

Enslaved Women's Fugitivity

S IX MONTHS AFTER SELF-EMANCIPATED CRISPUS ATTUCKS, whom many consider the first casualty of the American Revolution, was killed by British troops in the Boston Massacre on March 5, 1770, a twenty-three-year-old woman, her eight-month-old daughter, and her husband escaped from bondage in Leacock Township, a farming community with over 11,000 acres of arable limestone land that had been settled by emigrants from northern Ireland, two-thirds of whom owned slaves.[1] It was a relatively warm Thursday, the 13th of September, and the trio had been planning their evening escape since February, when the young mother had given birth, and dreamed of a time when she and her daughter would be free. She wore "good clothes," carried "two long gowns, and had new low-heeled shoes."[2] There were no free Blacks in Leacock at the time.

This unnamed fugitive slave and her daughter and husband made plans to escape to Philadelphia. The Philadelphia–Lancaster Old Road would have been a risky route for the trio but was worth the risk if it brought them closer to freedom. The revolutionary spirit was alive in Leacock Township as early as 1770. David Watson, the enslaver of the fugitives, was one of sixty men elected from Lancaster County to represent Leacock Township in defense of American liberty. The fugitives found reinforcement of their belief that they had a right to freedom after overhearing Watson's conversations that colonists were enslaved and had a right to liberty from Great Britain. For reasons unknown, Watson did not name the escaping trio. Perhaps he surmised that given the small Black population in Leacock Township (348 in 1790), a general description of their clothing would suffice. Their namelessness served as an erasure of their identity. Yet these revolutionary abolitionists provide a searing example of the ways in which freedom-seeking women advanced their liberation.[3]

Enslaved women ran away. Women in bondage were not content, and running away, or flight, was one of the ways in which they registered their protest. Slaveholders lived with this inescapable reality on a consistent basis, and they did everything they could to get their property returned. Posting advertisements in newspapers was the most pervasive method used to secure the return of runaway women. Runaway slave advertisements were a regular feature of print culture throughout the era of slavery. Newspaper advertisements leaned heavily toward the physical, offering detailed information about the facial and bodily features of slaves; their origin and ethnicity; where they may have gone; and rewards for their return. The advertisements also reflected on-the-ground collective transformations of names and ethnic changes and identities. In other words, the fugitive body became a living and moving text of victimization, protest, and personhood.[4] As articulated by historian Marisa Fuentes, "fugitivity in this context denotes the experience of enslaved women as fugitives – both hidden from view and in the state of absconding. It also signifies the fragile condition of runaways who came into visibility through runaway advertisements."[5]

Enslaved women and girls ran away as soon as they set foot in the Americas. Some escapes were collective; others were individual. While some newly arrived women escaped immediately, others did so within a few weeks of arrival and others escaped months later. On June 16, 1733, fifteen-year-old Juno arrived on the slave ship *Speaker* in Charleston, South Carolina. She had arrived from Angola along with 316 other enslaved men and women (out of 370; 54 died during the Middle Passage). Two weeks after being sold to a planter from Dorchester, she escaped.[6] Similarly, fourteen-year-old Lucia, who arrived on a slave vessel in Savannah, Georgia and whose country marks were evident on each of her cheeks, escaped in 1766.[7] Newcomers like Juno and Lucia were likely caught in the act of escaping days later. Despite the pervasiveness of the escapes, very little documentation exists about the personal experiences of women who attempted to flee.

Running from Bondage seeks to lift the veil on freedom-seeking women during the Age of Revolution. Although it is based on scores of cases in which enslaved women absconded or *attempted* to flee bondage, *Running from Bondage* neither attempts to relate all documented instances of fugitivity nor is it about all enslaved women in the British North American colonies. The individuals studied here share one key characteristic: they attempted to flee bondage. I argue that enslaved women's desire for freedom for themselves and their children propelled them to flee slavery during the Revolutionary War, a time when lack of oversight, and opportunity due to the presence of British troops, created spaces for them to invoke the same philosophical arguments of liberty that White revolutionaries made in their own fierce struggle against oppression. The desire for freedom did not originate with the American Revolution. However, the Revolution certainly amplified the quest for liberty. At stake in this discussion of fugitive women is demonstrating that Black women's resistance in the form of truancy and escape were central components of abolitionism during the Revolutionary Era. Thousands of women of diverse circumstances escaped bondage despite their status as mothers and wives. In fact, motherhood, freedom, love, and family propelled Black women to escape bondage during the Revolutionary Era, a time when, as historian Matthew Spooner argues, the chaos of war made women's flight possible due to the breakdown of oversight and colonial authority.[8] The war produced chaos that preoccupied enslavers and diverted attention away from the daily full-time control of slaves. There were in fact two wars being waged: a political revolution for independence from Great Britain and a social revolution for emancipation and equality in which Black women played an active role. I therefore challenge Black women's lack of representation in studies of Revolutionary America and the ways in which Black women enter history. By excavating the story of fugitive enslaved women, Black women's integral role in the eighteenth-century abolitionist movement is manifest.

The boundaries of slavery and enslaved women's manipulation of space continue to generate interest. Enslaved women challenged enslavers' control of their movements through everyday acts of resistance such as truancy and through flight. Fugitive women pursued alternative physical environments in what historian Stephanie Camp terms a "rival geography, alternative ways of knowing and using plantation and southern [and northern] space that conflicted with [enslavers'] ideals and demands."[9] I have adapted the term "rival geography" to refer to the movement of bodies, objects, and information *away* from plantations and the spaces of enslavers. This rival geography threatened the system of slavery and provided fugitive women autonomous spaces to resist enslavers' efforts to control their bodies and contain their movements. Containment, a principle of restraint, existed on farms, plantations, and areas controlled by enslavers. This geography of containment was elastic for enslaved women during the Revolutionary Era when more opportunities to leave farms, plantations, and enslavers' homes existed.[10] Running away was a strategic act and represented a central expression of human agency. Flight served as a method of fighting against an oppressive system.[11]

To understand women's lives in, and resistance to, slavery requires examining their efforts to escape bondage, and symbolically how what they wore and carried with them in the process of absconding were political acts that challenged enslavers' powers. Political acts of resistance, such as flight, and women's thoughts about resistance are in constant dialogue. Although the flight of enslaved women was one of institutional invisibility in that there was no formal organization, no leaders, no manifestos, and no name, their escape constituted a revolutionary social movement in which fugitive women made their political presence felt. In fact, fugitive women displayed a radical consciousness that challenged the prevailing belief that enslaved women could not gain their freedom through subversive actions. The wars that enslaved women waged during the American Revolution grounded the Black radical politics that informed their postwar struggles.

As a consequence of slave flight, many colonies passed laws to control the movement of enslaved women and men. Between 1748 and 1785 Virginia, for example, passed laws prohibiting and punishing "outlying" and "outlawed" activity. In 1748, Virginia distinguished between outlying runaways and outlawed escapees by making truancy (or outlying runaways) a capital offense.[12] In Williamsburg, Virginia, Rachel, who was "big with child," had experience with both truancy and escape. In November 1771, she fled from bondage to ensure that her child would be born free.[13] Similarly, eighteen-year-old Lydia ran away twice, seeking to reach Williamsburg.[14] The movements of Rachel and Lydia away from plantation spaces illustrates the creation of a rival geography in which both women moved through southern spaces to attain freedom. Through flight, they created spaces for private and public expressions of freedom.

Colonial Black resistance in the form of self-emancipation was a form of abolitionism. In "mining the forgotten" women who appear in runaway slave advertisements, historians recover Black resistance. Historian Manisha Sinha's study of abolitionism, *The Slave's Cause*, has advanced new perspectives on Black abolitionism that challenge the idea that White philanthropy and free labor advocates were responsible for the abolitionist movement. Key to her book is the argument that "slave resistance, not bourgeois liberalism, lay at the heart of the abolitionist movement." Sinha revives the early perspectives advanced by scholars such as C.L.R. James and Benjamin Quarles, who viewed runaway slaves as the "self-expressive presence [without whom] antislavery would have been a sentiment only."[15]

AN UNDERSTUDIED PHENOMENON

This book builds on the histories of how the American Revolution impacted slavery and freedom by highlighting the experiences of enslaved and fugitive women. Although numerous books have been devoted to the Revolutionary Era and its impact on slavery, none focus singularly on fugitivity by enslaved women in the thirteen colonies and their links with the wider Atlantic world. The first historian to seriously study the issue of slave resistance during the Revolutionary Era was Herbert Aptheker in *American Negro Slave Revolts* (1943). Aptheker's research was groundbreaking because it illuminated the colonists' fear that the British would wage war under an anti-slavery banner that would lead to "20,000 slaves" running to the British lines within a few weeks.[16] Benjamin Quarles in his classic study *The Negro in the American Revolution* (1961) makes clear the contradiction of the colonists' fight for their liberty from Great Britain while maintaining the institution of slavery when he states, "In the Revolutionary War the American Negro ... personified the goal of that freedom in whose name that struggle was waged."[17] Quarles argued further that the American Revolution constituted the first large-scale slave rebellion. Post-Quarles, Gerald Mullin's research on Virginia for the period 1736–1801 uncovered 1,280 runaways, or an average of 19.7 per year, with the majority occurring during the Revolutionary War. Philip Morgan in his analysis of South Carolina from 1732–1782 collected advertisements describing the flight of 3,558 slaves, or 69.8 per year. Not only did these historians use all extant newspapers, but the slave populations of Virginia and South Carolina were comparatively large, with Virginia's slave population totaling 188,000 in 1770 and South Carolina's slave population totaling 57,000 by 1760.[18]

Given America's Revolutionary heritage it is not surprising that slavery has long captured the collective historical consciousness of the nation. Students and faculty alike continue to ponder the imponderable: the relationship between slavery and the kinds of freedom enshrined in the Declaration of Independence and the U.S. Constitution. Historians Ira Berlin, Ronald Hoffman, David Brion Davis, Sylvia Frey, Woody Holton, Gerald Horne, Gary B. Nash, Simon Schama, and Cassandra Pybus have examined the transformations wrought by the American Revolution on the institution of slavery.[19] In each of these studies, the agency of enslaved women and men is paramount. In his thought-provoking essay "On Agency," historian Walter Johnson contends that historians' over-emphasis on agency, which refers to the self-directed actions of slaves, minimizes the brutality that enslaved people faced. In addressing the agency of enslaved women during the Revolutionary Era, in this study I present fugitive women as the architects of their own actions who challenged their enslavers' power and perceptions. Hence, I do not "give" agency to enslaved women, but simply recognize the agency that they created themselves. Recognizing how power shaped agency and vice versa, this study balances agency with manifestations of freedom.[20]

The most salient examination of Black agency in the Age of Revolution is Sylvia Frey's *Water from the Rock: Black Resistance in a Revolutionary Age*. Frey argues that the Revolutionary War in America's Southern colonies, rather than being merely a struggle between colonists and Englishmen, was a three-sided affair between Black slaves, White Americans, and the British, with each faction playing an independent and important role. She also concludes that republican political theory and Christian religious belief played huge, crucial roles in the thinking of African Americans as they struggled against slavery during this time. Frey notes that when the Revolution began, many slaves in the South took advantage of the situation to declare their freedom. They appealed to the British to guarantee their liberty, even though they realized that Britain was itself deeply involved in the slave trade, and large numbers of slaves fled to the "protection" of British armies. Also, some of them escaped to remote places to form maroon colonies, while others fomented full-scale rebellion. They continued into the next decades to resist slavery in the name of the liberation rhetoric of the Revolution and the individual dignity taught by Christianity. Taking Frey's argument further, Woody Holton's *Forced Founders* argues that slaves engaged in insurgency long before Lord Dunmore's official offer of freedom and that their actions, along with the fear of general emancipation, united free Virginians in advocating for independence from Great Britain.

In his study, *The Forgotten Fifth: African Americans in the Age of Revolution*, Gary Nash contends that one-third of all fugitives were women, a far greater number than in previous patterns. Who were these women? What obstacles did they face in attempting to flee bondage? Were they successful? The voices of enslaved women escaping bondage during the eighteenth century are silent, with few exceptions. As Marisa Fuentes has argued, these silences in the archive of bondwomen in slave societies bury the narratives of the most subaltern.[21] The overall invisibility of fugitive women seems to be due in part to the fact that women in general are often overlooked in studies about the enslaved population. Such male-specific analyses do not correspond to the reality, whether in North America or in the rest of the hemisphere.

FUGITIVITY AND LINKS WITH THE ATLANTIC WORLD

Slavery, as Dale Tomich argues, was one "of the strands that wove the histories of Europe, Africa, and the Americas, creating at once a new unity and a profound and unprecedented divergence in the paths of historical development of these regions and their people."[22] Slavery was foundational to European expansion projects, and its growth became inseparable from inter-imperial competition that turned the Atlantic into a theater of war in the eighteenth century. With this process came opportunities for free and enslaved African populations who in most cases were clearly aware of, and central to, the political conflicts of the age. With increasing frequency scholars have recognized the impact that the Age of Revolution had on slavery. Latin American historians from Gilberto Freyre to Frank Tannenbaum to Herbert S. Klein and Ana Lucia Araujo have studied slavery in Spanish and Portuguese colonies, as have scholars of the Caribbean islands. Barbara Bush has commented of West Indian slave women that "popular stereotypes have portrayed them as passive and down-trodden work horses who did little to advance the struggle of freedom." The "peculiar burdens" of their sex allegedly precluded any positive contribution to slave resistance.[23]

However, enslaved women in the British Caribbean exasperated their enslavers in countless ways. They shirked work, damaged crops, dissembled, and feigned illness. They also ran away. Enslaved women ran away for a variety of reasons. They sought to put pressure on their enslavers to sell them or improve conditions. They also ran away to visit kin or friends. Many attempted to merge into the free Black and urban communities, where they often found employment. Historian Gad Heuman suggests that runaways were less concerned about freedom than with preserving some sort of autonomy within slavery itself, which raises the question of the degree to which enslaved women could control and affect aspects of their enslavers' world.[24]

Young men without family ties predominated among runaways in the Caribbean; however, according to historian Barbara Bush, 40 percent of runaways in the Caribbean were women. Women took their children with them far more frequently than did men. However, if caught, both mothers and children were forced to wear collars, and running away with children meant that the women were more likely to be caught.[25] French historian Arlette Gautier suggests that women may not have had less desire to run away, simply less opportunity. Advertisements in the *Jamaican Mercury* and *Kingston Weekly Advertiser* (the *Royal Gazette* after 1790) provide important insights about women's family connections and their status and value. A number of slave women ran away with their children or other close relatives, an indication of strong familial bonds. Other runaways were suspected of having fled to join spouses or other kin from whom they had been separated, and often the advertisers alleged that their runaways were being harbored by kin or friends in distant parts of Jamaica. Thus, a significant number of women, African and creole, were among the lists of runaways.[26]

Slave imports from the Caribbean to the North American mainland increased during the eighteenth century. According to David Eltis's slave trade database, nearly 140,000 Africans were imported from Africa as well as the Caribbean between 1711 and 1740.[27] What is true about the Atlantic during this period is that absolute differences or actual boundaries were not real since we are talking about a deeply interconnected world. Illustrative of this is Margaret Grant, a fugitive slave from Baltimore, Maryland who had also experienced slavery in Barbados, Antigua, and the Grenadines and who escaped slavery at least twice.[28]

REVOLUTIONARY WOMEN

During the American Revolution, one-third of runaways were women and more than half fled in groups rather than alone. By contrast, prior to the Revolution, nearly 87 percent of colonial runaways were male, and about two-thirds fled alone. Roughly 25 percent fled in family groups consisting of husbands, wives, and young children.[29] Enslaved women pursued multiple avenues to gain freedom during the Revolutionary Era. Some, like forty-year-old Sarah of Pennsylvania, made plans to reach New York City on the eve of the Revolution on October 24, 1769, where ships headed for other northern ports docked. Others, like twenty-three-year-old Bellow, who was born in Barbados, sought to find refuge away from her enslaver's home on Broad Street in New York City on April 28, 1770. Others, like "Free Fanny," claimed freedom by running away on Christmas Day 1770 from her enslaver's estate in Essex, Virginia.[30] To migrate to another city or colony may seem to have been an improbable proposition for women in bondage. Going to town or to another colony implied that they had knowledge of the geography and topography of the area.[31] The enslavers of eighteen-year-old Lydia (mentioned earlier) remarked that she had traveled the road to Williamsburg several times and was familiar with the route since she had attempted escape on more than one occasion. The escape of many enslaved women was polycentric (having more than one center) in that they attempted to flee more than once.

Southern cities and Northern colonies were open spaces for freedom-seeking women during the Revolutionary Era. They could find refuge with the British, escape to Black enclaves in the cities and pass as free women, as well as find refuge with Native Americans. In some cases, women found refuge in the woods and swamps because "there was no other place of concealment and freedom for them."[32] They experienced what Damian Pargas describes as an "informal freedom," spaces within slaveholding regions where enslaved people attempted to escape by blending in with the free Black population.[33] As they experienced this "informal freedom," women truants in rural areas embraced the ecology. Women had knowledge of the fauna and flora, the animals and plants they would find, and what vegetation they should not eat. They also had familiarity with changes in the weather and had family and friends nearby.

In Virginia, 12,000 runaway slaves were with Lord Cornwallis's army by the middle of June 1781. In total, it has been estimated that Virginia lost 30,000 slaves during the Revolutionary War.[34] Virginia's fugitive slaves did more than serve soldiers as porters and body servants. They contributed substantially to Cornwallis's new style of warfare. Cornwallis encouraged bondwomen and bondmen to leave their enslavers, thus threatening Virginia with complete economic ruin. Virginia's fugitives also served Cornwallis in a more deliberate fashion. Runaways acted as spies and guides for the British. They frequently showed British soldiers where fleeing enslavers had hidden their valuables and livestock. In fact, African Americans delivered so many horses to Cornwallis that General Lafayette exclaimed, "Nothing but a treaty of alliance with the negroes can find out dragoon horses, and it is by those means the enemy have got a formidable cavalry."[35] The militia was Virginia's last remaining line of defense. The strength and speed of British forces terrified Virginia's citizen-soldiers. Militiamen were reluctant to take up arms lest they provoke the British into destroying their homes. The militiamen also feared leaving their families alone with their slaves. "There were ... forcible reasons which detained the militia at home," explained Edmund Randolph, who had been a Virginia delegate to Congress.

"The helpless wives and children were at the mercy not only of the males among the slaves but of the very [slave] women, who could handle deadly weapons."[36]

The frequency of flight by groups of slaves in Virginia is noteworthy and is indicative of the complexities of escape. A total of 329 acts of collective escape appear in runaway advertisements from the 1730s to 1790.[37] (A group is defined by Aptheker as three or more slaves.) In many cases during the Revolutionary War, fugitive women ran away with their husbands and children. In July 1778, Mary Burwell placed an advertisement for the return of Venus, Zeny, Nelly, and Jack, who escaped slavery in Prince William County and were seen in Isle of Wight County, Virginia. Jack and Venus were husband and wife and Zeny was the mother of Nelly. The group had plans to reach Williamsburg, which served as a departure point for many fugitives who intended to walk the four miles to Burwell's Ferry on the James River. Fugitive women who survived the war, perhaps four of every six, confronted several obstacles to freedom after the war. Among the obstacles was the pressure placed on the British by American diplomats to return fugitive slaves to their enslavers.[38]

Urban and rural enslaved women, literate and illiterate, were swept up by the force of revolutionary ideology. In a period of history when written communication was still hindered by undependable mail service and a paucity of printers and publishers, more people probably heard the news of Lexington and Concord from riders on horseback than read about it in newspapers. Black women had the means to maintain a vital oral tradition through the "common wind," the tradition of carrying oral communication that Africans retained in America. Table talk listened to by domestic slaves or conversations overheard by slave attendants was quickly transmitted to other slaves and disseminated to other quarters and plantations. Two of Georgia's delegates to the Continental Congress, Archibald Bullock and John Houston, confided to John Adams that the slave network could carry news "several hundreds of miles in a week or fortnight."[39]

The flight of enslaved women indicates that they did follow the progress of the war, and fully appreciated its implications for their own lives. Foremost among the implications of the war was American freedom. When the British launched their southern strategy in Georgia and

South Carolina in 1778, women escaped following the arrival of British forces. Among these fugitives were Renah, Sophia, and Hester and her son Bob.[40] Their escape, like that of many others, found its strategy and meaning in patterns of African resistance where self-reliance and survival strategies prevailed. As in the West African societies from which they were transported, kinship relations informed the social, religious, and political foundation of slave communities. Kinship relations, both fictive and non-fictive, were crucial to the achievement of short-term and long-term political objectives which included flight.[41]

General Henry Clinton's Philipsburg Proclamation in 1779 offering freedom to slaves willing to help the British led to the escape of scores of women. About two-fifths of those who escaped following the proclamation were women. Many of the women brought young children with them or had children while under British protection. Children born in British camps were free. Once under British protection women served as cooks, servants, laundresses, or did general labor.[42] Although the possibilities for maroon types of resistance were limited in the British American colonies, the expanse of unsettled frontier and a comparatively large amount of swampland in the South Carolina and Georgia Lowcountry, Florida, Louisiana, and the Great Dismal Swamp offered sanctuary for marronage. Marronage refers to the establishment of fugitive slave communities in the woods, swamps, and mountainous regions of the Americas. Renah, Sophia, Hester, and Bob were believed to be headed to St. Augustine, Florida where the Spanish offered freedom to fugitive slaves and where maroon societies were established.[43]

In their attempts to rid themselves of chronic runaways through sale, or to retrieve offenders through public notices, eighteenth-century enslavers acknowledged the intelligence, resourcefulness, and boldness of bondwomen. As historian Jacqueline Jones argues, descriptions of enslaved women "belie the conventional stereotypes that became popular during the early nineteenth century which portrayed Black women as obedient, passive, and lacking in imagination or strength."[44] Revolutionary Era runaways included Milly, "a sly subtle Wench, and a great Lyar"; Cicely, "very wicked and full of flattery"; and Hannah, "very insinuating and a notorious thief."[45] Women condemned "as guileful, cunning, proud, and artful often assumed the demeanor of free

Blacks, a feat accomplished most often in cities, and with the help of relatives, both slave and free."[46] These examples must be juxtaposed with the experiences of most enslaved women, who made the calculated decision to remain in their enslaver's household "and thereby provide for loved ones in less dramatic, though often equally surreptitious ways."[47]

The extraordinary flight of women during the war years also contributed to a crisis of confidence in the postwar era. The exodus of slaves "engendered by the British invasion and occupation created a severe labor shortage that destroyed the basis of the South's productive economy and weakened the wealth and power of its richest families."[48] In its postwar recovery effort, planter-merchants sought to rebuild the collapsed economies through the massive importation of African slaves and by enacting repressive slave codes. Planter-merchants also formulated a patriarchal ideology, which drew upon scripture and revolutionary ideology to proclaim that the social order was authorized and decreed by God, nature, and reason. Enslaved women found ways to challenge this patriarchal ideology in the postwar period through various stratagems, which included flight.

The story presented in these pages is unique. It examines the ways in which women's escape undergirded notions of womanhood, motherhood, and freedom. The war bolstered the independence of fugitive Black women, gave them increased access to their families with whom they fled, and greater autonomy in their day-to-day lives once they reached safe havens. Women ran away during the Revolutionary and post-Revolutionary period to claim their liberty, an act which they viewed as consistent with the ideals enunciated in the Declaration of Independence. Underlying the causes of their flight were efforts to defend their bodies and womanhood against exploitation, as well as to protect their children from the deleterious effects of the institution of slavery.

During the Revolution, women not only ran away with immediate family members, but also in groups without established kinship relations. They correctly perceived that their best chances for freedom resided with a British victory and a disruption of the existing social order. In the north and south, women fled to urban centers, took refuge in British camps, aided the Loyalist cause as spies, cooks, nurses, and performed duties for the British Army Ordnance Corps. In the postwar period, most Black women did not seek freedom in the North, but instead pursued "informal freedoms" in urban cities such as Baltimore, Richmond, Charleston, Savannah, and New Orleans where they defined freedom in terms of family and mobility. In these cities, they relied on networks of acquaintances, marketable skills, clothing, and language skills to assume identities as free women and carve out free spaces for themselves.

SOURCES AND METHODOLOGY

This social history of enslaved women during the Revolutionary Era has a wide span; it focuses on the Southern and Middle colonies where British forces battled with colonists, but also examines cases from the New England region. This regional approach can vividly retrace the experiences of fugitive women because it conforms to the reality on the ground. The pre-Revolutionary period from 1770 to 1775 witnessed disruptions in the institution of slavery as enslaved women took advantage of every opportunity to escape bondage. Lord Dunmore's 1775 Proclamation and Sir Henry Clinton's Philipsburg Proclamation of 1779 offering freedom to fugitives who joined the British army further disrupted the plantation economy as enslaved women fled plantations to follow their partners, husbands, and sons.

The temporal scope of *Running from Bondage* is the pre-Revolutionary and post-Revolutionary period to 1800; and its organization is chronological and thematic – emphasizing the various routes to freedom taken by fugitive women – because it focuses on fugitive women's individual and communal experience. Their world is at the center of analysis. Two themes are central to this study: the creation of a rival geography through fugitivity and fugitivity as a revolutionary act of resistance. Although the evidence is fragmented, the experiences of fugitive women are far from unknowable. While the firsthand accounts of runaways who settled in the North and Canada comprise an extensive body of abolitionist literature during the antebellum period, the accounts of runaways during the Colonial period are limited to colonial newspaper advertisements for runaways. In reading newspaper advertisements for runaways, the silences within the advertisements require that I imagine the varied meanings and possibilities that are inherent in these silences. I therefore find it useful to read against the grain in order to augment the fragmented archives.

Runaways were by definition a select group. Certain segments of the Black population – the young, mulattos, African, West Indian – are over-represented. The ultimate value of runaway advertisements lies chiefly in what they can tell us about the life stories of individual slaves. Each advertisement "describes part of the story of a real person, not an abstraction. When further research in other sources is undertaken, these human stories can be fleshed out as real human beings begin to emerge from the records."[49] There are limits to the utility of the advertisements in understanding the lives of enslaved women. We do not know the ultimate fate of the majority of the individuals named in the advertisements. Enslavers did not place advertisements for every runaway since many were captured quickly. But given these limitations, the runaway and captured advertisements still offer a remarkable amount of information about individual human beings caught in a horrific system of bondage. And when augmented with other sources, such as petitions, letters, county books, parish records, official correspondence, diaries, and plantation records, the advertisements can begin to restore human dignity to a group of persons who have long been denied their dignity.[50]

Newspaper advertisements map fugitive women's geography, detail individual stories, and go to the very reason for attempted escape. A number of other sources help reconstruct fugitive women's stories in their own voices and the voices of their relatives and friends. Trial records are an important source of first-person accounts. I concur with historian Sylviane Diouf that such documents must be handled with caution, as defendants and prosecutors may have been inclined to distort, lie, and minimize or overstate facts and claims. The threat and actual use of torture, sometimes bluntly acknowledged by prosecutors, must add a layer of circumspection to the person's account. But invaluable information can be gathered by paying attention to details.[51]

The four documentary volumes of Lathan Windley's *Runaway Slave Advertisements: A Documentary History from the 1730s to 1790* are an invaluable resource. Volume one, which details Virginia and North Carolina escapees, includes for Virginia a total of 1,568 fugitives, of whom 184 were women (six are stated to be pregnant). Seventeen are noted as being children below the age of ten; the remaining 1,367 are men. Included in these totals are one woman described as a free Negro, one Indian woman slave, one Indian man slave, and seven White indentured servants. In the remainder of the first volume dealing with North Carolina (where the population was sparse and extant newspapers relatively few) there are a total of 105 fugitives, one of whom was a child, thirteen of whom were women (one described as pregnant), and ninety-one of whom were men.[52]

Volumes two and three are devoted to Maryland and South Carolina, respectively. The number of fugitives being sought by advertisements in Maryland totaled 1,290, of which 134 were Black women (four described as pregnant), eleven were children, and thirty were White indentured servants. A total of 1,115 Black male runaways were advertised in the state of Maryland. The number of fugitives sought in South Carolina totaled 3,746, of which 698 were women (fourteen listed as pregnant) and 122 were children. A total of 2,926 Black men were advertised as fugitive slaves in South Carolina from 1732 to 1790.[53]

Volume four reprints slave advertisements from the few extant newspapers in Georgia, where slavery was illegal until 1750. From the first available advertisement in 1763 through 1790 there were a total of 1,233 fugitives. Of these, 229 were women (one was pregnant and one was Indian) and 64 were children, including eight specifically listed as infants. A total of 940 were Black men. The overall totals for the five areas through 1790 are: women, 1,258; children (under ten), 215; men, 6,439. (See Table 0.1.) Altogether, a total of 7,942 women, men, and children were advertised as fugitives. These data by no means reflect the totality of slave flight, as newspaper files are not complete and enslavers tended to place ads only when fugitives were missing for many days or even months. Also, newspapers were published in the few urban centers of the period so that plantations or homes near such centers were the main sources of advertisements.[54]

Antebellum memoirs and interviews of former runaways are also a rich source of information. Ona Judge, a fugitive slave of George Washington,

TABLE O.1 *Fugitives in the Southern colonies,*
1705–1790

	Female	Male	Children
Virginia	184[a]	1367	17
Maryland	134[b]	1115	11
North Carolina	13[c]	91	1
South Carolina	698[d]	2926	122
Georgia	229[e]	940	64
Total	1258	6439	215

a. Six women were pregnant.
b. Four women were pregnant.
c. One woman was pregnant.
d. Fourteen women were pregnant.
e. One woman was pregnant.
Source: Herbert Aptheker, "We Will be Free: Advertisements for Runaways and the Reality of American Slavery," Occasional Paper No. 1, Ethnic Studies Program, University of Santa Clara, 1984.

told her story to abolitionist Thomas H. Archibald forty-nine years after her escape. Her story appeared in the *Granite Freeman* in May 1845. A second interview with Ona Judge appeared in the *Liberator*, the nation's most powerful abolitionist newspaper, in 1847. Judge's interviews, according to Erica Armstrong Dunbar, are quite possibly the only existing recorded narrative of an eighteenth-century fugitive.[55]

***

In fleshing out enslaved women's fight for freedom, this book seeks to answer several key questions. How did Black women advance their own liberation during the Revolutionary Era? What regional variations and similarities existed in the flight of enslaved women? How did fugitive women engage with maroon societies? How does Black women's flight fit into the larger narrative of slave resistance? To emphasize the centrality of enslaved women who escaped bondage during and after the American Revolution, *Running from Bondage* directly engages archival silences within historical primary sources. Each chapter of this book begins with an event that foregrounds enslaved women's experiences with flight in what becomes an extended examination of fugitivity and the milieu of the Revolutionary and post-Revolutionary period. To uncover, re-create, and analyze the world of fugitive enslaved women, this book consists of five thematic chapters.

Chapter 1 provides an analysis of the status and position of enslaved women during the eighteenth century. The daily and seasonal work of enslaved women determined the boundaries within which women had to resist their bondage and their opportunities to do so. This chapter provides a broad understanding of enslaved women's labor in the southern and northern colonies as a basis from which to further examine enslaved women's fugitivity in subsequent chapters. This chapter demonstrates the diversity in enslaved women's experiences during the eighteenth century and the gendered resistance strategies they pursued to contest their bondage.

Chapter 2 is an examination of the pre-Revolutionary period. This chapter examines the flight of a mulatto woman named Margaret Grant who escaped slavery in Baltimore, Maryland in 1770 and 1773. This chapter examines the meaning of freedom through a delineation of acts of self-emancipation and places the story of Margaret in the context of the wider Atlantic world. Ideas about freedom are in many ways fruitful to investigate when analyzing the experiences of enslaved women. Bondwomen expressed their thoughts about freedom in private and public discourse throughout the era of slavery. Their involvement in conspiracies and acts of resistance such as running away is evidence of their willingness to fight for freedom no matter what the outcome.

Chapter 3 examines the ideas of the American Revolution and places fugitive slave women at the center of analysis. The impact of Dunmore's Proclamation and the Philipsburg Proclamation are examined. From plantations, women escaped to cities and towns, North and South; they fled poverty and malevolence. Following the pronouncement of the Philipsburg Proclamation, 40 percent of runaways were women. There were regional variations and similarities in the flight of enslaved women. In the Southern colonies, enslaved women pursued refuge in Spanish Florida and with British troops during the Southern Campaign; in the Chesapeake colonies, enslaved women fled to Pennsylvania and other northern destinations, often seeking refuge with British troops in the process of escaping; in the Northern and New England colonies, fugitive women sought refuge with the British during the war's early campaigns, but also endeavored to reach cities such as New York. In each of these regions, fugitive women also endeavored to pass as free women in urban spaces. Indeed, throughout the Revolutionary Era, enslaved women advanced their liberation through flight.

Chapter 4 examines the obstacles enslaved women faced in escaping bondage in post-Revolutionary America. The case of Elizabeth Freeman, an enslaved Black woman in Massachusetts who sued for her freedom, captures the tenacity of Black women, who not only resisted with their feet, but also used the courts to gain their freedom. By highlighting the case of Ona Judge, the fugitive slave of George and Martha Washington, this chapter brings to the fore successful escapes in which enslaved women overcame formidable obstacles to freedom.

Chapter 5 examines the gendered dimensions of maroon communities in America and the wider Atlantic world. Maroons were fugitives from slavery who established independent communities in swamps, deep woods, mountains, isolated islands, and other wilderness sanctuaries. Fugitive women joined maroon societies with their husbands and other family members. Runaways were a constant source of anxiety and fear. In the Caribbean and places such as Georgia, Florida, and the Gulf Coast and along the perimeter of the Virginia and North Carolina border in an area known as the Great Dismal Swamp, they were successful in establishing maroon societies. Such societies maintained their cohesiveness for many years. Given that the woods and swamps were spaces where the enslaved could exercise more autonomy than the fields and other open spaces on the plantation, fugitive women had more freedom in these spaces.

The enslaved women who escaped or *attempted* to escape bondage registered their hatred for chattel slavery and their desire for liberty – a desire so great they willingly braved danger to realize it. During the war, many chose death instead of returning to bondage. The goal of this study is to present an American Revolution that is inclusive of Black women. *Running from Bondage* broadens and complicates how we study and teach this momentous event, one that emphasizes the chances taken by the "Black founding mothers" and the important contributions of women like Margaret Grant to the cause of liberty. Wherever freedom is cherished, their struggle and sacrifice should be remembered.

CHAPTER 1

"A Negro Wench Named Lucia"

Enslaved Women during the Eighteenth Century

Absented from her master, a negro wench, supposed to be about 14 years old, named Lucia. She has a black stroke over each of her cheeks as a mark of her country; she has a very particular flesh mark on her upper lip right under the middle of her nose, it consists of a small round hollow spot, in the middle whereof is a smaller protuberance quite round and fastened underneath by a small shank. Whoever takes up said wench, and brings her to the subscriber, shall have ten shillings reward paid by John Reinier.

Royal Georgia Gazette (Savannah), November 19, 1766

L UCIA, A YOUNG GIRL TRANSPORTED TO THE GEORGIA Lowcountry during the 1760s, brought with her a deft understanding of her provenance. Prior to her forced migration, her father established her identity by placing "a black stroke over each of her cheeks" as a mark of her ethnicity.[1] Her family's conception of their historical reality no doubt included reverence for naming ceremonies, secret societies, and the rituals associated with such societies, including gendered roles, warrior traditions, and untrammeled freedom. For Lucia, running away was the final act of resistance to enslavement. It was a Pyrrhic victory against a system that sought to subsume her traditions and knowledge of herself. Within this system of inhuman bondage, however, enslaved Africans such as Lucia maintained some vestiges of freedom. They retained a sense of themselves and relied upon an informal network of both enslaved and free Africans for support, including the quasi-maroon communities developed by Africans who escaped enslavement.

Scholars of slavery have largely overlooked the experiences of fugitive women and girls during the eighteenth century. In explaining the low percentage of women in the runaway population, Stephanie Camp, in her work *Closer to Freedom*, has argued that motherhood and gender-based labor assignments kept the vast majority of enslaved women tied to plantations, forcing them to stay in bondage. Despite the limitations placed on enslaved women's resistance, they were able to contest their bondage through the liminal spaces of slavery. This contestation had significant consequences for their mobility and the actions that they pursued as slavery became entrenched during the eighteenth century.

SOUTHERN LABORS

Enslaved women in colonial America lived under diverse circumstances because bondage itself was based on distinct economic systems. While each system relied on enslaved labor, the Northern colonies emerged as "societies with slaves" rather than slave societies. In the Southern colonies, society became increasingly organized around slavery, which was central to its economic production. Most enslaved women lived on small family farms with their enslavers in the Northern colonies, whereas in the Southern colonies, cash crops such as tobacco, rice, and indigo led to a growing demand for plantation labor on large estates. In the first four decades of the seventeenth century, the largest number of enslaved Africans – 43,000 – were imported to the Chesapeake to plant and harvest tobacco. In the eighteenth century, South Carolina and Georgia colonists, aided by enslaved women and men, took the lead in planting rice and indigo. In the mid 1660s, South Carolina had begun to import slaves from Barbados, and by 1708 it became the only colony on the mainland with a Black majority.[2] On the eve of the American Revolution, there were 200,000 enslaved women and men in the Chesapeake colonies of Virginia and Maryland, comprising 40 percent of the population.[3] Georgia's Black population totaled 15,000 in 1773 (which was still equivalent to 40 percent of the population), and South Carolina's enslaved population totaled 82,000 by 1770 (60 percent of the population).[4]

Beginning in the seventeenth century, the English justified slavery by using concepts of race that defined Africans as "the other." According to scholar Zakiyyah Jackson, Western science and philosophy viewed Black people as empty vessels, as non-beings, and as ontological zeros. Positioned at the intersection of race and gender, African women were integral to the imposition of a racial and sexual hierarchy on the part of Europeans to establish racial and sexual differences. In order to justify the enslavement of Africans, "Europeans focused on gender and sexuality as markers of civilization, negatively contrasting African women's apparent licentiousness with European women's supposed chastity."[5] Historian Jennifer Morgan explains, "African women's 'unwomanly' behavior evoked an immutable distance between Europe and Africa on which the development of racial slavery depended."[6] Europeans viewed African women as particularly suited to both agricultural and reproductive labor.[7]

Planters argued that African women were an exception to the gender division of labor in order to exploit their productive and reproductive potential. In 1643, Virginia lawmakers concluded that English gender roles did not apply to African women and levied a tax on African women's field labor, categorizing them as laborers with the same productive capacity as men. This tax on African women's labor, according to Kathleen Brown, "created the first legal distinction between African and English women and was the foundation of a race-specific concept of womanhood."[8] Racial animus excluded Black women from ever being viewed as "good" wives and mothers and permanently relegated them to the status of "nasty wenches" associated with the agricultural labor and sexual promiscuity considered unsuitable for White women. During the first decades of the seventeenth century, the term "wench" had applied to English women of low status. By the 1730s, European colonists used it almost exclusively to describe women of African descent.[9] Cynthia Kennedy explains, "The term 'wench' set apart slave women as subservient laborers (an underclass) and denigrated them as a lower form of female, utterly distinct from white ladies and, therefore, legitimate targets of sexual exploitation by their owners."[10]

According to historian Betty Wood, many women enslavers, like their male counterparts, used "the sexually loaded and socially contemptible word *wench*, a term that would never have been applied, except perhaps in jest, to any white woman, however humble her social status."[11] The desire to distance themselves from their enslaved counterparts made White women even more reluctant than White men to grant enslaved women the respect of referring to them as women. In her examination of runaway slave advertisements in Lowcountry Georgia newspapers during the post-Revolutionary period, Wood found that female enslavers were more likely than their male counterparts to designate enslaved women as wenches.[12]

As the number of enslaved persons increased in the eighteenth century, Virginia and other Southern colonies enacted a series of codes and laws designed to prohibit interracial marriage and formalize legal enslavement. Virginia laws provided important benchmarks for the status and treatment of slave women that other colonies replicated. For example, in 1662, Virginia passed a law mandating that enslaved children would follow the legal status of their mother as slaves, following the Latin dictum *partus sequitur ventrem.* This law gave slave-hungry enslavers every incentive to sexually assault their female slaves in hope of procuring valuable child slaves. Moreover, Virginia deemed the paternity of slave children meaningless in its attempt to diminish enslaved fathers' influence over their enslaved offspring. Such slave laws were in contrast to "legal customs affecting white society, and they permanently affected enslaved women's lives. Slaveholders increasingly began to regard their female slaves as both laborers and potential reproducers for white men's future economic enterprises."[13] The South's economy grew increasingly dependent on slavery, in contrast to the Northern colonies, where slavery was less legally defined and less significant to economic development.

Enslavers emphasized the moral and physical differences between Black and White women and categorized Black women "legally and culturally as productive, reproductive, and sexual property."[14] Elite White women were key agents in emphasizing these differences, "as their ability to maintain this racially defined concept of womanhood necessitated their distinguishing themselves from their enslaved counterparts."[15] Enslavers expected enslaved women to produce more than White indentured servants because they perceived Black women as physically stronger than White women. Conterminously, enslavers viewed enslaved women's work to be worth only three-quarters of that of enslaved men, while they regarded children as a "half-share" by the age of nine or ten. In the Southern colonies, enslaved women "were given the most tedious and monotonous forms of fieldwork, including preparing ground, digging ditches, hoeing, and weeding."[16] Slaveholders also expected women to clean communal areas such as stables. In the minds of enslavers, "Black women were capable of hard physical labor and were consequently a source of rising profits. Some slaveholders took pride in the ability of their female slaves to labor as hard as did their male counterparts."[17]

Enslavers valued enslaved women primarily as laborers who were forced to work like men in the fields, yet they experienced labor differently than did men because of their sex. On tobacco, sugar, and later cotton plantations, enslaved women worked in gangs from sun-up to sundown. In the rice country of Georgia and South Carolina, labor was organized under the task system. "Enslaved laborers completed daily work assignments based on portions of an acre, from one-half to one-quarter, designated according to age and ability. Gender was not a factor in assigning tasks, and many women designated as 'full hands' were expected to do the same amount of labor as did men."[18] Women were the majority of prime field hands on large Lowcountry rice plantations and they engaged in preparing the fields, sowing, cultivating, harvesting, and cleaning rice, and maintaining plantation irrigation systems.[19] A small percentage of enslaved women were given skilled work. They wove baskets and made quilts, drawing on the skills they had acquired in Africa, while others worked in plantation dairies or raised poultry. Some women also became midwives or "root doctors."[20] Frequently, enslavers expected women to use these more advanced skills in addition to the field labor required of them. They expected enslaved women to weave, sew, and quilt at night and to labor in the fields or the plantation house during the day. Women's experiences differed markedly from those of enslaved men, most of whom were expected to use their skills as carpenters, blacksmiths, shoemakers, and bricklayers instead of laboring in the fields.[21]

While the task labor system offered a degree of freedom, it was not always beneficial for enslaved women. The health of women working on Lowcountry plantations remained poor, since they were forced to return to field labor soon after giving birth. Women also suffered from a variety of ailments, which included fallen wombs, spinal injuries from back-breaking work in rice fields, fevers, pulmonary illness, rheumatism, and foot rot caused by standing knee-deep in water. Moreover, new mothers took longer to complete their assigned task due to the need to stop working to feed their infants. New mothers, as well as pregnant and elderly women, suffered from exhaustion that slowed their pace of work. On many plantations, children aged two to twelve months frequently died as a result of being underweight and exposed to malaria, influenza, whooping cough, lockjaw, and winter fevers. For women, slavery was even more terrible since overt resistance was not a viable option. Retribution through physical violence such as whippings, more abuse or threats, as well as moral anguish, which included separation from their family or surroundings when sold away, remained omnipresent. Sexuality, as historian Catherine Clinton has argued, was a central and significant element in the system of power devised by the slave society.[22]

Cruel and unusual punishments provided the impetus for flight from plantations. The task labor system served as the cornerstone of Lowcountry plantation management; however, implacable hostility was coeval with this labor system. Severe beatings, whippings, and floggings were concomitant with chains, irons, and incarcerations. The threat of retribution through physical violence such as whippings or the moral anguish that would result from separation from their family or surroundings if they were sold away was present. Under these conditions, enslaved women seized opportunities for self-emancipation. The sea islands provided fluid egress for runaways to flee to the nearby pine lands, as well as to seek refuge with the Seminoles in Spanish Florida.[23] In Lowcountry South Carolina and Georgia, 927 enslaved women ran away between 1730 and 1790.[24]

For many women, the task labor system allowed them to manipulate their time to secure their own economic and social spaces. Women could plant and tend gardens as well as raise livestock; however, control and coercion remained central elements of this system. Slavery was a "system of many systems" that affected women on multiple levels. As Deborah Gray White has argued, "women deliberately dissembled their objective reality and masked their thoughts and personalities in order to protect valued parts of their lives from white and male invasion."[25] However, the hidden realm of women's lives was the primary domain in which women resisted the process of reduction. Their political, social and economic struggle for full humanity is captured in their narratives which reveal that women's domestic responsibility informed their social reality. Within slave communities, women emerged as cultural interlocutors. They maintained a place of honor and degrees of political power derived from the contributions which they made to the material and cultural life of the quarters. Women sustained family and kinship networks, anchored slave communities, and shouldered the dual burden of field labor for their owners and domestic responsibilities for their households on a daily basis. The status of women in slave communities increased as a result of their work as nurses, midwives, and educators.[26]

On wheat and tobacco plantations the gang system led to greater separation of men and women than under the task labor system. Enslaved women worked under the supervision of a Black slave driver or White overseer, performing different work than men for at least five days of the week. For instance, women worked as gatherers and stackers, whereas men harvested wheat with a scythe. Men carted and plowed while women put up fences, cleared stables, and leveled ditches. Tobacco had a shorter annual cycle than rice and required less heavy labor at certain times, but the work on tobacco was steadier, requiring transplanting, debugging, "topping," "suckering," curing, and packing. Tobacco growing also required plowing and the use of carts for hauling, which remained the domain of enslaved men. This sexual division of labor altered the everyday working lives of enslaved people. For women, working with other women provided support and camaraderie but also left them more vulnerable to sexual assault from enslavers and overseers.[27]

According to an eighteenth-century planter, tobacco was "a plant of perpetual trouble and difficulty." It was fragile and required tedious cultivation. Enslaved women labored from first daylight in the morning until sundown in the evening, usually in small, interdependent groups where their labor was closely monitored by the planter or overseer. George Washington, for example, required his slaves at Mount Vernon to "be at work as soon as it is light, [and] work till it is dark."[28] In the winter months, it was not unusual for women to even work by candlelight into the evening hours, curing, stripping, and packing tobacco. The planting cycle for tobacco began in January as enslaved people cleared or burned the land and prepared the soil for early planting. Between February and March, women sowed tobacco seeds in specially prepared beds of mulch. Transplanting began in April and the workload steadily increased as new fields were cleared and prepared to receive the transplanted tobacco plants. During the summer months, women were kept busy weeding, transplanting, replanting, and removing ravaging caterpillars from the tobacco leaves. Harvesting took place from August to October; however, drying, stripping, and packaging kept women busy through December, after which the cycle repeated itself.[29]

Gender-based labor assignments fostered female unity since working in female gangs, as well as working under the task labor system, allowed Black women to develop an independent female culture. Within their community, women held their own definitions of Black womanhood, "based upon African cultural traditions reshaped to accommodate the realities of their experiences in slavery. Black women rejected the notion that femininity required chastity, submissiveness, and weakness. Instead, they valued labor performed for their families and communities, prided physical and emotional strength, recognized female leadership, and celebrated resistance."[30] Historian Brenda Stevenson argues that enslaved women "revered resistance as a female trait, which enabled them to protect their most fundamental claims to womanhood ... their female sexuality and physicality, and their roles as mothers and wives."[31]

During the second half of the eighteenth century, Virginia's enslaved population grew due to a combination of the continued importation of enslaved people across the Atlantic and natural increase, as enslaved women bore more children than was necessary to replace the preceding generation. Likewise, the South Carolina slave population began to experience natural increase in the second half of the eighteenth century. Black and White women's fertility rates rose over the Colonial period from forty-two births per one thousand in 1670 to fifty-eight per one thousand in 1789. Still, enslaved children's lives remained fragile, and many infants fell prey to early mortality. Enslaved women also bore their first children at a relatively young age, typically aged sixteen, and children were born close together, mostly twenty-five to thirty months apart.

Therefore, the majority of enslaved women gave birth about every other year and bore many children over their lifetime, not all of whom survived.[32]

As the slave population increased, planters began valuing enslaved women for their productive and reproductive abilities. Thomas Jefferson declared that "a woman who brings a child every two years [is] more profitable than the best man on the farm [for] what she produces is an addition to the capital, while his labor disappears in mere consumption."[33] Jefferson was not the only slaveholder who valued a self-producing labor force. A planter in 1719 declared as he purchased two fifteen-year-old girls that "nothing is more to the advantage of my son than young breeding negroes."[34]

Enslaved women were at risk of sexual assault and physical violence by enslavers because they often lived and worked within the plantation house. Colonial mistresses could be particularly cruel when they suspected their husbands of engaging in illicit sexual relationships with their female slaves. In 1748, Hannah Crump of Lancaster County, Virginia was accused of murdering a woman named Jenny, who was enslaved by her husband. Hannah suspected that the two were intimately involved, and Jenny bore the brunt of her wrath regardless of the forced nature of Jenny's relationship with Hannah's husband.[35] Likewise, William Byrd recorded several extramarital affairs with female domestics, despite being in his late sixties. Having relationships with enslaved women whom he kept in his house allowed Byrd to affirm his sexual prowess and illustrates the power of White men in colonial American society. The mental and physical violence enslaved women faced within White people's homes grew more pronounced over time.[36]

The South Carolina Stono Rebellion of 1739 affected enslavers' attitudes toward reproduction. Led by Angolan slaves who killed twenty-one Whites, the revolt heightened fear within White society about the continued importation of Africans who could foment rebellion. Hence, rather than importing slaves from Africa, enslavers sought to encourage enslaved women's fertility as a more facile way to increase the colonies' supply of slaves. A decade after the rebellion, colonists raised the duties on imported slaves to prohibitively high levels, which caused the importation of enslaved women and men from Africa and the Caribbean to the

Carolinas to decline to one-tenth of the rate of importation that prevailed during the 1730s, which had been 1,000 per year.[37] This effort by lawmakers served to halt the importation of new Africans to ensure that imported slaves would never constitute so high a proportion of the colony's population as they had in the late 1730s.[38] Childbirth was thus used by enslavers to maintain, if not increase, the slave population.[39] The encouragement of frequent pregnancies led to conflict between enslaved women and enslavers as women resented their interference in matters related to their choice of spouse and the number of children they bore. Enslaved women also grew more exhausted as they balanced the demands of frequent childbearing with exacting physical labor.[40]

Enslaved women's bitterness and resentment toward callous and interfering enslavers led them to resist their oppression in various ways, including trying to limit the number of children they bore and escaping their bondage. Evidence suggests that "female slaves brought knowledge of plants that could induce miscarriages with them from West Africa, which some women used to restrict the number of children they bore as a result of white men's sexual abuse."[41] Others aborted pregnancies simply because they did not want to raise their children as chattel. According to Emily West, running away from hated enslavers was easier for bondwomen during the Colonial period than for those who lived during the antebellum years of slavery, "because over time white society grew more adept at tracking and capturing runaway slaves," especially following the Revolutionary War.[42] During the Colonial Era, small groups of runaways known as maroons existed in the swamplands of the Carolinas and along the border of Virginia and North Carolina as well as elsewhere in the colonies. Spanish Florida also became a haven for runaway slaves. Two women, an infant girl, and eight men were among the first recorded groups of slaves to escape from Carolina to Florida in 1687. After escaping by boat to St. Augustine, the two women worked as domestics for the Spanish governor and subsequently converted to Catholicism. This began a pattern of flight south where fugitives sought freedom with Spanish authorities.[43] They based their flight on a 1693 edict in which the "Spanish Crown offered freedom to all fugitives – men as well as women – who converted to Catholicism. Thereafter, Spanish officials in Florida provided 'Liberty and Protection' to all slaves who reached St. Augustine, and they consistently refused to return runaways who took refuge in the colony."[44]

Enslaved women who were mothers fleeing bondage in colonial times disrupts the narrative that all female slaves with children were bound to their enslavers through their offspring. For example, the *South Carolina Gazette* on June 3, 1760 advertised that twenty-three year old Martilla ran away with her child "about twelve months old."[45] Both were bought at the sale of Mrs. Mary Baker's Estate and were well known in Charlestown where her enslaver believed "she is supposed to be harboured [*sic*]."[46] Men were most likely to flee together, while women either ran away alone or with family members, including mothers, children, and husbands. In some cases, men ran away with their children. In 1772, for instance, South Carolina enslaver Mrs. Dellahow reported "that two sensible Negro fellows," Ramspute and his son George, had run away, and were probably "harbored with his wife in Charleston."[47] Similarly, "Bristol and his thirteen year old son" ran away from John Rawn in April 1767.[48] Runaway slave advertisements were also placed for couples, which is an indication that fugitive couples' marriages were just as important to them as their freedom.[49] Overall, more men than women escaped bondage. In South Carolina, from 1732 to 1737, males outnumbered females by three to one. Seventy-seven percent of runaways advertised in colonial South Carolina during the 1730s were men.[50] While this pattern persisted through the century it was not unique to South Carolina. According to Herbert Aptheker, in Virginia from 1705 to 1790, 1,367 men attempted to escape bondage, compared to only 184 women.[51] However, these figures are not definitive as not every runaway generated an advertisement. It is thus feasible that the actual number of runaways was at least double the extant number since not all newspapers were published consistently and many enslavers did not advertise for the return of runaways. In fact, many enslavers refused to pay the newspaper advertisement fees. Not only did they have to worry about paying publishers for the space, but they also had to "pay the informer (black or white), the warden, and the person who initially delivered the fugitive to the warden."[52] Delivery of the runaway was expensive.[53]

The scholarship on enslaved women has frequently focused on how women's work as unskilled laborers bound them more firmly than men to plantations and limited their options for resistance.[54] On large plantations, enslaved men were given skilled positions, such as craftsmen, that granted them a degree of mobility as they were often hired to work on neighboring plantations. Additionally, men "held positions as coachmen and boat hands that took them throughout the countryside and to town. As a result, men were able to gain a sense of geography, making them much more capable and successful runaways."[55] Betty Wood concluded that women did not run away in similar numbers to men because their labor did not take them off the plantation as often.[56]

Enslaved women had as much incentive to run away as did men, perhaps even more. Certainly, women were bound more tightly than men to plantations. The focus on plantations, however, obscures those women whose labor brought them throughout the countryside and into cities, facilitating their ability to run away. Many enslaved women did have skilled positions that granted them opportunities to travel. On large plantations, some women worked neither in the fields nor in plantation homes, but rather in the areas between the two. Women held positions as "poultry minders, dairy women, gardeners, nurses or midwives. Although these positions did not carry the same prestige as men's skilled positions, they granted women a degree of independence and mobility."[57] Midwifery skills took them throughout the countryside as they traveled to treat women on other plantations.[58] An example is fifty-year-old Sally who was well respected among the Black and White communities as a "doctress." Sally gained confidence from her healing skills and mobility, in addition to the fact that she could read "tolerably well." She left her owner on four occasions, traveling through the countryside, passing "by the name of Free Sally" and was able to support herself by employing her healing skills.[59] According to her enslaver, "some white persons have employed her by sending their own negroes to her."[60]

Many plantation women, under the task labor system, traveled to urban markets on Sundays to sell eggs, poultry, and crops produced in the internal slave economy during the free time the system permitted. As in Africa and the Caribbean, the important role played by Black women in the Charleston and Savannah markets "enabled the creation of networks between rural and urban enslaved women and encouraged a Black female forum on current events."[61] In addition to money and goods, women returned to plantations with "information about the outside world gleaned from conversations with urban residents, black and white, free and enslaved, as well as travelers and black sailors who brought news from the larger Atlantic world. The knowledge, mobility, acquaintances, and confidence gained through their experiences in the market facilitated women's resistance."[62] For instance, a "tall, fine looking brown girl," Sarah Washington laughed and talked "very loud[ly]," and was "inclined to be impudent."[63] Her enslaver noted that, prior to her escape, she had been "in the habit of going to Summerville to buy vegetables, which she sold in the streets of Charleston."[64]

Gender shaped both the work women were assigned and also the punishment used to enforce their labor, and gender did not exempt enslaved women from harsh punishment. To the contrary, slaveholders and overseers often punished enslaved women even more severely than they did men due to gendered assumptions of slave resistance and the woman's place.[65] Formerly enslaved James recalled, "The women are always beat worse than the men. The more they whip the men, the more likely they are to run away into the swamp, but the women don't run away so much."[66] However, Ruth did run away. Some advertisements contained explicit instructions for the type of punishment a White citizen should mete out for any slave caught without a pass. Enslaver Rebeccah Marsey stated, "whoever picks up Ruth, give her fifty good lashes."[67]

Deborah Gray White maintains that "the violence done to Black women might well de-center lynching as the primary site and preeminent expression of white (sexual) anxiety on the black body."[68] "Through the physical abuse and sexual assault of black women, [enslavers] and overseers asserted their authority over (and simultaneously expressed their fear of) both enslaved women and their male relatives. By beating enslaved women in front of their male relatives or forcing men to beat women, slaveholders undermined both women's roles as wives and mothers worthy of patriarchal protection and men's roles as husbands and fathers who have the right to defend their women."[69] The enslaved woman's body thus became the site of "interracial masculine conflict."[70]

In his examination of enslaved men's deemasculinization, Thomas Foster argues that enslavers regularly denied enslaved men autonomy in decisions regarding courtship and intimacy, which rendered them powerless to protect their wives from abuse.[71] However, in discussions on the abuse of enslaved women, it is essential to consider the woman's perspective. Enslaved women were abused physically, sexually, and psychologically, as enslavers "attacked their roles as women, denied them male protection, and often forced their male counterparts to be agents in their abuse. Sexual violence also informed enslaved women's resistance as they struggled against assaults on their bodies, womanhood, and psyches."[72]

Overseers and slave drivers viewed sexual access to enslaved women's bodies as one of the privileges of their authority as the division of the labor force into sex-segregated gangs left women alone in the fields.[73] Semi-nudity of enslaved female field hands added to their vulnerability. One former slave recalled, "Our clothes were rags, and we were all half naked, and the females were not sufficiently clothed to satisfy common decency."[74] The nature of enslaved women's work placed them in situations where they had to bend over to tend crops and often needed to lift their skirts when working in muddy or flooded fields.[75] The exposure of enslaved women made them more susceptible to sexual assault, which often led to violent altercations when women attempted to resist. John Hope Franklin and Loren Schweninger have argued that "young men were more willing than women to challenge the overseer's authority."[76] Women, however, did fight back, "resisting not simply physical punishment but also sexual or sexualized assault."[77] Recalling the story of a physical altercation between her grandmother Sylvia Heard and the overseer, Celestia Avery stated:

> Grandmother Sylvia was told to take her clothes off when she reached the end of a row. She was to be whipped because she had not completed the required amount of hoeing for the day. Grandmother continued hoeing until she came to a fence; as the overseer reached out to grab her she snatched a fence railing and broke it across his arms.[78]

By running away, enslaved women took ownership of their bodies and resisted sexual assault and White men's claims to unlimited access. Enslavers who sexually abused enslaved women became irate when they ran away. Enslaver John Champney believed that fugitives who hid on the outskirts of Doctor Striving's plantation in South Carolina were "providing a sanctuary for a runaway named Diane," whom Champney wanted back "dead or alive."[79] Jennifer Fleischner has argued that sexual exploitation was a "soul-murdering physical and psychological assault against the slave's identity" and that "the concept of 'family,' however configured, was a crucial counterforce to the soul-murdering abuse and deprivation under slavery."[80] Enslaved mothers instilled their daughters with a positive view of Black womanhood that negated the racialized and gendered notions of the slavocracy.[81] Leslie Schwalm contends that women "were the primary figures … in imparting to children the skills with which they, their kin, and their community might survive (and resist) lifelong enslavement."[82]

Motherhood inspired women to escape as many women ran away in an effort to maintain ties to their children or escaped in response to the death or sale of a child.[83]

Although childbearing and childcare responsibilities bound women more tightly to plantations than men and was a factor in a woman's choice to run away, enslaved women with children did flee, particularly during the American Revolution. According to Deborah Gray White, most male runaways were aged sixteen to thirty-five, the years when most women were pregnant, nursing, or caring for at least one small child. Although this may have hindered women from escaping, in some instances, the gender ideals within the "black community also informed women's decision to flee, as motherhood was central to enslaved women's definition of womanhood and abandoning a child was socially unacceptable."[84] Consequently, there were numerous cases where fugitive women fled with their children.

NORTHERN LABORS

The experiences of enslaved women in Northern cities and rural spaces differed considerably from Southern plantation slavery. The majority of Northern enslaved women lived in small households with their enslavers. Roughly fifteen thousand Black women lived in the North on the eve of the American Revolution, the majority of whom were enslaved. At this time, there were fifty thousand Blacks living in the North, comprising 4.5 percent of the total population. "The dividing line between slavery and freedom was more flexible and malleable in the North than on

Southern plantations. As a result, more Northern Black women moved out of bondage and into freedom."[85] In New England, enslaved women sought their freedom through legal manumission, as well as flight. They were viewed both as persons before the law and as property. "Being defined as persons before the law provided more opportunities for enslaved women to become free through the courts than anywhere else in the British North America colonies."[86] Women in bondage understood their enslavement as dispossession and being robbed of their families since they were threatened by sale or feared sale would come. In New England's port cities, Black women's ability to reproduce was more often seen as a liability than an asset for enslavers since most New England slaveholders owned only one or two slaves, who lived in the attics of their enslavers' homes.[87]

The Northern economy was also more diversified than the Southern plantation-centered economy. In some of the most agriculturally productive rural areas of Connecticut, Long Island, the lower Hudson River valley, and southern Pennsylvania, Black people made up as much as half of the workforce in the decades after 1750. Certain industries, such as ironworking in Pennsylvania or tanning in New York, relied heavily on slave labor and enslaved people worked in the carrying trade and around shipyards in Rhode Island and Massachusetts. In the Northern colonies, enslaved women grew a variety of crops including wheat, while others worked in the dairy and cattle industries, raised other livestock, and worked as craftswomen.[88] The vast majority of enslaved women labored as domestics in their enslavers' homes. This entailed spinning yarn and other thread, soap and candle making, gardening, childcare, food preparation and cooking, and making and mending clothes. Owing to an increased reliance on slave labor, enslaved women monopolized places in the kitchens and pantries of Northern farms. In rural Pennsylvania, New York, and New Jersey enslaved women worked in the fields part-time.[89] Black women had to contend with constant surveillance, the drudgery of unrelenting domestic labor, disruptions to family life, and barriers to education.[90]

Like their Southern counterparts, enslaved women in Northern colonies resisted bondage and slaveholders' efforts to control their mobility in what Stephanie Camp refers to as "geographies of containment."[91]

Containment was a core part of slavery and enslavers sought to control the movement of bondwomen. Following the New York slave conspiracy of 1712 in which the main arsonists were allegedly women, legislators in New York enacted a law for "preventing, Suppressing, and punishing the Conspiracy and Insurrection of Negroes and other Slaves." This law sought to discourage the importation of Africans by placing an excessive tax on imports and permitted any punishment for the offense of arson to include burning, hanging by a chain, and being broke on the wheel.[92] Northern enslaved women also resisted bondage by attempting to run away. In 1758, a Westchester County, New York slave named Bridget conspired with six others to run away but was caught and punished. Similarly, Lucretia who spoke "broken Dutch and English" and was "great with Child" ran away in New York City on May 1, 1763.[93] According to her enslaver, she was entrusted to sell various goods in the city and, like other enslaved women who had mobility, took advantage of the opportunity to escape bondage. Northern enslaved women also fought to maintain their families, to live in communities of their choosing, and to share culture across generations.[94]

The Northern free Black population declined in the first half of the eighteenth century as a result of efforts to limit manumissions. The free Black female population that existed in the North was the result of either being born free, manumission, or self-purchase. Prior to 1780, New York, New Jersey, Pennsylvania, and the New England colonies curbed manumission by requiring slaveholders to post heavy bonds for the good conduct of former slaves and to support those who might rely on public charity. "During the sixty-five years between 1698 and 1763, only ninety slaves were manumitted in Philadelphia; the number in New York was even smaller. Aged and sickly, many of these women and men were released by [enslavers] who had effectively emancipated themselves from the support of laborers deemed nonproductive."[95] As the free Black population declined, its prosperity waned and White northerners began equating bondage with Blackness. Northern lawmakers reinforced that presumption by circumscribing the freedom of free Blacks. "In various northern colonies, free Blacks were barred from voting, attending the militia, sitting on juries, testifying in court, and holding property."[96] In several places, "free Blacks were required by law to carry special passes to travel, trade, and keep a gun or a dog."[97] They were judged in special courts, along with slaves, and could be punished like slaves for certain offenses. The punishment meted out to free Blacks often drove them back into bondage. In Pennsylvania, a law enslaved those free Blacks found to be without regular employment, and who "loiter[ed] and mispen[t]" their time.[98]

Creating a community of Black women was more difficult in the New England colonies due to the uneven ratio of men to women. Most slaves lived in seafaring cities, which had a largely male enslaved population throughout the eighteenth century. In the New England countryside, enslaved women lived isolated lives dwelling miles from another Black person. According to Michael Gomez, a Black community can take shape even without a shared work life or common residence as long as "Black folk could get from one farm to the next on a regular basis and within a reasonable time."[99] According to historians Catherine Adams and Elizabeth Pleck, "even by this standard, a community of Black women did not exist in rural New England since they encountered other Black people on an irregular basis."[100]

The northern system of slavery placed enslaved women in menial and servile tasks considered women's work. In elite households, a mistress assigned an enslaved woman or girl the task of polishing silver or furniture. In some instances, wives of great men of wealth had an enslaved lady's maid who aided them with "their clothes, hair, drew their baths, and mended clothes. Some [enslavers] preferred to have a servant girl shave them rather than going to the barber."[101] Enslaved women who lived in town might be sent to the store to pick up a skein of thread or a yard of ribbon.[102] However, most mistresses used enslaved women "not as their personal attendant but as a domestic menial sweeping, emptying chamber pots, carrying water, washing the dishes, brewing, taking care of children, cooking and baking, spinning, carding, knitting and sewing."[103]

Slavery in the Northern colonies has been viewed as benign; however, despite not having the rigidity of Southern plantations, Black women, men, and children were cruelly treated by enslavers. The account of slaves "who were branded by their enslavers, had their ears nailed, fled, committed suicide, suffered the dissolution of their families, or were sold" refutes the myth of the "kind master."[104] Enslavers behaved in a way that belied their benevolent views of themselves. They lashed out at bondwomen when "they were angry, filled with rage, or had convenient access to a horsewhip."[105] In the Massachusetts Bay colony, two women, Maria and Phillis, were found guilty of killing their enslavers in 1681 and in 1755, respectively. As punishment, their corpses were set aflame to convey the message that the killing of a master would not be tolerated in the colony.[106] In the case of Phillis, there were two accomplices, Mark, an enslaved man, and another woman, who was punished by banishment to the West Indies. Mark was hung, his body covered in tar, and "suspended on chains at Charlestown Common." Mark directed his *Last & Dying Words* to Black women, stating "my Fellow Servants, especially the Women, take warning from me, and shun those Vices which have prov'd my ruin."[107]

Northern judges, like their southern counterparts, used a racial double standard with respect to murder and other offenses. Bondmen and bondwomen who took the life of a slaveholder were treated as though they had killed nobility while enslavers who killed their slaves were not punished. There were laws that made the murder of a slave a capital crime; however, according to Catherine Adams and Elizabeth Pleck, no enslaver was ever put to death for killing a slave.[108] In 1767, the enslaver of Jenny in Newport, Rhode Island "flogged her so badly that she was crippled and had trouble walking. Her owner was never brought to trial and it was Jenny who was hauled to court for the death of her infant, a crime she could have committed as revenge for prior ill-treatment."[109] In 1761, a nine-year-old enslaved girl in New London, Connecticut was punished with a two-foot-long horsewhip. She lived for four days before dying. A court failed to exact any punishment on the enslaver because it believed that her death was unintentional.[110]

Despite living in "societies with slaves," communities in which slavery represented a marginal part of life, enslaved women in the Northern colonies were not content with their enslavement. Although many were probably better fed and clothed than enslaved women in the South, they were far from being happy and content with their status. While New England, for example, had a much smaller slave population than Virginia, its newspapers reported almost twice as many runaways between the 1730s and 1750s. Between 1700 and 1789, over eight hundred runaway slave advertisements appeared in New England newspapers; 7 percent were fugitive women and girls.[111]

GENDERED RESISTANCE

Throughout the first half of the eighteenth century, enslaved Black men performed much of the physical labor slavery demanded. This was the case throughout the Northern and Southern colonies. The sex ratio in Virginia for imported males and females was two to one. In Surry County, Virginia, the ratio was 145 men to 100 women and in St. George Parish, South Carolina, it was 129 to 100. The uneven sex ratio made colonial slavery different for Black men and women. According to Deborah Gray White, "it was much harder for a man to find a wife than for a woman to find a husband."[112] Moreover, a significant number of men could expect to die without ever having a spouse. Those who did manage to marry often wed women living on other plantations. On colonial plantations, both married and unmarried men lived together in small groups.[113] These conditions served to foster strategies of resistance among men.

Typical acts of resistance for both women and men included feigning illness, destroying crops, stores, or tools, and sometimes attacking or killing overseers. Running away was perhaps the most ubiquitous form of resistance for women and men, as newly arrived Africans and seasoned Caribbean slaves came from turbulent, fragmented societies where flight was common. In eighteenth-century Virginia newspapers, male runaways were described as truants who usually returned voluntarily. However, there were accounts of "outlaws" who refused to give themselves up, and fugitives "who visited relatives, went to town to pass as free, or tried to escape slavery completely, either by boarding ships and leaving the colony or banding together in cooperative efforts to establish villages or hide-outs on the frontier."[114] To discourage runaways, the Virginia House of Burgesses passed "An Act Concerning Servants and Slaves" in 1705. This act defined enslavement as limited to persons of African descent and encouraged Whites to "take up runaways" with bounties paid in tobacco to persons who captured runaway slaves.[115] Similar laws on slave movement were enacted in North Carolina in 1715, which were further strengthened in 1741 with a reward system incentivizing the return of fugitive absentees, outliers, and maroons. The laws also created public gaols.[116]

Slavery was the vilest form of captivity, whose roots strengthened during the eighteenth century. Slavery meant "cultural alienation, reduction to the status of property, the ever present threat of sale, denial of the fruits of one's labor, and subjugation to the force, power, and will of another human being."[117] It mandated the strictest control of the physical and social mobility of enslaved people as the accoutrements – shackles, chains, passes, and slave patrols – demonstrate. Enslaved people everywhere were forbidden by law and common practice to leave their enslaver's property without a pass and slave patrols ensured abidance to the law and to plantation rules. Short-term runaways caused the greatest consternation to authorities in Virginia, who made truancy a capital offense in 1748. Local authorities who captured outliers had the authority to "dismember" or "kill and destroy" them. Lawmakers modified this punishment on the eve of the American Revolution in response to egalitarian thinking and also due to the financial loss to enslavers, who demanded compensation. The modified law stated that death could occur if the truant engaged in mischief and compensation for the death of a slave would not be paid by the public.[118]

South Carolina passed its first "Act to prevent Runaways" in 1683 and adopted an "Act for the Better Ordering of Slaves," modeled on the Barbadian laws, in 1691. Article IX of the Act required the sheriff to organize a party of twenty men to "pursue, apprehend and take the said runaways, either alive or dead."[119] Escaping with the intent to leave the colony was punishable by death, as was running away for the fifth time. The death penalty could be substituted by cutting off the Achilles tendon. Fugitive men who were captured were to receive "forty lashes and face branding for the first offense and be castrated if they were over sixteen and repeat offenders."[120] Fugitive women would be whipped, branded, and have their ears cut off.[121] Following the 1739 Stono Rebellion lawmakers passed a new comprehensive code which among other things "listed the generous rewards whites and free Indians could receive if they caught a runaway who had been absent six months on the south side of the Savannah River. They would receive fifty pounds for a man; twenty-five for a woman and boys over twelve; and five pounds for children provided they were alive."[122]

South Carolina and Virginia set the pattern for the rest of the slave South, where principles of restraint and confinement wove a continuous thread through the variations of regional space. Enslaved women everywhere were forbidden from leaving their enslaver's property without written consent and knowledge of managers and overseers. Authorities dictated that passes must express their names, from and to what place they were traveling, and the time granted by their enslavers. Passes were enormously powerful as they "were animated by the power of enslavers and overseers. They spoke for slave managers and acted on their behalf, directing and overseeing the movement of enslaved people."[123] Enslavers put the principles of restraint into practice in everyday life, adding to them their own plantation rules in building "geographies of containment."[124]

In South Carolina, recently imported African men were frequent runaways who often cooperated in their efforts to abscond. From the early 1750s, enslavers started advertising for the return of groups of men who shared ethnic identities. They included four "new Gambia men" who ran away in 1765; three Angolans, "all short fellows"; six other Angolans, purchased in the summer of 1771 and runaways by November, "so they cannot as yet speak English"; and four men from the "Fullah Country."[125] In some cases, those that fled were family members. Women fled with their husbands, as was the case of Satira and the unnamed wife of Prince, who fled together in December 1752. Satira's husband George had received many whippings as indicated by "marks of a whip on his back and belly."[126] Fugitive women and men found refuge in the "Black Settlements" that had formed forty miles south of Charleston and consisted of African fugitive slaves who specialized in raiding Georgia plantations across the Savannah River. Another center for escaped slaves was Thompson's Creek, located west of the Peedee River in South Carolina. Both settlements were well supplied with axes and other tools, pots, pails, and blankets.[127]

Slave rebellions and rumors of slave rebellions illuminate the networks that enslaved women created to secure their freedom. On December 7, 1774, four enslaved women conspired with "six negro fellows" to kill a master and an overseer. According to the *Georgia Gazette*, the group, who were enslaved by Captain Morris of St. Andrew Parish, killed the overseer, murdered the wife of Captain Morris, and severely wounded a carpenter and a boy who died the next day. The group then marched through the countryside and attacked neighboring plantations, seriously wounding the owners of two plantations and killing one of their sons. The authorities meted out severe retribution on the leaders of the revolt by burning them alive. The St. Andrew Parish Revolt increased White anxiety and demonstrated the tacit network of communication between enslaved women and men to plan and organize a successful revolt. In the aftermath of the revolt, residents of St. Andrews adopted a set of anti-slavery resolutions which pledged to manumit "our slaves in this colony for the most safe and equitable footing for the masters and themselves."[128]

Enslaved women and men were fully aware of the difficulty in organizing a successful revolt on a large scale and turned to other forms of resistance such as arson and poisoning. Charges of arson or poisoning brought slaves before courts, which consisted of local slave owners. On the eve of the American Revolution, an unnamed enslaved woman in Savannah, Georgia confessed to having attempted to poison her enslaver and his wife with arsenic. She was given a short trial and was condemned to be burned alive on the Savannah Common. Execution was the punishment for arson and poisoning and while most defendants were hanged, in some cases they were burned alive, and always in public to deter other slaves.[129]

***

Enslaved people were more valuable than land throughout the eighteenth and nineteenth centuries. Between 1770 and 1810, slaves as capital were worth 2–3.5 years of national income. By 1775, slave ships had carried 160,000 Africans to the Chesapeake colonies, 140,000 to the Carolinas and Georgia, and 30,000 to the Northern colonies. Twenty percent of the mainland colonies' 2.5 million inhabitants were enslaved by 1775.[130] Slave labor was essential to the North American colonies. Tobacco shipments from the Chesapeake funded trade throughout the colonies. Low country rice planters were the richest elites of the period, and commercial sectors of the Northern colonies depended heavily on carrying plantation products to Europe.

New England slave traders, who maintained a thriving shipbuilding industry, were responsible for the hundreds of thousands of Africans brought to the colonies before 1800. Slave value was roughly double the national value of housing and, in the South, "slave capital largely supplanted and surpassed landed capital."[131] By 1830, aggregated slave property was valued at $577 million, which amounted to 15 percent of the national wealth.[132]

Black women were enslaved in diverse settings. They labored in rural and urban, coastal and inland environments in the North and South; and worked on small family farms and large plantations. The intersection of enslaved women's productive and reproductive capabilities, and the exploitation of both, shaped their experience of slavery and informed their resistance. As they were denied the privileges of womanhood reserved for White women, enslaved women labored in the fields like men, did grueling work as domestic servants, and performed other tasks that consumed their daily lives. Not only were they forced to engage in taxing physical labor, but enslavers asserted their power over women by attacking their bodies and womanhood as they endured brutal, sexually sadistic punishment, while living under the constant threat of sexual assault. Enslaved women also struggled to balance their roles as laborers while being denied the privileges of motherhood. Yet motherhood and gender-based labor assignments motivated many enslaved women to escape.[133] This fact distinguished women's resistance from that of men who absconded. At the beginning of hostilities with the British, enslaved women, in greater numbers than in previous years, self-emancipated by running away to gain their freedom. One such woman was Margaret Grant.

CHAPTER 2

"A Mulatto Woman Named Margaret"

Pre-Revolutionary Fugitive Women

Run away, on Saturday ... Margaret Grant, a mulatto, about 20 years of age, 5 feet 1 or 2 inches high; had on and took with her sundry womens apparel, but has since disguised herself in a suit of men's blue cloth clothes, attending as a waiting boy on the above John Chambers. She is an artful hussy, can read and write, has been in Barbados, Antigua, the Grenades, Philadelphia ...

Virginia Gazette, April 5, 1770

ON SATURDAY MARCH 10, 1770, MARGARET GRANT, A TWENTY-year-old mulatto woman living in Baltimore, Maryland, ran away from her enslaver Mordecai Gist. Margaret's escape presented a conundrum. She was not dressed as a woman. Instead, Margaret escaped wearing a blue suit of men's clothes. She further camouflaged her identity by acting as a waiting boy to an escaped English convict servant named John Chambers. Described as an "artful hussy," Margaret had also reportedly experienced bondage in Barbados, Antigua, and the Grenadines. In addition, she was literate.[1]

Margaret's story – though scattered and fragmented – offers a constructive narrative that can be used to examine several aspects of her lived experience. First, her story does not begin at birth, but when her name first appears in the written record. Margaret's life story begins with a runaway slave advertisement that provides a window into her birth and escape. She was a mulatto, which typically referred to the offspring of an interracial relationship between persons of European and African descent. She had experienced slavery on three Caribbean islands prior to her arrival on the North American mainland. On these Caribbean islands she became familiar with marronage and petit-marronage. She was enslaved in South Carolina and Philadelphia in the late 1760s. She could read and write. She was sold to an enslaver in Baltimore in 1770, where she attempted to escape slavery. She forged an alliance with an English convict servant to facilitate her escape. She was sold again because of her attempted escape. She escaped again in 1773.[2] She was resourceful and determined to end her enslavement. Fugitive women like Margaret pursued alternative environments through a "rival geography, alternative ways of knowing and using plantation and southern [and northern] space that conflicted with planters' ideals and demands."[3] Margaret's story stands as a microcosm of the lives of other fugitive women in pre-Revolutionary America. Indeed, enslaved women such as Margaret were a dynamic force when measured against the contingencies of Revolutionary America.

The half-decade prior to the outbreak of the American Revolution can be viewed as an epic struggle between slavery and freedom. This epic struggle manifested most stridently in the border states, where the status between slave and free regularly blurred. Maryland's middle-ground position exemplifies this better than any other colony. The years prior to the outbreak of the American Revolution gave impetus to the anti-slavery movement. During the pre-Revolutionary period James Otis, a leading theoretician of the Revolution, denounced slavery, affirmed the inalienable right of enslaved women and men to freedom, and by implication, upheld their right to rebel against enslavers. In his 1772 *Oration Upon the Beauties of Liberty*, the Reverend Isaac Skillman demanded the immediate abolition of slavery and also asserted the right of the enslaved to rebel, stating such an act would conform "to the laws of nature."[4] These same years witnessed the height of Philadelphia Quaker Anthony Benezet's anti-slavery work, as well as that of Benjamin Franklin and Benjamin Rush. Historian David Brion Davis has aptly termed Benezet a "middleman of ideas." In his *Short Account of That Part of Africa Inhabited by the Negroes*, published in 1762, Benezet included a passage that denied that any sort of legal title could be held in man, and that therefore any pretended sale of a slave must be "ipso jure Void."[5] Philadelphia physician Benjamin Rush and Benjamin Franklin also joined in the colonial debate against slavery. Thomas Paine's *African Slavery in America*, published in 1775, equated slavery with murder, robbery, lewdness, and barbarity.[6] Similar sentiments were expressed by Abigail Adams in September 1774 as she told husband John, upon the discovery of a slave conspiracy in Boston, that "it always appeared a most iniquitous scheme to me to fight ourselves for what we are daily robbing and plundering from those who have as good a right to freedom as we have."[7]

There were many instances of organized protest against the institution of slavery during the pre-Revolutionary period. On November 5, 1766, Massachusetts slaves attempted to bring a trespassing suit in the local courts against their enslavers in an effort to challenge the entire legal concept of slavery. Although the court action proved futile, John Adams reported that there were many such actions brought before the court. Enslaved women and men also used petitions to the legislatures in their appeal for liberation. In April 1773, a petition was presented to the Massachusetts General Court appealing for the possibility for slaves to earn money with which to purchase their freedom. Two months later, bondwomen and bondmen presented a petition to Governor Gage of Massachusetts and the General Court to grant them freedom and land, asserting that "they have a natural right to be free."[8] Expressions of anti-slavery sentiment and petitions to the legislature were ubiquitous in the colonies. Concomitantly, running away or flight was also a prevalent action undertaken by enslaved women like Margaret Grant who were inspired by the rhetoric of the American Revolution.

***

MARGARET'S LANDSCAPE OF RESISTANCE

Until March 10, 1770, Margaret lived as a domestic enslaved woman in Baltimore, Maryland. Like other enslaved domestics in Maryland, Margaret lived in a home that included White convict servants like John Chambers, who arrived in the colony in 1764 as a result of being convicted of highway robbery in England.[9] Baltimore, established in 1729, was created as a port for shipping tobacco and grain. Local waterways were also used to harness flour milling. At the beginning of the American Revolution, it was a bustling seaport and shipbuilding center. Baltimore clippers plied the seas and trade extended to the Caribbean. By 1770, sixty vessels engaged in trade with the British Caribbean from Baltimore Harbor.[10]

The Chesapeake Bay was the most valued possession of the colony. People traded and traveled on it; they fought and frolicked on it; its inlets and estuaries were so numerous and accommodating that every planter had navigable salt water at his front door. The backwoods were the wilderness and consisted of any unsettled region removed from the navigable waters. On the eastern shore, planters had barges propelled by oars driven by enslaved Africans. In 1770, the population of Maryland consisted of 50,000 Blacks and mulattoes and 130,000 Whites.[11]

The Maryland Black Code was established in 1650 and regulated interactions between Black people in the colony and Whites. The code did not distinguish between Black and White servants until Blacks outnumbered indentured servants and convicts. It was then that the code gradually increased in detail and severity. At first enslaved men were not prohibited from bearing arms and even participated in the militia during the Native American Wars. In the end, Black assemblages were prohibited even on Sunday and if they occurred, they were broken up with the lash by constables. The penalty for a Black man or woman striking a White person was to have their ears cropped. Persons encouraging "Negro" meetings were fined 1,000 pounds of tobacco. Free Blacks or mulattoes who had immoral intercourse with a White woman would be sold as slaves and enslavers received full compensation for the death of a slave by hanging. Clergymen who married free Black men or women to Whites were fined 5,000 pounds of tobacco, while the "Negro or mulatto so marrying became a slave for life."[12]

In order to encourage the capture of runaways it was the custom in the colonies to advertise them with a reward for their apprehension, by both handbills and advertisements in the newspapers. These advertisements were the best business for the newspapers. Each advertisement was inserted six times in the *Maryland Gazette*. Over 150 runaway advertisements appeared yearly in the *Gazette*. Of these runaways, one-third were enslaved women and men, one-third were convicts, and the rest indentured servants and redemptioners.[13]

Between the 1718 Transportation Act, which established a bonded system to transport criminals to the colonies, and the American

Revolution, 50,000 convicts were transported to the American colonies, compared with 278,000 enslaved women and men. Sheriff's deputies and rangers were kept busy in pursuit of runaways; nor could anyone safely harbor runaways. There was a fine of 100 pounds of tobacco for every hour a runaway was harbored and a severe whipping for every servant or slave who harbored a runaway. Persons dealing with servants or slaves without written consent of the master were fined 2,000 pounds of tobacco. Indentured servants and convicts stealing their masters' goods were adjudged felons who would be whipped, pilloried, and fined fourfold the value of the goods in additional servitude.[14]

Maryland, like other colonies, relied on all forms of forced labor – convict, indenture, and slave. All convicts and indentured servants were considered runaways if located ten miles from their home without the permission of the master. A 1641 law made it a felony punishable by death for an indentured servant to run away. By 1750, the law had been modified to have ten days added to their term of service for each day absent. Persons who harbored runaways were fined 500 pounds of tobacco (they were whipped if unable to pay the fine) for each 24 hours and Indians who caught runaways were given a match-coat (blanket) for each runaway captured. Transported European servants without indentures were sold for a period of five years if aged 22 or older. If between 18 and 22, they were sold for a period of six years; European servants 15 to 18 years of age were sold for a period of seven years. The punishment for convicts included whippings, being placed in the pillory, and putting them to work on the chain gang on public roads, where they were chained by the ankle and waist and overseen by an overseer. The Maryland penitentiary system was not begun until 1810.[15]

Enslaved women and men faced severe penalties for running away and other infractions that violated colonial laws. In Charles County, Maryland an enslaved girl was "whipped and her ears cropped close" for perjury in 1755. In Talbot County an enslaved man's "right hand was cut off," and he was hanged and dismembered for killing the overseer. In 1747, an enslaved man was executed in Annapolis for horse stealing.[16] A 1715 Maryland law made it illegal for Black women to engage in intimate relations with White men. In other parts of the colonies, laws mandating the capture, maintenance, and punishment of runaways were passed.

Colonial slave laws were concerned with regulating the movements of the enslaved, a concern based on the "pragmatics of social control and in the ideological nexus of human beings who were both real and chattel property."[17] Many enslaved women traveled outside the confines of plantations and farms. As they moved from place to place, they likely carried with them the belief that movement was their right; freedom of movement did not crumble in the face of regulatory attempts to limit it. In fact, slave laws illuminate the extent to which enslaved women and men were moving all around the colonies. The gathering of Black people in private and public places formed an essential part of their lives in the colonies.[18]

***

Runaway advertisements provide insights into the ways slaves and servants were known and surveyed. They indicate forms of control and modes of categorization and portrayal that were common in the culture of the colonies. Such representations were as much a method of detection as a formal method of description. The language in these advertisements reveals conventional ways of looking at subalterns, providing evidence of the kind of surveillance and classification enslavers used. Some enslavers maintained detailed records on their workforce. George Washington issued orders that thorough descriptions of his slaves be kept. Such practices served a dual purpose: the maintenance of inventory lists and the identification of those who escaped. It was customary to keep these records in a slave society to recapture human beings who were liable to "steal themselves." This system of surveillance was the outcome of the commodification of labor through the ownership of enslaved bodies.[19]

The culture of surveillance in relationships of power had as its object inspecting the body of the subaltern. The distinctive features were recorded for detailed public records, which could then be circulated and used by controlling authorities as a means of identification. In the colonies, enslaved women were objects of private inspection and classification. Their appearance, character, and culture were made public through descriptions in newspaper stories produced by enslavers. Their bodies were "marked by their working lives, accidents, punishments, and personal choices of decoration. They were fashioned by individual

circumstances and personalities, providing a summation of life experience up to that point."[20] Enslavers had a powerful need to know the
bodies of those they owned.

These vivid accounts of running away offer more than just the personal details resulting from the enslaver's physical surveillance. They also
offer a window into the extent of resistance to unfree labor. Rebellion was
the most extreme form of collective resistance. The prevalence of runaway advertisements in newspapers from New York to the Carolinas
suggests that for enslaved women either short term or permanent escape
was a common form of resistance. Control of the workforce was not
absolute and some enslavers tolerated the absence of enslaved women
to allow them some freedom. But American society, particularly in the
Chesapeake colonies of Virginia and Maryland as well as in the Carolinas,
was organized to publicize and recapture those who overstepped the
boundaries of the enslaver's tolerance.[21]

Enslaved women frequently ran away prior to the American
Revolution. One such woman was Flora, who escaped from South
Carolina and had plans to reach Spanish Florida. Flora's flight was
abetted by a network of communication between Black people. She
escaped a week after a Spanish expedition, which included a free
Black man, arrived in Charleston. The unnamed free Black man
conversed with Black Charlestonians and drew the ire of Whites,
who believed he was enticing enslaved women and men to escape to
Spanish Florida. Between 1732 and 1739 slave owners in South
Carolina placed 195 advertisements in the *South Carolina Gazette* for
runaway slaves. Of the 252 escapees, 61 were women.[22] According to
Jennifer Morgan, while men tended to escape in groups, women
almost always fled alone in the years prior to Revolution.[23] Yet there
were instances when women escaped collectively. Delia and Clarinda
fled together and shouldered the risk of running with their
children.[24] Jennifer Morgan has postulated that "children could
either propel women to run or compel them to stay. Family could
act as both a pacifier and as an instigator of action."[25] Among the
concerns of women who fled were taking additional clothing into
which to change in order not only to have garments to wear but also

to subvert the descriptions enslavers placed in newspapers, to avoid capture.

BODY PRESENTATION

Fugitive slave women like Margaret wore garments similar to those of the rest of the working population. The clothing given to enslaved domestic women by their enslavers was usually made of cheap homespun material. Typically, females usually wore a petticoat and a dress or gown. In spite of the limitations imposed by their position as slaves many women took a great deal of care of – and pride in – their attire. Slave owners made precisely this point in their runaway notices.[26] When Margaret Grant ran away for the second time in 1773, she had on, for example, "a white Holland jacket, new gray half-thick upper petticoat, and white country kersey under ditto, much worn ..., osnabrig [sic] shift, lawn cap, a white linen handkerchief, or a blue spotted ditto, ..., much worn high heeled leather shoes, with white metal buckles."[27] A second fugitive woman, who had given birth eight months prior to her escape, was described by her enslaver as having "good clothes, two long gowns, and new low heeled shoes."[28]

Forty-year-old Edith ran away dressed in a "striped Virginia cloth petticoat and waistcoat." However, like many women who escaped, according to her enslaver, "it is likely she has changed her dress, as she carried sundry other cloaths [sic] with her, and a new Dutch blanket." Forty-year-old Sarah "took some clothes with her and had on good shoes tied with strings."[29] Similarly, "Free Fanny" had on "when she went away a Negro cotton petticoat and jacket, oznabrig [sic] shift, and a pair of old shoes." Her enslaver imagined "she has altered her dress." In some cases, women fled without shoes. When twenty-three-year-old Bellow fled, she had on a "blue stripped Homespun Petticoat, a blue coating waistcoat, lined with Oznabrugs [sic], a blue cotton romall [sic] handkerchief tied about her head, and a red and white cross bar'd Handkerchief round her Neck, without shoes or stockings."[30] Other advertisements, such as that for Isaac Varian's slave Molly, who was "very fond of dress," help to suggest the important role clothing played in the lives of some women.[31]

Charles Alexander Warfield, of Anne Arundel County, Maryland, offered eighty silver dollars reward for the return of the runaway slaves Dick and Lucy. Lucy had with her:

> two calico gowns, one purple and white, the other red and white, a deep blue moreens petticoat, two white country cotton do, a striped do, and jacket, and Black silk bonnet, a variety of handkerchiefs and ruffles, two lawn aprons, two Irish linen do, a pair of high heel shoes, a pair of kid gloves and a pair of silk mitts, a blue sarsanet handkerchief, trim'd with gauze, with white ribbon sew'd to it, several white linen shirts, osnabrigs for two do, hempen rolles petticoat, with several other things that she probably will exchange for others if in her power.[32]

The sheer quantity of clothes owned by Lucy is striking, as is the quality of many of the items, including the "high heel shoes," which were a recognizable insignia of gentility.[33]

West Indian fugitive women were often noted for their distinctive appearance in runaway advertisements. A thirty-seven-year-old runaway, Peggy, who was born on St. Eustatia, was described as dressing "in the style of the West Indian wenches."[34] In addition to incorporating combinations of clothes and colors in the West Indian style, women also used handkerchiefs as head coverings. Historian Charles Joyner, in his study of South Carolina, argued that "the white bandanna handkerchiefs commonly worn by women reflected continuity with African tradition and demonstrated a high degree of personal pride."[35] The handkerchiefs fulfilled a similar function in New York, where colors other than white were used: "Suke generally wore a black handkerchief; Isabella wore a striped one on her head and another on her neck."[36]

The hairstyle of women was the most important factor contributing to their distinctive appearance. These hairstyles reflected continuity with an African past as illustrated by the styles of Mary, who wore her hair "braided in several parts of her head," and Caty, who had short hair but wore "a braid of long hair tied to her head."[37]

For many Whites, the sight of a well dressed slave woman aroused suspicion that she might be involved in illicit activity. The South Carolina Negro Act, 1735 referred disapprovingly to the number of Negroes who wore "clothes much above the condition of slaves, for the procuring whereof they use sinister and evil methods."[38] According to Shane White, there is considerable evidence that enslaved women did steal clothes. On some occasions they took clothing belonging to other slaves; Cloe's enslaver surmised that "her unwillingness to return now is not less owing to the shame of seeing the negroes whom she deprived of their cloathes [sic] than the dread of correction."[39] More typically, however, enslaved women stole from Whites. Mary was imprisoned in the gaol "for stealing cloths from sundry persons." According to the jailer, "there are many clothes still in my custody, supposed to be stolen."[40]

Clothing was integral to the system of rewards and punishments that made the plantations and the institution of slavery run smoothly. South Carolina planter Henry Laurens told John Owens, his overseer, that "Sam, Scaramouche, or any other Negro who has behaved remarkably well" should be rewarded, and suggested that Owens "distinguish them in their cloathing [sic] by something better than white plains."[41] The overseer saw to it that Laurens's most trusted slaves received quantities of blue cloth and metal buttons. Enslavers also allowed enslaved women to "earn small amounts of money on the side, either through doing extra work on their own or adjoining plantations, or by raising vegetables, poultry and the like on small plots of land not needed for commercial production."[42] This happened in the South Carolina low country under the task system; however, many enslaved women throughout the mainland colonies had similar, if more limited, opportunities. In some cases, women were able to spend this extra money on clothing.[43]

Enslaved people traded clothing in an informal economy that followed the colonial elite and middle classes' concerns with consumption and fashion. Clothing was valued by bondpeople for its own sake, and since it was readily disposable, it could function as a form of currency. The Maryland enslaver of twenty-one-year-old Jacob was unable to say which clothes Jacob was wearing, as Jacob had "lost his own at cards just before he went away." Jacob's enslaver did not bother itemizing his runaway slave's clothes "as he had doubtless disposed of all but those he needed immediately." In fact, Jacob had "offered some for sale, a little before he went off, for hard money."[44]

Through an underground economy, enslaved women bought, sold, bartered, and traded items of questionable origin. Some enslaved women, as they departed, grabbed an armful of their enslavers' clothing in order to finance their flight. In some cases, these items ended up on the backs of other slaves.[45] According to historians Shane White and Graham White, opportunities to acquire additional clothing were more numerous in urban areas. In the cities, "the sphere of conspicuous display was larger, and the ability to earn extra money greater."[46] This was most notable in Charleston. In 1772, travelers to Charleston perceived "a great Difference in Appearance as well as Behavior, between the Negroes of the Country, and those in Charles Town." Although the former were "generally clad suitable to their Condition," the latter were "the very Reverse, abandonedly rude, unmannerly, insolent and shameless."[47] The aggregation of several thousand African Americans, many of whom were allowed to hire out their own time and hustle around the markets of Charleston, contributed to the often commented-on dress and demeanor of Charleston Blacks. Enslaver John Garden recognized the link between hiring out a slave in the city and her consequent control of her own appearance. When he advertised for his runaway Amey in 1773, Garden simply noted that she "had a variety of cloaths" [*sic*] as she had "been hired out in Charles-Town for some years past."[48]

In cities such as Charleston and Baltimore the connection between well dressed African American women and the sexual depredations of White men was felt to be evident. In 1744, less than a decade after the passage of the South Carolina Negro Act, the Grand Jury complained that clothing restrictions were being ignored: "it is apparent, that Negro Women in particular do not restrain themselves in their Cloathing [*sic*] as the Law requires, but dress in Apparel quite gay and beyond their Condition." The Grand Jury suggested that the source of this unseemly display was either theft or "other Practices equally vicious." Twenty-five years later, visitors to Charleston lamented that "many of the Female Slaves [are] by far more elegantly dressed, than the Generality of White Women below Affluence," which was attributed to "scandalous Intimacy" between the "Sexes of different Colours."[49] Miscegenation had its roots in the slave trade, where African women experienced sexual violence from White enslavers. Margaret, who likely was a product of this sexual violence, perhaps observed the terror of this violence through her travels to three Caribbean islands.

MARGARET AND THE ATLANTIC WORLD

The eighteenth century represented the peak period for slave imports from the Caribbean. A very large proportion of the increase in the Black population to the North American mainland resulted from extensive importations of new slaves from West Africa as well as the Caribbean. Approximately 177,000 slaves were imported between 1741 and 1770 from West Africa and the Caribbean.[50] Margaret would have spent the formative period of her youth laboring in Barbados, Antigua, and the Grenadines prior to being brought to the North American mainland. As a young child in the Caribbean she would have engaged in tasks such as weeding, grass picking, digging drains, and planting.[51] She would have also heard stories from elders within the slave communities of women and men who ran away into the limited forested areas, hid in gullies and caves scattered across the islands, and formed temporarily the semblance of a petit marronage rebel culture, which involved short-term flight for days or weeks.[52]

Marronage was common in New World slave societies. Although the landscape of eighteenth-century Barbados, Antigua, and the Grenadines did not permit maroon development on a large scale, petit marronage was common. Running away consisted largely of "individual responses to situations of impending threat or great tension, which provided at best a few months' respite from the rigors of the system, although some slaves stayed at large for a number of years."[53] According to William Dickson, secretary to the governor of Barbados and a contemporary observer of slave life, only death was seen as worse than being transported from the island of Barbados.[54] Whether Margaret left Barbados with her enslaver or was sold is not known. The fact that Margaret had been enslaved on three islands may be an indication that she was viewed by her enslavers as recalcitrant and troublesome.

In 1765, Margaret was transported by a vessel bound for Charleston, South Carolina. As an enslaved woman in South Carolina, Margaret would have experienced the vicissitudes of an inhumane system. During the 1760s, Charleston was an urban city and the center of the rice and slave trade in the Lower South. Enslavers traveled long distances to buy bondmen and bondwomen in the city of Charleston. Margaret would have also observed Charleston's free Black community, which had established close relationships with Whites. Thomas Cole, Sr. of Charleston, for example, was a free mulatto bricklayer. At his request, two prominent White Charlestonians purchased Cole's wife and two children and then transferred the family to Cole, who paid for them the purchase price with interest.[55]

In Charleston, Margaret would have observed free Blacks claiming other bondmen and bondwomen as their property. Sabinah, a free Black woman in Charleston, owned three slaves and used them as collateral to secure a loan. According to the available data in 1790, 59 of the 586 free Blacks residing in South Carolina owned 357 enslaved men and women.[56] Yet, the historical records are silent regarding how long Margaret lived in South Carolina or where she resided. We do know, however, that she was sold again, and by 1767 was living in Philadelphia.[57] By 1765, 100 slaves were imported annually to Philadelphia from the West Indies and South Carolina.[58]

Like other Mid-Atlantic colonies, Pennsylvania prospered due to slave labor, despite having relatively few slaves. To be an enslaved woman in early Pennsylvania and other British colonies, one had "to work hard, be flexible, and think shrewdly."[59] African American women generally spent most of their lives as domestics since innkeepers and widows of Philadelphia needed help with housekeeping and childcare duties and thus preferred slave women to men.[60] Margaret would have been among the women laboring in White households, caring for young children, and perhaps dreaming one day of her freedom from bondage. By the eve of the American Revolution, slavery had expanded in Pennsylvania. By 1770, there were 6,000 slaves living in Pennsylvania.[61]

From Philadelphia, Margaret was sold to Mordecai Gist in Baltimore, a merchant who later became a general in command of the 2nd Maryland Brigade during the Revolutionary War.[62] Enslavement in Baltimore provided spaces for Margaret to claim her freedom. Initially, Baltimore was less a place where goods were made than a conduit through which goods made elsewhere moved. In the eighteenth-century, as Maryland tobacco sailed out of the Chesapeake Bay, other ships arrived carrying sugar from St. Kitts, linens from England, indentured servants from Germany, and enslaved men, women, and children from West Africa and the

Caribbean. With a population of 6,000 by the time of the American Revolution, Baltimore had developed into a city whose physical infrastructure of wharves, streets, and canals made it a hub of the Chesapeake economy.[63] The shipping docks in particular provided spaces for runaway indentured servants like John Chambers, who absconded with Margaret, to board vessels headed north to Philadelphia and other Northern cities.

Based on evidentiary information drawn from slave advertisements, a majority of women who escaped from urban spaces were engaged in domestic labor. Many of the advertisements praised the domestic skills of enslaved women. Jasper Farmer boasted that his fifty-year-old slave was an "excellent cook." A notice in the *Brunswick Gazette* noted that a twenty-year-old enslaved woman was "well calculated for doing the business of the kitchen." Fugitive women's skills as cooks could be leveraged to secure work as domestics in freedom. In non-urban spaces, women were escaping both domestic labor and agricultural labor. In outlying areas of cities, enslavers tasked women and girls with tending to fields and in the Southern colonies producing labor-intensive crops such as rice and tobacco.[64] In Northern and Mid-Atlantic cities, slavery depended upon Black women not for their ability to reproduce but for the most arduous kinds of domestic work. Preparing meals, cleaning, and sewing were taxing in the eighteenth-century. "Without the luxuries of running water or electricity, the work required lifting heavy buckets of water and cooking in hot kitchens or freezing sheds. For most Black women who labored as domestic slaves, their bodies were broken and their time was not their own."[65]

Much of the evidence about naming patterns for bondwomen points toward an overall process of acculturation and anglicization. When Margaret acquired the surname "Grant" is not known. The use of the surname, however, is indicative of the fact that Margaret sought to portray a sense of dignity that may have been viewed as inappropriate to her servile status. Margaret's use of a surname represented a sign of freedom. In America's patrilineal culture, surnames flowed from paternity and from exclusive marriage, which were both formally denied to slaves. Out of 150 advertisements for runaway enslaved women from 1770 to 1775, only nine appear with a surname. It should be noted, however, that many enslaved people used surnames without their enslaver's knowledge.[66]

The voices of enslaved women do not always exist where we would like. We gain momentary access to their bondage through behaviors, bodies, and other characteristics captured in newspapers.[67] For example, Kate, a thirty-year-old woman, ran away from her enslaver, who lived near Georgetown on the Potomac. She went to South River about thirty miles away, where she had formerly lived. Friends concealed her there. Her enslaver feared that since "she had been a great Rambler, and is well known in Calvert and Anne Arundel Counties, besides other parts of the Country," Kate would "indulge herself a little visiting her old Acquaintances, but spend most of her time with her husband at West River."[68] Twenty of 233 Maryland runaways (9 percent) left masters to join their spouses. Sue and her child Jem, eighteen months old, ran away from Allen's Freshes to Port Tobacco, Charles County, a distance of about ten miles, "to go and see her husband."[69] Enslaved women who wanted to run away would find "kinfolk, friends of kinfolk, or kinfolk of friends" along their route who willingly would harbor them for a while. As kinship and friendship networks grew larger, the proportion of runaways in Maryland who were harbored by others for significant periods of time increased.[70] Margaret and John may have been aided by such a network.

MARGARET AND JOHN'S ESCAPE

Historical details illuminating whether Margaret received assistance from friends in planning her escape are unrecorded. However, the fact that she concealed her identity by dressing as a waiting boy to John Chambers reveals that she had assistance from Chambers and possibly others. Margaret was well known in "Baltimore town," as the advertisement for her return revealed. John Chambers, who absconded with several pieces of Gist's clothing, including "nine ruffled shirts, a brown bush wig, a pair of single channel boots, and a blue cloth great coat,"[71] could have provided the men's suit that Margaret wore during their escape; or perhaps Margaret, who had access to her enslaver's clothes as a domestic enslaved woman, took the blue suit on her own. However Margaret secured the clothing, Chambers sought to ensure their flight would be successful by also stealing cash worth 150 pounds. In colonial Baltimore, where the majority of people were of Euro-American ancestry, white skin offered no escape from drudgery. As Seth Rockman states, "even in a city with slavery, low end jobs were not easily coded Black or white."[72]

Interracial relationships were not uncommon in colonial Maryland. In Prince George's County Court, Catherine Graham, an indentured servant, admitted on June 28, 1732 that she had a child by "Negro or Mallatto Nasy." The court sold her six-week-old daughter to be bound out until the age of thirty-one. Three years later, on March 25, 1735, Catherine again admitted in court that she had an illegitimate child by "Negro Taff." She was ordered to serve her master for an additional seven years; her child was bound out until the age of thirty-one and Taff was ordered whipped. In November 1737, the court ruled that Catherine's son, Moses, "Begotten by a Negro," be sold into servitude. A year later, on November 28, 1738, Catherine confessed she had a child by Yarrow, a "Negro" slave. The court sold her and her four-year-old son Dick into servitude. In March 1737 and October 1738, Catherine confessed to having two illegitimate children: Ann (born February 28, 1737) and Charles (born October 1738). On August 25, 1747, the court sold Catherine Graham to the sheriff, Osborn Sprigg, to serve twenty-eight years as punishment for committing five counts of interracial fornication and bastardy.[73]

Perhaps John Chambers and Margaret Grant developed a relationship that was in part based on their mutual status as unfree labor. As Marisa Fuentes observes, "discussions of Black women, free or enslaved, using White men as an avenue to freedom often erase the reality of coercion, violence and the complicated positions Black women were forced to inhabit in this system of domination."[74] While this observation is true, the existence of Black women who may have entered relationships with White convicts or indentured servants, who were also unfree, requires further interrogation of what it means to use White men who share a mutual status as unfree labor. What is at stake in these interpretations of female slavery is teasing out how discourses of "resistance," "sexual power," and "will" shape our understanding. Margaret's inner self, her fears and confidences, remain difficult to retrieve using documents produced within a slave society limited by capitalist and elite perspectives.[75] Gist's description of Margaret as "an artful hussy [who] can read and write" informs us that she was a shrewd and cunning woman who knew the power of being literate, but who may have also used John Chambers to escape bondage.[76] Gist's description also implies that Margaret would use her skills to transform herself into a free woman once she and John Chambers reached their destination.

Alliances with White servants began as soon as the first Africans arrived in Jamestown, Virginia in the seventeenth century. In addition to Margaret, "a lusty negro woman named Rhoad," who changed her name to Nancy Bannaker, fled with an Irish servant on April 15, 1775, four days before the first shots of the American Revolution were fired at Lexington and Concord. Her enslaver's sexualization of her body in the advertisement speaks to the power that is present in the making of archival fragments at Nancy's historical moment. Integral to debates on "enslaved agency" and resistance in contemporary scholarship on slavery are the ways in which agency has been gendered and sexualized concerning enslaved women and women of color in slave societies and their sexual relations with White men.[77]

For Margaret and John, Baltimore's shipping industry would provide the clearest avenue for escape. As stevedores and day laborers loaded barrels of flour, tobacco, whiskey, salt fish, and butter onto schooners, Margaret and John could have found passage on a vessel commandeered by a Baltimore waterman headed to Philadelphia or New York. In addition to carrying American produce abroad, Baltimore ships specialized in re-export, carrying trade commodities like sugar and coffee from the Caribbean and South American colonies to various European nations and other parts of the British colonies.[78]

The historical record closes on John and Margaret's escape but reopens in Margaret's case in 1773. While it may be nearly impossible to string together events in a neat narrative of what happened to John Chambers and Margaret Grant after their escape, Margaret was caught and sold to George Ashman sometime between 1770 and 1771.[79] As was the case with most runaways, they were either physically punished for their behavior or sold away. For twenty-year-old Margaret, this would be one of several sales in her young life. Margaret would spend nearly three years laboring as a domestic for George Ashman in Baltimore County. She cooked meals, sewed clothes, washed and ironed clothes very well according to Ashman. When permitted, Margaret also traveled from Ashman's residence near the Gun Powder meeting house to Baltimore to visit with friends with whom she had developed long-standing relationships. On April 21, 1773, Margaret decided she would not return to Ashman's residence.[80] At the age of 23, now pregnant, she made the decision that her days of toiling for Ashman would end and that her child would be born free. Whether Ashman or someone else was the father of Margaret's baby is not known. What is known is that slavery was a system that depended upon the systematic sexual exploitation of enslaved women. The core experiences of women like Margaret were shaped by sexual violence and impossible choices, which are not necessarily fully elucidated by progressive notions of agency.[81]

Margaret's actions indicate that she knew her "soul value." According to historian Daina Ramey Berry, "soul value" refers to "an intangible marker that defied monetization yet spoke to the spirit and soul" of who she was as a human being. Soul value "represented the self-worth of enslaved people." For some, like Margaret, this meant that she would not comply with slavery.[82] The escape of Margaret and other bondwomen during the Revolutionary Era constituted a major refutation of slavery. The American Revolution, which inspired enslaved and free African Americans to claim greater rights for themselves, created both psychological and physical freedom for those who "pretended to be free" or who simply fled to create their own liberty.[83] Women ran away more frequently during the Revolutionary Era than at any time before or after the war due to the breakdown of oversight and state authority. In addition to Margaret, Sarah, a pregnant woman who changed her name to Rachel, ran away with her six-year-old son, Bob. Rachel's husband had joined the British Army and she intended to "pass herself as a free woman."[84]

Roughly half a million Black people lived in America on the eve of the war, representing 20 percent of the population, but only 5 percent of them were free. While the rise of hostilities affected some Black women's lives nominally, others played key roles in the Patriot protests against the British Crown, voluntarily or not. For example, during the "homespun" campaign owners forced enslaved women in port cities to spin and weave more cloth following a boycott of imported goods from Britain. Enslaved women used the rhetoric of the Revolution to boost their own arguments for freedom. Enlightenment ideas of liberty influenced Phillis Wheatley, an urban enslaved woman, who published poems supporting the Patriot cause and freedom for all slaves.[85] Throughout the American Revolution, Wheatley became actively engaged in the politics of freedom and slavery. In her poem to George Washington, written in 1775 and read mistakenly as pure flattery, she gently chides him for his order excluding African Americans, including those who had fought in the initial revolutionary battles of Bunker Hill, Lexington, and Concord, from the Continental Army:

> Shall I to Washington their praise recite?
> Enough thou knows't them in the fields of fight.
> Thee, first in place and honours, – we demand
> The grace and glory of thy martial band.[86]

Women who fled slavery during the Revolutionary War chose to find safe haven in the English "Black town" located in lower New York City. These Black "Loyalists" came from New Jersey, Virginia, Maryland, Pennsylvania, and Delaware. They included women and children and were among the first and largest recorded examples of a freedom-seeking Black migration.[87] Whether Margaret found refuge in lower New York City is not known. Direct evidence of where Margaret may have settled is veiled. However, her enslaver warned that she would attempt to leave Baltimore on one of the many ships that docked in the city, an avenue of escape she had tried once before.[88] Having lived in the city of Philadelphia previously, she would have found women with similar ambitions had she reached the city. During the 1770s and 1780s, more than 160 slaves escaped slavery in Philadelphia. While most runaways were men, some women escaped, seeking to reunite with husbands in New England and fleeing with children in tow.[89]

The Somerset Case (1772) in London also inspired enslaved women to run away. As a literate woman, Margaret would have read about the Somerset Case or heard talk of the case as she visited friends in Baltimore. It involved an eight-year-old African, James Somerset, who was sold into slavery in Virginia and purchased by Charles Stewart. Stewart traveled to Britain with James, his manservant, for business. When it was time to leave, James ran away and refused to return to America. Stewart had Somerset arrested and placed aboard the vessel the *Ann and Mary* to be transported to Jamaica and sold for his intransigence. Granville Sharp heard about the case from London's Black community and pleaded with Lord Mansfield, chief justice of the King's Bench (the highest common law court in Britain), to issue a writ of habeas corpus to prevent Somerset from being transported. Mansfield ruled that Somerset be discharged from slavery since there was no common law in England that provided for the enslavement of Africans for life as long as they remained in Britain and "no statute compelled him to return to America."[90] The Somerset decision and the arguments it spawned were promptly disseminated in the colonies. The *Virginia Gazette* and *Maryland Gazette*'s London correspondents followed the argument closely, and the papers published varying versions of Mansfield's opinion.[91]

In the Fall of 1773, the *Virginia Gazette* reported a Williamsburg couple attempted to run away in hopes of reaching Britain, "a notion now too prevalent among the Negroes, greatly to the vexation and prejudice of their masters."[92] South Carolina newspapers carried advertisements for runaway slaves who were inspired by Lord Mansfield. Among those who took flight was Bacchus, who stole money from his enslaver as back pay, changed his name to John Christian, and was expected to get on board a vessel headed for Great Britain "from the knowledge he has of the late Determination in the Somerset Case." Another notice for a runaway slave couple mentioned that they too "were on their way to Britain where they imagine they will be free."[93]

Prior to the Somerset Case, Jenny Slew of Salem, Massachusetts sued for her freedom in 1765. Slew, who was a free Black woman, had been kidnapped from her home in 1762 and enslaved by John Whipple. Harnessing her courage, Slew went to a local court with an appeal to restore what she claimed was her "birthright freedom." Slew won her case, and according to John Adams there were many similar cases brought before the courts. These freedom suits were invariably heard in the small country towns by non-slaveholders who, according to Adams, "never determined a Negro to be a slave."[94] In Boston, however, where many jurors owned slaves, enslaved women petitioned the legislature for their freedom.[95]

The majority of enslaved women did not wait for local courts to declare them free or send petitions to legislatures arguing their case for freedom. They took flight from plantations, towns, and cities. As Gary Nash posits, "flight *from* slavery" with the hope of passing as free women and "flight *toward* a force prepared to guarantee freedom" to those on the run were two strategies that women like Margaret pursued. Six months prior to the issuance of Lord Dunmore's Proclamation in November 1775, Dunmore wrote to the secretary of state in London setting out his plan to "arm all of my own Negroes, and receive all others that will come to me whom I shall declare free."[96] The official enunciation of Dunmore's Proclamation inspired both men and women to flee. Among the first to flee to Dunmore were eight of twenty-seven slaves of Peyton Randolph, the speaker of Virginia's House of Burgesses and one of Virginia's delegates to the Continental Congress. Three of the eight freedom fighters from Randolph's estate were women.[97] The flight of Randolph's slaves set the pattern that would continue over the next seven years: one-third of those fleeing to the British were women. In a list of eighty-seven slaves who fled to Dunmore, "twenty-one were women, twenty-three were girls under the age of sixteen, sixteen were men, and twenty-seven were boys under sixteen."[98] A majority fled as families, with one slave as old as sixty and six others infants.[99] Virtually no enslaved women were prepared to abandon their children to facilitate their own escape.

An unknown number of fugitive women also found refuge in the back-country and the coastal rivers and swamps, if they could not make it to the lines of the British. For many this informal freedom would prove to be temporary and tenuous. In Georgia, there had been runaway or maroon communities prior to the war that greatly alarmed Whites in the state. At least one of these maroon communities located near Savannah survived into the mid-1780s, supporting itself by growing its own foodstuffs and raiding outlying plantations. This community, which contained "a number of women," was organized on strict military lines under the leadership of two fugitive men, Lewis and Sharper (also known as Captain Cudjoe). In this maroon community, the "women planted rice" and "stayed in Camp." Whites attacked the community in 1787, killing Captain Cudjoe and capturing Lewis, who was later sentenced to death. The women were "ordered ... in the Canes" and did not take part in the fighting that ensued. Several, however, remained at large in the aftermath of the attack.[100]

Enslaved women formed significant bonds with one another in maroon communities, but they also forged bonds in planning escapes. Twenty-five-year-old Milly and twenty-three-year-old Betty lived on separate farms and escaped together in April 1774. Both women were captured and committed to the gaol in Prince George County, Virginia. The published advertisements for runaways provide evidence of the courage, resourcefulness, and determination displayed by Black women. Fugitives adopted different names and, whenever possible, changed their clothing in the hope of thereby avoiding detection. If challenged, they might try to pass as free Black women. Even when identified as runaways, some women refused to give up without a struggle. They may not have had the physical strength to overpower their captors but, if the opportunity presented itself, they seized the opportunity to escape. Sometimes this meant taking flight again in leg irons or handcuffs.[101] On at least one occasion some female runaways joined with male slaves in breaking out of the gaol.[102]

Margaret's flight coincided with increased debate on whether to end the slave trade to the colonies. This debate increased anti-slavery sentiment, particularly in Braintree, Massachusetts, which adopted a resolution in 1774 to abstain from the slave trade and to boycott all who engaged in it. On March 8, 1774, the Massachusetts Assembly enacted a law prohibiting the importation of African slaves. Within a year of this resolution, other colonies such as Rhode Island and Connecticut banned the trade. Rhode Island's act stipulated that "any Negro or mulatto brought into the colony would immediately become free."[103] In the Middle colonies of Pennsylvania and New Jersey the slave trade was on the decline before the war officially began. Pennsylvania passed a prohibitive tax in February 1773, imposing a duty of twenty pounds on every imported slave. A similar tax was considered in New Jersey; however, the New Jersey Council rejected the idea. In the Southern colonies, Virginia and North Carolina banned the trade in 1774 with Georgia following suit in 1775. The decision to ban the trade in the Southern colonies was not motivated by humanitarian concerns but rather was a part of the non-importation agreement against the

British Parliament. To this end, the Continental Congress prohibited the slave trade after December 1, 1774.[104]

***

The pre-Revolutionary years witnessed and facilitated not organized rebellion but the amplification of what was undoubtedly the most common expression of Black discontent and despair: running away. Although by no means indicative of the total number of runaways, newspaper advertisements provide the best source of information about this mode of enslaved women's behavior. It is conceivable that in 1775, mainly because of wartime dislocations and separations, more women than before the Revolution were actually running away. Much can be gleaned by examining the life of Margaret Grant, who came to maturity in pre-Revolutionary America. Her life story is embodied in runaway slave advertisements. On the eve of the American Revolution, thousands of enslaved women like Margaret absconded from their enslavers in search of freedom. As they forged expanded and alternative paths to self-liberation before, during, and after the Revolutionary period, enslaved women appropriated the tools of the master, which included his dress, to dismantle their enslavement. Margaret's escape generates new meaning and new tensions on fugitivity. Her escape represents a polycentric narrative of freedom in that she initiated escape multiple times. Although fragmented and representing lives that can never be fully recovered, close readings of runaway slave advertisements allow us to reconstruct these women's histories. Tracing the movement of enslaved women in, out of, and through spaces in colonial America and the Atlantic world provides an unmediated microcosm of Black female agency.

CHAPTER 3

"A Well Dressed Woman Named Jenny"

Revolutionary Black Women, 1776–1781

Runaway last September, from the subscriber, living upon Monk's Neck, about 13 miles above the town of Petersburg, a Virginia born negro wench named Jenny, who carried with her a child named Winney. The wench was very big with child when she went away, is about 25 years old, near 5 feet 2 inches high, and of a yellow complexion. She carried with her a green shalloon gown, a pale blue durants quilt much worn, a white Virginia cloth cotton coat and waistcoat, coat and waistcoat striped with copperas and blue, and another suit checked with blue. The child is between two and three years old, is of a yellower complexion than its mother, and clothed like her. As she generally goes well dressed, I expect she will alter her name and the child's, and will endeavor to pass as a free woman . . .

Purdie's *Virginia Gazette*, April 11, 1777

BY SEPTEMBER 1776, JENNY, A "WELL DRESSED" TWENTY-FIVE-YEAR-old enslaved woman who lived on a farm on Monk's Neck, thirteen miles from Petersburg, Virginia, was eight months pregnant. Over the past eight months, she had surely overheard her enslaver, Allen Freeman, discussing the ongoing crisis with Great Britain. She had heard of Dunmore's Proclamation through the enslaved internal communication network. She knew that if she were to reach the lines of the British Army, both she and her two-year-old daughter Winney could claim their freedom from bondage.[1] Allen Freeman would go on to serve in the Revolutionary War in defense of American independence. Throughout the early months of 1776, Virginians were feeling the impact of Dunmore's Proclamation. Enslaved men, women, and children were leaving farms and plantations to catch the breath of freedom. Monk's Neck, located in Dinwiddie County, where the nation's first free Black eighteenth-century rural physician Dr. Thomas Stewart resided, included several farms where tobacco, cereals, and grains were produced.[2] Jenny spent months planning her escape, intending to leave with her daughter at night to avoid detection. They would travel the road that hundreds of other fugitives walked to reach Richmond, the nearest city, to pass as free persons, in hopes of reaching a British vessel. She took several garments with her in preparation for the fall weather, which included "a green shalloon gown, a pale blue durants quilt ..., a white Virginia cloth cotton coat and waistcoat, [a] coat and waistcoat striped with copperas and blue, and another suit checked with blue." (Figure 3.1.) Her enslaver noted that her daughter is "cloathed [*sic*] like her and she generally goes well dressed."[3] At the time Allen Freeman placed the advertisement for Jenny on April 11, 1777, she had been a fugitive for seven months.

None of Jenny's probable movements, the impetus of her flight, or her experience in fugitivity, are recorded in the existing archives. Still, it is certain that the publicity and intention of the runaway ad challenged her concealment and freedom. If fugitivity is "the artful escape of objectification" (racial, commodified, legal/political), Jenny's disappearance was a defiant act against these constraints.[4] Fugitive women "subverted the very paradigm of enslavement – immobility, disembodiment, violation – and created an alternative self" by pursuing a rival geography.[5] The discourse of runaway advertisements remained an ever-looming and corporeal threat for the absconding slave. According to Marisa Fuentes, "this discursive power combined with the legal right of whites to interrogate, inspect, probe, and detain any Black suspect made fugitivity both an insecure and defiant status."[6] In Virginia, laws enacted in 1723 and 1748 prescribed punishment by dismemberment for attempts at escape. Consequently, fugitivity embodied both a critique of slavery and the precarity of the fugitive condition.[7] Yet, the Revolutionary War bolstered the independence of Black women, gave them increased access to their families with whom they fled, and greater autonomy in their daily lives once they reached safe havens.

3.1 Jenny, "a yellow Negro Girl," wears a chintz gown "with a large flower and yellow stripes," a pink coloured moreen petticoat, a "new black peeling bonnet," under "a chip hat trimmed with gauze and feathers," a white apron, and a "pair of blue worsted shoes with white heels"; she carries a piece of "new stamped linen, a purple flower and stripe ... She is very fond of dress ... she has gone either to New York or Baltimore." *New York Journal*, December 17, 1782. Illustration by Eric H. Schnitzer.

LANDSCAPES OF FREEDOM

At the time Thomas Jefferson penned the majestic words enshrined in the Declaration of Independence that "all men are created equal" and have a right to "life, liberty, and the pursuit of happiness," Samuel Hopkins in 1776 published *A Dialogue Concerning the Slavery of the Africans*, which became a leading anti-slavery tract of the Revolution. In this tract, Hopkins summed up the argument against slavery and anticipated later themes of American abolitionism. Hopkins equated the moral evil of slavery with the slave trade, which he classified as sin by emphasizing the link between slavery and racism, and called on the Continental Congress to abolish slavery throughout the United States.[8] Like Hopkins, many colonists had already begun exploring the relationship between slavery and the principles underpinning the American cause. In Massachusetts, James Otis, Nathaniel Appleton, the Reverend Samuel Webster, and John Allen condemned slavery's opposition to "the law of nature." Their views were echoed by Thomas Paine and Benjamin Rush in Pennsylvania, and were cheered on by English friends of the American cause, including Granville Sharp and Thomas Day. Enslaved women and men in Boston participated in this debate. Led by Sambo Freeman, a group of them petitioned the General Court for emancipation, arguing that "the efforts made by the Legislature of this province in their last sessions to free themselves from Slavery gave us, who are in that deplorable state, a high degree of satisfaction."[9] Another group of Boston Blacks reminded the Massachusetts legislators that "every principle from which America has acted in the course of her unhappy difficulties with Great Britain, pleads stronger than a thousand arguments in favour [sic] of your petitioners."[10]

In the spring of 1775, enslaved African Americans in Bristol and Worcester, Massachusetts, petitioned the Committee of Correspondence of Worcester to aid them in obtaining freedom. As a result of this petition, a convention was held in Worcester on June 14, 1775 at which it was resolved by the White residents that "we abhor the enslaving of any of the human race, and particularly that of the Negroes in this country, and that whenever there shall be a door opened, or opportunity present for anything to be done towards emancipation of the Negroes, we will use our influence and endeavor that such a thing may be brought about."[11] Petitions for freedom were ubiquitous in Massachusetts Bay Colony. In 1773 and 1774, enslaved women and men presented five petitions to the Massachusetts legislature and had them printed in newspapers and pamphlets. Drawing inspiration from the political ideology of the Revolutionary crisis, they made similar arguments in favor of their own natural rights. African Americans also brought freedom suits to court.

Reverend Jeremy Belknap of Boston noted the rising number of freedom suits brought by Massachusetts Blacks during the 1770s. In the two decades before 1783, thirty Black men and women sued their enslavers for their freedom in the Massachusetts courts, with only one unfavorable decision.[12]

In Connecticut, enslaved women and men petitioned the state legislature for their liberty, claiming that they were not only oppressed in their own burdens, but they contemplated with horror "the miserable Condition of Our Children, who are training up, and kept in Preparation, for a like State of Bondage and Servitude."[13] A few Connecticut petitions came from African Americans whose enslavers fled with the British. The slave Pomp sent a request in October 1779 to the legislature praying that the state would emancipate him after his enslaver Jeremiah Leaming voluntarily joined the British troops in Norwalk. Although Pomp, who was married to a free Black woman, ran away, he was still considered a part of the estate of Leaming under Connecticut law.[14] A month later, eight bondwomen and bondmen in Salem, Connecticut, enslaved by William Browne, petitioned the General Assembly for their freedom. Among them were Prue and her three children, who stated "that our good mistress, the free State of Connecticut, engaged in a war with tyranny, will not sell good honest Whigs and friends of freedom and independence, as we are."[15] Similarly an enslaved woman, Belinda Sutton, petitioned the Assembly stating that although she had been serving her enslaver for more than forty years, her labors had not brought her any comfort or security. She begged for freedom for herself and her "poor daughter."[16] Belinda was the mother of two children, Joseph and Prine. She recognized the vulnerable condition of enslaved women and girls by pleading for the freedom of her daughter. Belinda's enslaver, John Royall, willed her to his daughter "in case [Belinda] does not choose her freedom." Royall fled the United States for England during the Revolution, where he died in 1781. In a codicil to his will, John Royall granted Belinda and her children their freedom and a pension of thirty pounds for three years.[17]

The Black population of New England was relatively small, numbering 16,034 persons on the eve of the American Revolution.[18] Between 1774 and 1790, Connecticut's Black population decreased by 1,045 or

16.1 percent.[19] The reduction in population was caused not only by death through war and combat service, but also by Loyalist enslavers fleeing with their bondmen and bondwomen; however, some of the enslaved achieved self-emancipation.[20] Between 1700 and 1789, over 800 runaway slave notices appeared in New England newspapers.[21] A sample of sixty-two runaway advertisements from the New England region during the Revolutionary Era reveals that these fugitives came from thirty-seven towns. Massachusetts, with a Black population of 5,249 out of 349,094 in 1776, had the largest number of fugitives, at thirty-two. Half of these runaways came from Boston, which had a Black population of 682 in 1776. Connecticut, where eighteen runaways escaped from eleven towns, ranked second. In 1774, with 6,464 persons, Connecticut had the largest African American population in New England. The remaining fugitives came from New Hampshire and Rhode Island.[22] Of the sixty-two fugitives mentioned in these advertisements, eight were women or girls, while fifty-four were men or boys.[23] These figures are not surprising, given the fact that male slaves generally outnumbered females in New England. Furthermore, as domestics, Black women would be under close surveillance of housewives and hence had fewer opportunities to escape than did men, whose work frequently kept them outdoors.[24] Yet, enslaved women took advantage of every opportunity to escape bondage.

In the New England region, 1776 was a watershed year for escapees. As free Black men were welcomed to serve in the Patriot Army in 1776 following General George Washington's reversal of an earlier policy which prevented their enlistment, enslaved women made plans for their own declaration of independence from bondage.[25] Sarah Seheter, a Boston fugitive in 1776, had been in servitude in both Providence, Rhode Island, and Concord, Massachusetts. She had labored as a cook, laundress, and maid in the homes of prominent New England families. She was also skilled in the domestic arts of spinning, knitting, and weaving.[26] Drawing inspiration from the revolutionary climate which permeated Boston in 1775–1776, Sarah made a daring run for freedom. The Siege of Boston that lasted from April 19, 1775 until March 17, 1776 marked the opening phase of the Revolutionary War and proved an opportune time for enslaved women like Sarah to escape. Following the Battles of Lexington and Concord, on April 19, 1775, militia units in Massachusetts blocked land access to Boston. In the Battle of Bunker Hill, more than one hundred African Americans and Native Americans fought for American freedom.[27] Among the Black men were Silas Burdoo, who claimed in his pension application that "he had chased the British back to Boston and promptly reenlisted in May 1775, arriving in Charles Town common while the Battle of Bunker Hill was raging."[28]

As a British-occupied city, Boston and the surrounding area became the center of military action for ten months until the Continental Army, led by George Washington, forced the British to evacuate to Halifax, Nova Scotia.[29] Three-quarters of Massachusetts' Black population of 2,700 lived in the colony's three coastal counties – Essex, Suffolk, and Middlesex – in large measure due to the importance of slave imports to colonial shipping.[30] Among the enslaved women who escaped in the early months of the Siege of Boston was Flora, who carried her "small child" with her. Flora was accompanied by two enslaved men, Exeter and Ireland, both of whom carried guns and were "poorly dressed."[31] Their enslaver, William Gilliland, was a respected attorney in Essex County, Massachusetts, located thirty miles from Boston. Essex – which included Salem, Ipswich, Newbury, and Gloucester – maintained a thriving trade, shipbuilding, fishing, and whaling economy. In 1776, there were 1,049 African Americans in Essex, forming the second largest Black population in Massachusetts.[32] The Black population of both Essex and Suffolk counties decreased during the Revolutionary period. Suffolk County – which included the towns of Boston, Dorchester, Roxbury, and Braintree – experienced the steepest decline. In 1764, there were 1,351 African Americans, but their number declined to 682 by 1776.[33] This reduction was due to the flight of African Americans to the British Army in Boston.[34] Among those fleeing was twenty-four-year-old Nell, who fled on Saturday evening March 16, 1776. Like other women who fled, Nell took with her an assortment of clothes, which included four gowns, "a light blue quilted coat, a red coak, and a blue ridinghood [sic]" into which to change.[35] Coeval with Nell's flight, John Hancock, president of the Continental Congress, issued a proclamation on March 16, 1776 calling for a day of "humiliation, fasting, and prayer" to protect the colonies' freedom from British tyranny.[36] This irony would not have been lost on Nell, who recognized that this moment provided the most opportune time for her to escape, as the British Army began retreating from Boston on Sunday, March 17, 1776. Nell would have been among the fugitive slaves who fled Boston seeking refuge in other British-controlled environs. On Monday, March 18, 1776, General George Washington visited Boston and found that the city had "suffered greatly" but was not in as "bad a state" as he had expected.[37] Washington allowed British General Howe to sail away peacefully in exchange for Howe's pledge not to burn the city of Boston.[38]

Akin to slaves from Massachusetts, in 1776, those enslaved in Connecticut fled to British vessels in significant numbers. Three fugitives escaped to British vessels in New Haven and a number of Newport slaves also took refuge with the British fleet. Several fugitives from Colchester, Connecticut, joined the British Army in hopes of gaining freedom. Among those escaping was Nane, a twenty-seven-year-old woman who wore "a blue Callimanco Gown [sic]," and sixteen-year-old Cloe who had scars on her nose and ear, and burns on her foot.[39] Several fugitives were later recaptured by Admiral Esek Hopkins, commander of the Continental Navy. Hopkins arrived in New London, Connecticut, on April 8, 1776 after launching the Raid of Nassau, an attack on the British colony in the Bahamas on March 3, 1776.[40]

In other parts of the New England region women and girls also found opportunities to escape. Zil, a fifteen-year-old Rhode Island fugitive, seems never to have considered herself a slave, for her enslaver complained that "she pretends she is free."[41] Likewise, Cloe evidently evinced considerable interest in her personal attire for, according to her enslaver, she was generally "well dressed."[42] Young enslaved girls often formed alliances with White indentured servants. Ann Gorman, a White indentured servant girl in Portsmouth, Rhode Island, ran away in July 1773 and was seen in the company of an enslaved girl who ran away at the same time.[43] In other cases, enslavers commented on the past and present habits of young girls who escaped. Such was the case of Silvia, a seventeen-year-old enslaved girl who labored as a domestic in Providence, Rhode Island for the household of Peter Taylor, who described her as a thief with a "flippant tongue."[44] In planning her escape, Silvia contemplated what resources she would need to succeed. She had waited for the seasons to change from the harsh New England winter and surmised that she would need money, which she could procure from her enslaver. The community of free Blacks in Providence might also provide temporary shelter to Silvia, who escaped wearing "a plaid short gown, an old brown camblet short cloak, and a petticoat."[45]

After abandoning Boston, British commander Sir William Howe attacked New York City in the summer of 1776. Washington's army likewise moved from Massachusetts to Brooklyn to defend the city. Howe pushed American forces back as Washington retreated by crossing the Hudson River to New Jersey. Throughout the war, British forces occupied New York City and used it as a headquarters. Enslaved women and girls saw British occupation of New York as an opportune time to escape their enslavers. Both Diona and Phillis, aged eighteen and twenty-five respectively, fled, seeking refuge with British forces.[46] According to Graham Russell Hodges and Alan Edwards, a greater number of women fled their enslavers in New York and New Jersey in the 1770s than in the previous six decades.[47] After the defeat of Lord Cornwallis at Yorktown in 1781, Black fugitives flooded the city. In 1782, over two thousand fugitives arrived from southern ports to join hundreds of African Americans who fled across the Hudson River or from Long Island, creating one of the largest Black communities in the North.[48] Although only 314 runaway advertisements for New York exist, more than this number escaped into the city, and were later registered as a part of the Black exodus to Nova Scotia. When the British left the city in 1783, three thousand former slaves and free Blacks went with them, making it the largest single flight by chattel slaves in U.S. history.[49]

In Pennsylvania, slave owners did not fear that bondwomen and bondmen would flee to the British since they viewed themselves as humane. However, the flight of hundreds of enslaved men and women in the Philadelphia region to the British over the course of nine months from 1777 to 1778 indicates that large numbers of fugitives were willing to take their chances on freedom no matter what the outcome.[50] As the British occupied Philadelphia in 1777, twenty-year-old Peg escaped from her enslaver Persifor Frazer. Determined to reach New Jersey, Peg boarded a vessel bound for the state where she would pass as a free woman. Her enslaver had some indication of where she had gone, as nearly two years after her escape, he advertised that she had been seen in the markets of

New Jersey.[51] Many other enslavers expressed a great deal of certainty in their advertisements regarding fugitive women's path to freedom. According to enslaver David Kerr, forty-five-year-old Sue, who ran away from Greenbury's Point near Annapolis, Maryland, in 1780, "passed through Baltimore where she remained for some time, by the name of Free Poll."[52] Sue boarded a vessel headed for Philadelphia, where she settled and waited for her husband, Mark Stubbs, who was a free mulatto in Baltimore. Stubbs sailed to Philadelphia aboard the ship *Enterprize* and had planned to use his skills as a butcher to secure employment in Philadelphia.[53] A successful escape required luck and ingenuity, as being able to leave one's enslaver undetected was only the first step. Once a fugitive, women like Sue were viewed as potential prey for slave-catchers. An absconding fugitive woman faced being stopped and questioned and had to be ready with a plausible story to satisfy the whims of an inquisitive public.[54]

In the Age of Revolution, slavery was an explosive problem precisely because it brought to prominence fundamental issues few leaders were prepared to face. Indeed, throughout the nation's history, the presence of enslaved women and men was an irrepressible reminder of the systematic violence and exploitation which undergirded a society dedicated to individual freedom and equality of opportunity. As slave owner Benjamin Franklin warned, "slavery is such an atrocious debasement of human nature, that its very extirpation, if not performed with solicitous care, may sometimes open a source of serious evil."[55] Slavery contradicted the natural law principles of the American Revolution, which emphasized the ideals of liberty and natural rights that were used to justify revolution. Still, as David Brion Davis argues, analysis of the first great political struggle over slavery requires moving beyond a simple dichotomy of economic motives and humanitarian ideals. It is generally recognized that the economic structure and the degree of development governed the political response to slavery. No Southern colony or state moved toward general emancipation as a result of the American Revolution. Likewise, no northeastern colony or state contemplated a commercial boycott of the West Indies in order to disengage from the slave system. In Virginia and other Southern colonies, the hegemony of the planter class set boundaries on the idealism of the Revolution. It was

Virginia that produced the leadership that played a pivotal role in national politics in the Revolutionary Era, leading the revolt against England, providing much of the leadership of the Continental Army, and shaping the new government. This leadership was inculcated by natural rights ideology and saw clearly the necessity of abolishing slavery, but could not bring itself to do so.[56] In fact, in 1776, Thomas Jefferson, George Wythe, and Edmund Pendleton wrote a bill that emancipated all slaves born after the passage of the bill, provided for their education at public expense, and proposed their removal to a new land when they reached adulthood.[57] The trio had been charged with reformulating Virginia's laws; however, the bill was defeated. In the North, where there were many slave owners but not a distinct slaveholding class, idealism served a variety of purposes and mixed freely with objectives unrelated to social justice or the future of African Americans.[58] Slave labor in many northern towns stifled industry and the mechanical arts. As John Adams observed, the White workingman's hostility toward Black people could find "an outlet in opposition to slavery as well as in racial persecution."[59]

It has only been within the past five decades that historians have demonstrated how widely slavery was recognized as incompatible with the natural rights philosophy of the revolution. Bernard Bailyn in *The Ideological Origins of the American Revolution* (1967) argued that the contradiction between slavery and revolutionary ideology "became generally recognized" in the colonies.[60] Educated colonists had been influenced by Montesquieu's attack on slavery in the *Spirit of Laws* (1748) and by Adam Smith's condemnation of slavery in *Theory of Moral Sentiments* (1764). Massachusetts lawyer James Otis in his *Rights of the British Colonies* (1764) relied on Montesquieu's argument when he wrote that "The Colonists are by the law of nature free born, as indeed all men are, white or black."[61] Otis's pamphlet was read throughout the colonies and was joined by clerical attacks on slavery that stemmed from the Quaker argument that slavery was sinful and corrupted White colonists who turned Africans into a degraded and despised people.[62]

During the Age of Revolution, newspapers provided a means of rapid and widespread communication. As Robert Parkinson has argued, newspapers were the best medium at hand to make the American Revolution a common cause. Newspapers were critical of the Patriots' mobilization campaign as the pen and press had merit equal to that of the sword, as David Ramsay observed in his 1789 history of the Revolution. The colonial press expanded in the mid-eighteenth century as a result of both the Great Awakening and the Seven Years' War. The number of newspapers doubled in the decade before the Stamp Act and increased by more than 250 percent over the next ten years.[63] In the summer of 1775, newspaper printers throughout the colonies began relating events happening throughout North America, from the Canadian frontier to the islands off the Georgia coast. The majority of these stories were about the role African Americans and Native Americans might play in the upcoming war.[64]

Historians have estimated that five thousand African Americans served in the Patriot military during the Revolutionary War compared with an estimated twenty thousand who aided the British. In the Patriot Army, they served in integrated units; however, several were also members of active Black units, such as the "Attucks Company" in Connecticut and the "Rhode Island Black Regiment."[65] In 1778, North Carolina had a brigade with forty-two Black men on its roll and, in 1779, the Assembly promised freedom to all slaves who had enlisted. In the subsequent two-year period, laws permitting Black men, free and enslaved, to enlist were passed in Maryland. Although this was prohibited in Georgia and South Carolina, Black men from Virginia, North Carolina, and South Carolina did serve in the war, fighting at Charleston and Savannah for Patriot forces.[66] Some of these soldiers "received grants of freedom and land bounties or pensions as reward for their service."[67] In New York, New Jersey, Connecticut, Massachusetts, New Hampshire, and Rhode Island, Black men willing to serve in the army were placed in integrated units. Due to the growing manpower needs, a law was enacted in Rhode Island to raise a regiment of slaves in 1778. A large number of Black men served for longer periods, despite the typical three- to nine-month terms of many White soldiers. Based on a review of fifty Black pension files as part of his study of Black pensioners of the American Revolution, Robert Greene has indicated that Black pensioners served an average of 4.5–5 years during the war. Ultimately and ironically, African American Patriots contributed to what Gerald Horne refers to as the counter-revolution of slavery: the idea that the revolution was in large part a revolt against a "nascent abolitionist movement" in Britain.[68]

In a few cases, enslaved women who chose not to flee were hired out during the Revolutionary War and their service provided invaluable support to the Patriot war effort. Fifty-six-year-old Hannah worked with her husband Isaac as a cook at Valley Forge headquarters. Hannah was permitted to keep forty shillings a month from her wages for clothing and necessities. The remainder of her salary went directly to her enslaver, Rev. John Mason of New York. Mason allowed Hannah to purchase her freedom for fifty-three pounds, which Hannah did sometime between December 1778 and June 1780. On December 19, 1778 Mason wrote that he received thirty-two pounds New York currency in "full for my servant Hannah's wages who was in the service of His Excellency General Washington."[69] On a June 23, 1780 receipt for eighty-six dollars "in full for two months wages at His Excellency George Washington's family," Hannah signed the receipt Hannah Till with an X for her signature.[70] She discarded her enslaver Mason's name, which had been used on previous receipts. Hannah's husband Isaac would also purchase his freedom. After the war ended, Hannah and Isaac lived in Philadelphia at 182 South Fourth Street. General Lafayette, whom Hannah was loaned to during the war, later paid off the mortgage on Hannah's Philadelphia home. Hannah died in 1825 at the age of 104.[71]

Another woman with Washington's family at Valley Forge was Margaret Thomas, a washerwoman, seamstress, and free Black woman. Margaret was possibly married to William Lee, Washington's body servant. She received pay for providing sewing services to Washington in February 1776. After the war, Margaret lived with Isaac and Hannah Till in Philadelphia, an indication of the close bonds that developed during the war. Seeking to reunite William Lee with Margaret, Washington wrote to Clement Biddle in Philadelphia for assistance after Lee asked that Margaret be allowed to join him at Mount Vernon. William Lee had served Washington admirably during the war and Washington sought to reward his service. Biddle was asked to arrange transportation for Margaret Thomas from Philadelphia to Mount Vernon by sea or stage. Margaret Thomas, however, did not come to Mount Vernon to live in a slave society where her freedom might have been jeopardized.[72]

DUNMORE'S PROCLAMATION AND FUGITIVITY
IN THE CHESAPEAKE

Throughout the Revolutionary War, enslavers were concerned that enslaved women and men would run away to the lines of the British, particularly after John Murray, Earl of Dunmore and Governor of Virginia, issued Lord Dunmore's Proclamation in November 1775. Their fears were further fueled by the Philipsburg Proclamation issued by British Army General Sir Henry Clinton in June 1779. Both proclamations offered freedom to slaves who would aid the Loyalist cause. Enslaved women and men did not wait for Lord Dunmore to issue his proclamation. According to historian Woody Holton, the actions of enslaved women and men in Virginia inspired Dunmore to act. Rachel, a twenty-two-year-old domestic who fled from enslaver John Jones of Virginia in 1774 (Figure 3.2), embodied the actions enslaved women initiated to gain their freedom. Rumors of slave revolts and insurrections and an increase in criminal cases involving slaves in Virginia intensified in 1774–1775. As tensions between Patriots and Loyalists deteriorated in Virginia, Dunmore informed Peyton Randolph, the speaker of the House of Burgesses, that "if one senior British official were harmed, he would declare freedom to the slaves and reduce the city of Williamsburg to ashes."[73] Dunmore made good on his word on November 14, 1775. One-third of those fleeing to the British were women. Of the eighty-seven slaves who fled to Dunmore in the weeks following the proclamation's issuance, twenty-one were women, twenty-three were girls under the age of sixteen, sixteen were men, and twenty-seven were boys under sixteen. Many of the fugitives fled as families, with one woman as old as sixty, and half a dozen infants.[74] Over the course of one year, Dunmore estimated that two thousand enslaved women and men had reached his lines.[75] As a result of Dunmore's Proclamation, the colonies adopted a policy of removing the enslaved population from areas close to the British Army settlements. On April 10, 1776, the Virginia Committee of Safety ordered the removal of all enslaved persons above thirteen years of age from the eastern counties of Norfolk and Princess Anne further inland and away from British forces. A month later, the Congress of North Carolina ordered that enslavers compel all adult male slaves south of Cape Fear

3.2 Rachel, a "Negro Woman ... about 22 Years of age" wears two petticoats, "a blue and white flowered Linen Waistcoat, and a Felt Hat ... is apt to change her name." Purdie and Dixon's *Virginia Gazette*, February 10, 1774. Illustrated by Eric H. Schnitzer.

River to move further inland, "into the country, remote from the Sea."[76] In September 1777, the Council of Virginia, after bemoaning the fact that several slaves had fled, empowered the Governor to remove them whenever and wherever he desired. The Assembly of Virginia also passed an act making it possible for planters from other states to send their slaves to the interior of Virginia.[77] During the process of removal to the interior, enslaved men and women suffered from hunger and exposure. John Habersham, a patriot leader in Georgia, reported that he had lost several slaves to illness and starvation as they made their way to the Virginia piedmont.[78]

In response to Dunmore's Proclamation, the government of Virginia also passed an act in December 1775 permitting the sale, banishment, or execution of enslaved women and men attempting to flee. This law was enforced with the hanging of four captured runaways in March 1776 and the sale and transportation of twenty-five others in January 1776. The proceeds from the sale were given to the enslavers who lost their chattels on the condition that they supported the Patriot cause. The sale and banishment of enslaved men and women was not confined to Virginia. In New York, four women and men were sold in Albany for attempting to gain their freedom, while three others involved in fleeing received fifty lashes each.[79] In Georgia, Black boat pilots were confined in August 1776 and a guard boat started patrolling along the Savannah coast to prevent enslaved women and men from reaching Cockspur Island, where British vessels were stationed. In St. Mary's County, Maryland, an officer posted guards to prevent enslaved women and men from reaching the British by boats and canoes in March 1781. African Americans in St. Mary's County had been reaching British ships in sufficiently large numbers to prompt the Governor of Maryland to request sixty more guards to patrol the region to prevent the flight of slaves.[80]

Estimates on the number of fugitive women and men who joined the British following Dunmore's Proclamation vary considerably, but according to Benjamin Quarles about 800 succeeded in reaching freedom three weeks after the issuance of the Proclamation. Dunmore, in fact, used between 300 and 400 runaways at the Battle of Great Bridge in Norfolk County.[81] When Lord Dunmore abandoned the tidewater region for the security of his ships after mid-December 1775, fugitive women and men who sought his protection secured boats and sailed into the rivers and the Chesapeake Bay. Inspired by the promise of freedom, they were desperate to reach the British. Nine runaways, two of whom were women, attempted to sail in a small boat from the Eastern Shore to Norfolk. Coming ashore at Old Point Comfort, they were pursued and fired upon. Although two of the men were wounded, three fugitives subsequently boarded a Virginia vessel believing that they had reached one of the British ships. Upon discovering that the vessel was not British, the fugitives vowed to spend "the last drop of their blood in Lord Dunmore's service."[82] Dunmore's pursuit of the war along Virginia's unprotected coasts was short-lived. After a smallpox epidemic ravaged his forces and killed scores of fugitives on Gwynn's Island, he sailed from Virginia and did not return. Fugitive slaves left on Gwynn Island included a child who sought nourishment from the breast of its dead mother. Dunmore, invariably, refused sanctuary to fugitive slaves unless he could use them in his military campaigns; refuge was also denied to slaves of Loyalist followers who refused to abandon their slaves. However, hundreds of enslaved women and men responded to Dunmore's Proclamation. Even more fled when the British returned in 1777 and 1781.[83]

The experiences of fugitive women and girls point to the tensions inherent in fugitivity between the rejection of the notion of being owned as property and the tenuous position of moving through public spaces. Closer examination of 141 runaway advertisements featuring women published between 1736 and 1801 in Virginia reveals that enslavers knew their slave women better than they knew the men. This is demonstrated by the fact that only half of enslavers who publicized runaway men knew where they were going compared to two-thirds of enslavers who mentioned the destination of fugitive women.[84] A majority of the women featured in the advertisements worked in homes rather than in the fields and were therefore more likely to be known to their enslavers. Phillis, who was enslaved by Robert Carter, ran away in October 1773. She was described as a "middle sized Negro woman, about 35 years of Age" with a "few specks of black about the lower part of her face, some scars on her breast," and "a very impertinent countenance."[85] The agent for Robert Carter, John Draper, went further to describe Phillis as "fond of liquor and apt to sing indecent and sailor songs." Phillis had intended to pass for a free woman and made plans to leave Virginia by ship.[86]

In other advertisements, enslavers expressed who had assisted fugitive women and girls in their escapes. Fanny, for example, escaped on October 18, 1773 at the age of fourteen or fifteen. Her mother Joan was enslaved in Middlesex County, Virginia, on the Eastern Shore and labored as a cook. Fanny was sold by Augustine Smith and lived in York County, located in Tidewater Virginia. Fanny found refuge with Moses, an enslaved young man who lived on the estate of attorney Peyton Randolph, before attempting to make the forty-four-mile trek to reunite with her mother in Middlesex. One-fourth of the women who fled in Virginia left to visit their husbands, parents, or children, whereas two-fifths went to town to pass as free. Fifteen percent of fugitive women either left with another man or attempted to board a vessel leaving the colony.[87] Along the coastal waterways of Virginia, fugitives "cut boats loose from the moorings or stole them from unattended barns, then sailed, rowed, or paddled to British naval vessels cruising close to the shore."[88] Of the 141 fugitive women whose escape was advertised, 38 were committed to jail, 25 ran away with men (both Black and White), 3 were accompanied by children, and 6 were pregnant.[89]

The frequency of flight by groups of slaves in Virginia is noteworthy and is indicative of the complexities of escape. Runaway advertisements from the 1730s to 1790 featured 329 acts of collective escape.[90] A group is defined as a minimum of three slaves. Frequently, fugitive women ran away with their husbands and children. In July 1778, a married couple, Jack and Venus, escaped slavery with mother and daughter, Zeny and Nelly, in Prince William County and were seen in Isle of Wight County, Virginia. The group had plans to reach Williamsburg, which served as a departure point for many fugitives who intended to walk the four miles to Burwell's Ferry on the James River. British forces, led by Sir Henry Clinton, had implemented a plan that called for a series of coastal raids to choke off the Chesapeake's export trade of tobacco and produce. By May 1779, five sloops and twenty-eight transports with eighteen hundred troops had anchored in Hampton, Virginia.[91] For many fugitives, travel from Virginia to Pennsylvania via vessels located in Hampton, Virginia proved to be a viable method of egress from the colony. This was the case for a fugitive woman and her three children who escaped to Lewis Town, Pennsylvania from Hampton, Virginia in 1778.[92]

The scars from whippings, beatings, and branding as evidenced in the details provided in the runaway advertisements signify the basic brutality of slavery on Black women's bodies and reveal enslavers' ways of seeking to contain enslaved women. In this context, the body is read as a text to understand the tangible effects of slavery. Kate, a twenty-six-year-old fugitive woman from Hanover, Virginia, had "many scars about her neck and breast." According to her enslaver Leighton Wood, "her back will prove her to be an old offender" [and she] "has lost a piece of one of her ears," which was the penalty meted out for escaping at least three times.[93] Kate ran away with her husband Will, who likewise bore the brutal marks of slavery as he had "a large scar behind one of his ears and down the side of his neck occasioned by a burn."[94] Will and Kate had plans to reach the French Army, whose officers often protected runaway slaves by refusing to return them to their enslavers. Will in fact expressed his intention to join the British Army.[95] In other cases, young girls experienced whippings, as was the case for fourteen-year-old Hagar, who was encouraged by her parents to run away. Hagar's enslaver William Payne of Baltimore reported that she had "a scar under one of her breasts, supposed to be got by a whipping" [and] "an Iron Collar about her neck."[96] Escapes may have been difficult for fugitive women encumbered by iron collars and leg irons, but many ran away despite being attached to these restrictive devices. Eighteen-year-old Nancy of South Carolina, for example, escaped "with an iron hoop around her neck" in February 1788.[97]

Representations of fugitive women's bodies in newspaper ads allow us the opportunity to interrogate their physical condition. The advertise-ments are filled with evidence of the basic brutality of slavery insofar as that brutality left physical marks. Enslaver William Allegre reported that his six-foot-tall female fugitive, who was twenty-two years old, had a large scar, "as long as one's finger above her breast."[98] Allegre did not name this fugitive woman, but indicated that "she holds her head pretty high when she speaks," and was seen with a fellow named Will, "who stole her" in Nansemond County, Virginia, in April 1775.[99] Similarly, thirty-year-old Lucy, who ran away in September 1777, had a scar "between her eyebrows and another under her left breast."[100] Not surprisingly, women who ran away had experienced whippings and other forms of punishment, which served to intensify their pursuit of freedom during the Revolution. In fact, fugitive women as well as their enslavers provided information on their motives and activities as runaways. Although enslavers were mislead-ing when they portrayed women's character, they proved to be well informed about fugitive women's whereabouts, as they had often received information from other slaves, townspeople, and officials by the time they advertised the escape.[101]

The health of fugitive women provides a glimpse into the unpredict-able and often dangerous environments that they confronted. According to runaway advertisements, fugitive women survived smallpox, had poor teeth, whip marks, burns, brandings, wounds, and leg injuries due to which they often limped.[102] Sally, who ran away in October 1777 from Fredericksburg, Virginia, lost her front teeth and had been seen in both York and Williamsburg, Virginia. She escaped with another Black woman and both were likely passing as free women. Their enslaver, William Smith, noted that a community of free Blacks in Albermarle County, which included Charlottesville, harbored and assisted fugitive women who escaped and assisted them in passing as free women.[103]

In other cases, women ran away in hope of reuniting with loved ones. This was the case for forty-year-old Hannah who ran away on December 1, 1778 from Petersburg, Virginia. Described as having "a small beard under her chin and a scar on one of her arms below her elbow," Hannah was headed to the estate of Robert Pendleton in Paspotank County, North Carolina, the place from where she was sold.[104] Fugitive women in Virginia would travel along the rivers in a southeasterly direction, often using the peninsula formed by the York and James Rivers. Twenty-eight-year-old Cuthie of Mecklenburg, Virginia, followed this route when she escaped in December 1777. A year after her escape, her enslaver, Robert Munford, was still searching for his fugitive. According to Munford, she had several clothes into which to change and was likely headed for York County, where she had several relations. Like other enslaved women, Cuthie bore the marks of bondage, and had a "large scar on the outside of one of her legs" and a "remarkable gap between her two lower fore teeth."[105] The advertisements for runaways published in Virginia newspapers from 1730 to 1790 featured 1,568 fugitives, 184 (or 12 percent) of whom were women (six were stated to be pregnant).[106]

In other areas of the Chesapeake, British forces launched a land assault through Maryland to Pennsylvania that culminated in the occupation of Philadelphia in September 1777. British forces, in fact, defeated American forces at Brandywine with the assistance of Black guides. Throughout Maryland, enslaved women used the chaos of war to claim their freedom, often by passing as free women. From Baltimore came Peg, whom her enslaver suspected would "pass for a free woman" and would be carried off by a sailor.[107] In other cases, women gained access to horses to facilitate escape, as did Sarah from Frederick, Maryland. Fluent in both English and Dutch, Sarah and her six-year-old son took an assortment of clothing, bedding, and "a large sum of money" from her enslaver George Somerville on

January 14, 1778.[108] Her escape had been planned with the assistance of Valentine Lind, a local tailor with whom she had a relationship and who Somerville believed would act as her husband. From Frederick, the trio would have likely traveled to Baltimore, which had a large free Black population and where interracial relationships were common.[109] Fugitive women like Sarah and Peg recognized the importance of being near bodies of water where ships could provide further transport out of bondage. Like Sarah and Peg, Monica of St. Mary's County, Maryland had planned to use the Chesapeake Bay to escape. Her enslaver Abraham Clarke surmised that she would "pass for a free woman, and may endeavor to procure a forged pass and go off by water."[110] The number of fugitives featured in advertisements in Maryland in the 1730–1790 period totaled 1,290, 134 of whom (or about 10 percent) were Black women (four described as pregnant), 11 were children, and 30 White indentured servants.[111]

Enslavers assumed that Philadelphia was the most likely destination for fugitive women from the Chesapeake states. Enslavers in Maryland often advertised for the return of runaways in the *Pennsylvania Gazette*. Fugitives Rachel and Toney were believed to be in Philadelphia by their enslaver. They had escaped from Cecil County, Maryland in the spring of 1779 with their young child. Their enslaver, John Hall, believed that they had secured a pass, would change their names, and pass as free persons.[112] The unauthorized writing of passes for enslaved women and men was common throughout the eighteenth century. As Hugh Rankin has remarked "the greatest forgery problem . . . continued to be forged passes used by runaway slaves and indentured servants. As late as 1795, Ishmael Lawrence was indicted and found guilty of feloniously forging, uttering, and distributing freedom passes to slaves, and was fined ten dollars."[113]

ENSLAVED WOMEN AND THE SOUTHERN STRATEGY

Fugitive women that attempted to escape bondage in the early years of the war formed only the first wave of what became a massive self-emancipation after the war stalemated in the North in 1779. In 1778, the focus of the war shifted to the deep South, to Georgia and South Carolina, where the British had three objectives. They hoped to exploit the social tensions between backcountry farmers and wealthy planters, enlist southern Loyalists, and disrupt the economy by encouraging slaves to escape. In 1779, British forces occupied Savannah, Georgia, where free Black men, such as Henri Christophe and André Riguad, from St. Domingue fought with the French and American armies during the siege of Savannah; and in May 1780, Sir Henry Clinton captured Charleston, South Carolina. General Henry Clinton's proclamation offering freedom to slaves willing to help the British led to the escape of scores of women. About two-fifths of those who escaped following the proclamation were women. Many of the women brought young children with them or had children while under British protection. Children born in British camps were free. Once under British protection women served as cooks, servants, laundresses, or did general labor.[114] From the plantation of Joseph Gibbons in Savannah, eighteen enslaved women and men escaped following the arrival of the British. Among these fugitives were Renah, Sophia, and Hester and her son Bob. The group was believed to be headed to St. Augustine, Florida, a haven for runaway slaves.[115] British strategists chose Georgia, which had a substantial Loyalist population, as the base from which the Southern states could be severed from the North. Attacking by land and sea from East Florida, the British gained control of Georgia in a month. For fifteen thousand Georgia slaves this victory was hollow since most of them were owned by Loyalists. The fate of those owned by Patriots who fled the state was tied to that of their enslavers, who took most of their slaves with them. William Moultrie, an American officer, witnessed "the poor women and children, and negroes of Georgia, many thousands of whom I saw . . . traveling to they knew not where."[116]

The appearance of British troops in the vicinity of Savannah provided a degree of safety and prompted many women to take flight. Thirty-four-year-old half-blind Hannah Lining and her sixty-two-year-old mother Dinah, along with numerous other enslaved women, escaped to the British. Hannah, who escaped slavery once before in 1761 but was recaptured, knew that her escape this time would be different. While it is not known how long mother and daughter were planning to run away or why they did so together rather than in male company, we do know that, in 1780, British soldiers passed close to the Lining plantation where they labored and the circumstances appeared right to flee. Hannah and

Dinah traveled with British forces until October 31, 1783, when "they were evacuated from the port of New York on board the brig *Elijah*" and sailed away to "begin in a new life in Port Mouton, Nova Scotia."[117]

Despite the obstacles enslaved women and girls faced in Georgia, many attempted to flee bondage. Fanny, Sall, and Nan fled their enslavers in Savannah in 1779. Nineteen-year-old Sall was likely late in her pregnancy when she ran away, as her enslaver described her as "big with child."[118] Fourteen-year-old Nan ran away with Charles, who was the same age. Both Nan and Charles were described as well-known in the city of Savannah, where they could be harbored or concealed. Harboring runaways meant giving them shelter and protecting them from would-be apprehenders. Enslavers feared that runaways would receive such benefits most readily in towns with large free Black populations. Fugitives were concealed for a number of reasons. Sometimes refuge was given to allow the runaway time to escape to another state. In other instances, runaways were kept clandestinely by others.[119]

Fugitive women often attempted to leave the colonies by securing boats. Fugitives who were able to reach port towns like Savannah had a much better chance of escaping out of the colony. Four fugitives escaped from St. Johns River in Florida, and were believed to be headed for Savannah. They escaped with a canoe and a rifle and were described as being good boatmen. Among this group was Mary-Ann, who "spoke good English" and wore a "blue petticoat and white jacket."[120] Many of the fugitive women who were successful in running away often found refuge and protection in forests, swamps, creeks, and rivers characterizing the topography of the South. Newly imported African fugitives in particular were accustomed to the forest life and, as one historian has noted, "it was not great hardship to them to live for months or years in camp in the swamps."[121] Newly imported Clarissa and her comrades, Aaron and Peter, escaped from their enslaver's plantation near the Little Ogeechee River outside of Savannah in August 1779. Peter and Clarissa, described as from the "Guinea country," and Aaron of the "Ebo country," may have tried to reach the South Carolina side of the Savannah River, where runaway slaves had established camps.[122]

Invariably, women fugitives sought out towns where they could pursue diverse objectives for running away. Savannah and the outlying areas of the city thus proved an opportune environment for runaways. In Sunbury, Georgia, a "negro girl, 16 years old and Guiney born," escaped from the Ogeechee River ferry en route to Savannah still wearing handcuffs.[123] Similarly, Sally and her two mulatto children found refuge in the woods near Savannah as their enslaver, Alexander Wylly, promised severe prosecution to any person harboring or concealing them.[124] In several instances, newly arrived Africans saw enslavement as a problem to be solved collectively. On June 20, 1779, thirty-six Africans, twelve of whom were women, ran away from their enslaver Benjamin Edings on Edisto Island, South Carolina.[125] Proximity to rivers and other bodies of water facilitated escape for runaways adept at navigating canoes.

For newly enslaved Africans, planning an escape involved utilizing networks on the plantation. These networks centered upon shared occupations as well as common origins. On Mark Carr's plantation near Sunbury, Bridgee, a "prime sawyer," who spoke fluent Portuguese and Spanish, organized other sawyers on the Carr plantation. He also included his wife Celia in his plans to escape slavery. After inflicting "several outrages" near the ferry, the group cut away a chained canoe at the Sunbury wharf and made their escape northward.[126] In October 1780, a plea came from John Rose of Savannah for the apprehension of three male and three female slaves, including "a girl of fifteen years." One of the women, Phebe, had five children with her, "one of them at the breast." The other, Juno, had two children with her.[127] One of the fugitives, Jemmy, was described as wearing "old soldier's clothes."[128]

The exact number of fugitive women who joined British and Hessian forces as they advanced to Savannah and Charleston may never be known. However, toward the end of the war, over four thousand slaves of "both sexes and all ages" were believed to have accompanied General Cornwallis on his march north.[129] In some cases, women spent a few days or weeks with the troops, as was the case for Kate. Kate had followed the British Army in 1779 and had been recaptured on Edisto Island, after being separated from the regiment.[130] Like Kate, Sally took advantage of the British advance on Savannah to take flight. Sally had been captured in Guinea as a young girl and was brought to Savannah. Like Hannah and Dinah, she "managed to reach New York City – how and when we do not know – and at the age of twenty-three, was taken on board the Hesperus, which set sail for St. John, New Brunswick on July 29, 1783."[131]

Many enslaved women – whether married, single, or widowed – fell in love during the journey or gave birth while traveling with their regiments. Phillis Clarke, who ran away from her enslaver at the beginning of the war, met her partner Pompey, who was the servant of Dr. William Clarke from Massachusetts, while both were working for the general hospital department. At the end of November 1783, Phillis and Pompey left New York on board the *Danger* for Port Mouton, Nova Scotia.[132] According to Betty Wood, for women who gave birth during their time with the British Army, only in cases where the woman's husband is mentioned can we be reasonably certain of paternity. Regimental records remain silent on the issue of miscegenation between women of color and the officer class or with soldiers of the line. We can infer, however, that interracial sexual relationships formed, but whether they were on a significant scale is not known.[133]

Runaway slave advertisements provide a glimpse into the thoughts and aspirations of enslaved Africans. An examination of 270 advertisements for runaway slaves reveals, for example, that 126 advertisers designated fugitive Africans by nationality and included detailed descriptions of country markings.[134] Sydney, a young woman whose country marks were evident on her breast and arms, and who spoke "no English," took flight from the home of Elizabeth Anderson, well dressed with a cloth gown and coat.[135] Like many other new Africans, Sydney was unfamiliar with the environment in which she lived. Still, she assumed that she could successfully find refuge from the oppression of bondage in a city, and deftly concealed her country marks and her identity as a fugitive as she moved through the streets of Savannah. From the advertisements for runaways in Georgia published in 1763–1790, 1,242 enslaved persons attempted to escape, 229 of whom, or 18 percent, were women (one was pregnant and one was Indian) and 64 were children, including 8 specifically listed as infants.[136]

In South Carolina, the dialectical relationship of slave resistance and the British strategy of racial manipulation climaxed with the Philipsburg Proclamation issued in Philipsburg, New York, which offered freedom to slaves, but upheld the institution of slavery. On June 30, 1779, British

General Sir Henry Clinton issued the carefully worded Proclamation warning that "all Blacks taken in rebel service by British armies would be sold for the benefit of their captors. Those who deserted the rebels for British service were promised full security to follow within these Lines, any occupation which [they] shall think proper." The Philipsburg Proclamation, like Dunmore's Proclamation, was a military measure designed to counteract the use of Black men by the Patriot army. As Sylvia Frey has argued, this "dynamic converted the Revolutionary War in South Carolina into a complex triangular process involving two sets of White belligerents and at least twenty-thousand – probably more – Black slaves."[137] Following Clinton's Proclamation promising Blacks emancipation, the British military employed Black women to cook and wash clothes.[138] Following a five-month delay caused by the Franco-American assault on Savannah in 1779, Clinton launched an offensive against Charleston in December 1779.[139] Some fugitive women, in exchange for their freedom, carried intelligence to the British. Governor John Rutledge of South Carolina wrote to General Francis Marion advising him that:

> Any person who go[es] to town or the enemy without a permit from you or an officer must be treated as carrying intelligence to the enemy and will suffer accordingly. *Any woman* who will go to town or in the enemy's post without leave, must not be permitted to return. Severe examples must be made of the negroes who will carry any provisions of any kind, aid or assist, or carry any intelligence to or for the enemy; agreeable to the laws of this State, all such negroes shall suffer death.[140]

After the British captured Savannah and began their invasion of South Carolina in 1779, Continental officer John Laurens of South Carolina urged his father, rice planter Henry Laurens, who had served as President of the Continental Congress, to put forth a plan to Gen. Washington that would allow enslaved men to earn their freedom by serving in the Patriot army. Henry Laurens, who owned 260 enslaved persons, told Washington that, with the "aid of three thousand Negro troops the British could be driven back and even out of East Florida."[141] Although Washington was skeptical of the plan, Laurens continued to petition the Congress to buy the release of three thousand slaves in South

Carolina and Georgia with the aim of freeing them at the end of the war. Congress refused to put the measure into effect without the consent of the South Carolina Assembly, which bitterly opposed the plan. Congressional deference to South Carolina was an early example of federal acquiescence to state power when it came to protecting slavery-as-property. The British succeeded in occupying South Carolina until the end of the war.[142] It seems likely that word of Laurens's plan reached the ears of enslaved women and men in South Carolina and Georgia, who understood that their prospects for freedom changed radically when British schooners and barges began maneuvering up the region's rivers. Many of the White males "had run away" leaving behind their wives, children, and slaves.[143]

This propitious circumstance prompted many enslaved women to escape, to the consternation of their enslavers. South Carolina planter, William Snow, warned his overseer about the possibility of slave flight in anticipation of the British arrival when he wrote, "if they are not well secured [they] will get away." Snow warned that Ruth, in particular, would run off "for she is an arch bitch."[144] A family of ten in South Carolina led by a fifty-six-year-old "Ebo" woman called "Old Ross" escaped from the plantation of Mrs. Mary Thomas in 1780. Accompanying Ross was her daughter, thirty-six-year-old Celia, Celia's six-year-old daughter Elsey, Celia's husband Cato and her sister Country Sue, Kate of the "Angola country," Scipio, Rose's son Dick, Town Sue (described as "smart and sensible"), and "a waiting boy," Will.[145] Similarly, Betty escaped with her husband Hercules and their five-year-old son Winter.[146] In both cases, parents clearly wished to keep their families together, even at the risk of being caught.

Planning and timing were an intricate part of every escape, and this was particularly true for fugitives who escaped in groups. Although run-away slave advertisements rarely mentioned that a fugitive had planned his/her escape, a degree of planning and forethought could be deduced from the extra clothing taken by fugitives mentioned in the ads. Clothing was brought along far more often than any other item. Since most of the fugitives ran away during the war and in hot weather, they carried extra clothing to keep warm at night on the long journey they anticipated. Clothing was also used as a means of disguise, as enslavers frequently noted that fugitives would change their clothing. If runaways did not take any additional clothing, they may not have traveled far.[147] To increase the likelihood of a successful escape and to expedite travel, some fugitives took horses and boats, as a further indication of planning and fore-thought. Fugitives who took boats had access to the many rivers and waterways of South Carolina and Georgia. Moreover, when boats were used, it usually meant that fugitives were escaping in groups. In South Carolina, ten fugitives took with them "a large canoe 22 feet long and 5 feet wide, with all their cloaths [sic], blankets, pots ... ."[148] Among the fugitives were three girls – Daphne, Sabina, and Rachel – and their mother Alcie. The ten fugitives had escaped from Wadmalaw Island and were headed up the Ponpon-River to Chehosse Island where they would establish a camp.[149] Of the 1,004 women listed as fugitives in the South Carolina newspapers between 1732 and 1782, 113 (or 11 percent) were accompanied by their children.[150]

Men, women, girls, and boys of all ages and circumstances moved like a tidal flood toward the British army in South Carolina. Although Clinton tried to limit the impact of the Philipsburg Proclamation, enslaved peo-ple throughout South Carolina self-liberated, creating chaos for ensla-vers and the armies. In the spring of 1779, a British army commanded by General Prevost "overran most of the coastal area between Savannah and Charleston. The troops and their Indian allies raided coastal plantations and some further inland, including one belonging to Thomas Pinckney." According to Pinckney, the British "took" nineteen of his slaves, leaving only "the sick women, and the young children, and about five fellows who are now perfectly free."[151] Following the British departure, Pinckney's overseer, who had been hiding in the swamps, returned to the plantation. Pinckney mused that he hoped "he will be able to keep the remaining property in some order, though the Negroes pay no attention to his orders."[152] At Wadboo Barony, the ancestral home of Sir John Colleton, one of the original proprietors of South Carolina, few slaves remained on the plantation, and "in the breakdown of authority that followed the surrender of Charleston, they acknowledged no subjection to the Overseers."[153]

Charleston remained a prominent destination for fugitive women. While some women escaped to Charleston to be near family in the city, others chose Charleston as their destination because it provided an opportunity for them to pass as free women. Moreover, fugitive women could also seek to leave the colony aboard the many vessels that docked in the city and, as the British launched their offensive to capture Charleston, the city would serve as a base for British forces. Nan of Edisto Island, for example, was believed to be headed to Charleston, where she had relations, in 1779.[154] Likewise, Cloe, who spoke "pretty good English," was seen in the company of Nero, who was also a runaway. Both were headed toward Charleston.[155] From Beaufort came thirty-year-old Beck, who survived smallpox and was seen in Charleston a few days following the issuance of the Philipsburg Proclamation.[156] For Judy, passing as a free woman became the objective of her escape. On June 17, 1779, she escaped from her enslaver's residence near the fish market in Charleston. Described as "very artful" with country marks on her arms, she was extremely valuable to her enslaver, who offered a reward of fifty pounds and an additional reward of one hundred dollars for her return.[157] In addition to English, fugitive women like Nancy were also conversant in French. At age thirty-five, Nancy made plans to escape from her enslaver John Gregg by boarding a vessel leaving the colony.[158] Perhaps Nancy was brought to South Carolina by French forces who brought Haitians to assist the Patriots in the defense of Savannah; or perhaps she came to South Carolina from the French Caribbean via the inter-colonial trade with the mainland. Regardless of how Nancy arrived in Charleston she, like other fugitive women in 1779, was resourceful and determined to take advantage of the fortunes of war to secure her freedom.

To contain the impact of the Philipsburg Proclamation, the British military command moved quickly to confine massive slave resistance to the relative safety of military service and thereby forestall the disintegration of the plantation economy. But, Black women and men found ways to serve in all of the civil departments of the British army. Next to engineering, the Royal Artillery was the largest employer of emancipated men and women. Artificers such as carpenters, wheelers, smiths, sawyers, and collar makers repaired and built wagons, mended equipment and arms, made platforms, and attended to numerous other tasks associated with the artillery. Black men and women made musket cartridges for ordnance. The quartermaster and barrack master departments employed hundreds of Black artificers and laborers in constructing barracks and in building and repairing boats and wagons. "Commissaries used Black workers to butcher livestock and to pickle, barrel, and store meat for use by the troops. The hospital department also employed Black men and women in a variety of capacities. Men served as orderlies, women as nurses in hospitals."[159] According to reports in the *Royal Gazette*, 666 formerly enslaved women and men worked in the various departments of the British Army in Charleston. Lt. Gen. Alexander Leslie noted that "there are many negroes who have been very useful, both at the Siege of Savannah and here [at Charleston]."[160] In addition to work in the Royal Artillery, "Black men, women and children served as guides, since they had intimate knowledge of the terrain, which proved to be indispensable to the British. They were familiar with the woods because they were permitted to set traps. They knew the river crossings and the roads because it was customary in South Carolina to use slave labor for building and maintaining the road system."[161] It was also common in the pre-Revolutionary war years for slaves to go visiting with a pass from their enslaver or to move about on their enslaver's business. Many Lowcountry slaves also raised livestock, and women in particular grew provisions in their own small garden plots for sale or barter in markets away from the plantation.[162]

In many instances, fugitive women were successful in reaching the British. Eighteen-year-old Marsley was seen "resid[ing] with the troops on James Island" in South Carolina according to her enslaver Hester Graham.[163] In some cases, when they did reach the British, they were recaptured. Tom, Hester, and Celia were taken from a British ship and were confined to a jail in Philadelphia.[164] Many of the thousands of runaways who were successful in reaching the British were shipped out of the country, especially during the evacuation of Charleston and New York at the conclusion of the war. Ralph Izard, a member of the Continental Congress, wrote to his wife in October 1782 that "if they have a sufficient number of transport, they will carry with them about twelve thousand negroes."[165] William Grayson, in correspondence to James Madison, in November 1785 reported that nearly 3,000 Black people were transported out of the U.S., including 1,386 men, 954 women, and 657 children.[166] During the evacuation of

Charleston and New York, slave owners in Virginia and South Carolina believed that their slaves would take advantage of the opportunity to leave the country. Robert Taylor, an enslaver in Smithfield, Virginia, wrote to Neil Jamieson: "when the British under General Leseley [sic] came to Portsmouth in October 1780, several of my negroes ran away ... . I apprehend are either now in Charles Town or New York."[167]

Mary Postill, an enslaved woman of a wealthy South Carolina planter, fled with her children to British-held Charleston, where the military gave her a certificate of freedom. When the American army reclaimed Charleston in 1782, Mary and her family went to St. Augustine, Florida as the hired servants of Jesse Gray, a Loyalist. In Florida, Gray took Mary's certificate of freedom and declared that she and her family were legally his slaves. Gray then sold Mary and her family to his brother Samuel, who emigrated to Canada. In Canada, Mary ran away with her daughters; however, Gray went to court to recover her and won the case, despite Mary testifying that she was a free woman.[168]

Loyal Whites in South Carolina demanded remuneration for their loss of property during the South Carolina offensive. Rather than provide Carolina Loyalists with large-scale permanent confiscation of land and slaves, the British assigned much of the property seized by the army from the patriots to Loyalist families for their use, including slaves. This system treated Loyalists as "trustees for the Crown to whose receiver they must be accountable for the profits of it."[169] In some cases, captured slaves were given to Loyalist Militia officers as a reward for extraordinary service. This was the case with William Henry Mills, a South Carolina Loyalist who fought with Major J. Wemyss in campaigns along the Pee Dee River. To compensate Mills for his loss to the rebels of "two sawmills, a grist mill, all of his plantation buildings, and fifty-seven slaves," Wemyss gave Mills one hundred slaves along with permission to stay at Laurens's plantation. Cornwallis, citing the expensive nature of the gesture, later rescinded the order.[170] Cornwallis, however, did support the sale of enslaved men and women to pay for army supplies. In his instructions to Lieutenant Colonel Charles Gray, Cornwallis tells Gray to "sell a Negro to help provide for yourself."[171] Thus, while the British proclamations spurred acts of self-emancipation, fugitive women were far from safe in the hands of the British.

The war in fact created a paradox, as enslaved women were faced with a fatal dilemma: to remain on the plantations and suffer the physical deprivations that it imposed during the war, or to risk death in a military camp or betrayal by British forces and still be a slave. A quarter of South Carolina's slave population, or twenty thousand, chose to defy the dangers and run away. Among them were Dinah and her nine-year-old child; Abby, who escaped with her daughter Bridget and an infant "at the breast"; Sally, who managed to reach Williamsburg, Virginia; Hagar and her twelve-year-old daughter Mary; and Haebe, who took her twelve-month-old child with her.[172] The advertisements featured in South Carolina newspapers between 1730 and 1790 called for the capture of 3,746 fugitives, 698 of whom were women (14 listed as pregnant) and 122 were children.[173]

FUGITIVITY AND THE FINAL CAMPAIGN

British raids up the Potomac River in Virginia in 1781 brought new opportunities for escape. Benjamin Fendall of Charles County, Maryland, reported that two enslaved persons from his estate, Adam and Chloe, "went on board the enemies [sic] vessels" while they were up the Potomac River on April 11, 1781.[174] When the British sloop *Savage* landed at Robert Carter's Cole's Point plantation, thirty-two men, women, and children ran to the vessel. The sloop also carried fourteen men and three women from George Washington's Mount Vernon estate. The presence of British forces along the coast prompted planters to move their slaves to the interior to prevent further escapes. This allowed General Charles Cornwallis to establish his headquarters at Thomas Jefferson's Elk Hill plantation in Goochland County, where "for ten days Cornwallis's troops, accompanied by escaped slaves, destroyed barns and rustled cattle, sheep, hogs, and horses."[175] When the British left, Black Sall, three of her children, and seven other Jefferson slaves joined them, while another eight fled his Cumberland plantation.[176] As British vessels continued their assault, all of the slaves of Edward Taliaferro and Richard Paradise eventually fled to the British. The governor of Virginia, Thomas Nelson, lost all but eighty to one hundred of his seven hundred slaves. According to the Hessian officer Johann Ewald, "well over four thousand Negroes of both sexes and all ages" were now a part of Cornwallis's British army.[177] Among them were Jack, Ned, and James, who ran away from Edenton, North Carolina, joined the British army at Portsmouth, Virginia. James "carried his wife and several other Negro women" with him.[178] The group likely boarded a vessel in Edenton headed for Portsmouth.

Escaped slaves from Thomas Jefferson and John Ball's Virginia plantations consisted of men, women, and children bound together by family and kinship relations. Among the twenty-three slaves who abandoned Jefferson's estate were ten adult women and three girls. Of the five female adults, two left with their husbands, one of them was accompanied by her children; another fled with three of her four children; and the remaining two, one of whom was married, left by themselves. Among the fifty-three slaves who ran away from John Ball's plantations in 1780 were eighteen women, which included eight mothers with children, some of the latter still infants. Charlotte, a childless woman, led a mass escape from Ball's Kensington quarter. She fled on May 10, with Bessy and her three children, but she was soon recaptured. A week later Charlotte ran away again, this time along with what Ball called "Pino's gang." The fifteen-member group that comprised Pino's gang escaped via Ball's flatboat and included Pino, his wife, their youngest daughter, and two of their granddaughters; their daughter Jewel, her husband Dicky, and son Little Pino; Dicky's sister, her husband, and their daughter; and Eleanor Lawrence, her husband Brutus, and their two daughters. Eleanor's sister Flora had also absconded to the British, along with an infant son two weeks prior.[179]

Abandoned British ships docked in places such as Annapolis, Maryland provided refuge for women and children escaping bondage. This was the case for an unnamed fugitive woman and her three children who left the home of enslaver Ann Tilly in 1781 and according to Tilly was "taken away by a mulatto man, the husband of the woman." Tilly, a destitute woman, petitioned the Maryland Assembly for aid in finding her slave woman. With permission from the government, Tilly boarded abandoned British ships lying in Annapolis in March 1781 to look for the woman she claimed as her property. By approving Tilly's petition to reclaim this fugitive woman and her children, the Maryland Assembly failed to recognize the impact of the Revolution on enslaved women. This unnamed fugitive believed, for instance, that the ideals of the Revolution included her right to live free with her husband and children. Freedom, however, proved elusive for this family as Ann Tilly succeeded in securing the fugitive woman and her children.[180]

The quest for freedom in the heart of Virginia's slavocracy was near its end in 1781. Cornwallis's army reached Williamsburg on June 25, 1781, where they occupied the town for ten days before ultimately reaching Yorktown, a small tobacco port, in August. En route to Yorktown, hundreds of escaped women, men, and children were struck by an outbreak of smallpox with dozens dying. At Yorktown, fugitives built fortifications for Cornwallis's seven thousand soldiers, who were preparing to battle French naval forces and American land forces. In the siege that began on September 28, 1781, hunger and disease became the enemy. With rations dwindling, to increase the chances of survival for his troops, Cornwallis expelled thousands of fugitives from his encampments. Half-starved fugitives sought refuge in the nearby woods, where they faced death or certain return to slavery. General Charles O'Hara, a senior officer in Cornwallis's army, recalled leaving four hundred fugitives, which included dozens of women, with provisions to get them through smallpox and placing them in "the most friendly quarter of the neighborhood," where he begged "local residents to be kind to the refugees he had once sheltered."[181]

The British surrender at Yorktown on October 19, 1781 ended the greatest tragedy of the American Revolution in Virginia. When American and French forces entered Yorktown, they found "an immense number of Negroes" lying dead "in the most miserable manner from smallpox."[182] Planters descended on Yorktown following the surrender and hired American soldiers to entice fugitives out of the woods. Among the soldiers who accepted pay was Private Joseph Martin. According to Martin, some of the American soldiers refused to hand over the former slaves of Virginia planter and legislator John Banister "unless he would promise not to punish them."[183] Thomas Jefferson estimated that about 90 percent of Virginia's 30,000 slaves who fled to the British died of smallpox and camp fevers. Although historians have determined that Jefferson's numbers are inflated, he was correct about the overall impact of smallpox on fugitives, especially his own. Of Jefferson's thirty slaves who fled to the British, at least fifteen (including women) died from typhus and smallpox. He recovered six fugitives after the surrender at Yorktown and sold or gave away most of them within a few years.[184] Women like Judy, who left with the British at Hanover Courthouse in May 1781, remained in Yorktown following the surrender, not sure what to do or where to go. Others like Kate, who had been with the British at Gloucester, returned to her enslaver, only to run away again a few months later.[185]

Only about two in every three fugitives survived the war, and their road to freedom was still fraught with obstacles, one of which was the pressure placed on the British by American diplomats to return fugitive slaves to their enslavers. The British refused these demands. When the British evacuated Savannah in July 1782, four thousand African Americans, most belonging to Georgia loyalists, sailed with them.[186] On November 30, 1782, the United States signed the Provisional Peace Agreement with the British. According to the Agreement, British troops were to withdraw from the United States, "set prisoners at liberty and do so without causing destruction, carrying away Negroes or other property of American inhabitants." Patriots and Loyalists both petitioned their governments for reimbursement for lost property.

In December 1782, the British fleet prepared the final stages of evacuation from South Carolina. Fugitives had to register with the British army and in some cases plead their case for freedom in the quasi-judicial proceedings established by Major General Alexander Leslie to compensate South Carolina loyalists.[187] British officers who heard the stories of the fugitives ruled in their favor, to the consternation of the loyalist Americans. Reports regarding the number of Black evacuees from South Carolina range from 5,327 out of a total of 9,127, to 10,000 and perhaps even 12,000.[188] In other cases, slaves who remained the property of their loyalist enslavers faced the real prospect of servitude in the West Indies, where loyalists leaving South Carolina had planned to settle. Staying "off the departing ships, not on them was their only hope for freedom."[189]

The last British vessel that departed Charleston, South Carolina arrived in New York City within a week of its departure in

December 1782. In New York, escaped women and men were sur-
rounded with fugitives from nearly every state who were waiting to depart
the U.S. for Nova Scotia and other regions. Among those leaving were
Jenny Toney, "worn out" from hard labor in Connecticut and Rhode
Island; Dinah Weeks, who had been enslaved in New York by Robert
Bruce; Jane Thompson, who left with her five-year-old grandchild and
who believed she was about seventy years old; and Sarah Jones, "a stout
wench" of about thirty-three years old who married Harry Washington,
a fugitive from George Washington's Mount Vernon plantation, upon
arrival in Canada.[190] About 2,960 others sailed for Jamaica and St. Lucia
in the Caribbean, where they faced the prospect of lifelong slavery. Those
who went to East Florida (St. Augustine) included 2,210 evacuees who
likewise faced continued bondage at a new location.[191]

East Florida was the last British territory in North America to be
evacuated. As a haven for runaways, by 1779 East Florida's Black population had quadrupled as a result of the large influx of Black fugitives and
kidnapped slaves after the British invasion of the South in 1779. The local
Assembly in East Florida consisted of the original White refugees from
Georgia and South Carolina. The Assembly authorized the governor "to
seize all fugitive slaves and employ them under white overseers in building fortifications for the defense of the colony."[192] In January 1782, the
British Crown designated East Florida as an asylum for Loyalists.
A preliminary peace treaty with Spain in January 1783 retroceded East
Florida to Spain. A struggle over the nine thousand Black people, the
majority of whom were fugitives, ensued between South Carolina and
Georgia enslavers and the British. A special commissioner, William
Livingstone, was sent from South Carolina to try to prevent the removal
of the fugitives. Dr. James Clitherall represented South Carolina Loyalists
and would assist in the recovery of slaves claimed by the citizens of South
Carolina. To settle the controversy, Governor Tonyn of East Florida
invoked a law making it "a felony to remove any Negro or to assist in
their escape on penalty of death without benefit of clergy and to require
all ships masters to post bond of 200 pounds upon entering any East
Florida port as surety against the illegal transportation of slaves."[193]

The evacuation of East Florida by the British brought the lives of
thousands of fugitives into freedom's purgatory. On August 29, 1785,

6,540 fugitives and enslaved persons left for different parts of the British Empire aboard the HMS *Cyrus*.[194] The majority of these Black émigrés were slaves forced by White planters to relocate with them, almost half of whom ended up in Jamaica and the Bahamas. The rest were scattered throughout the British West Indies, Europe, Nova Scotia, and Spanish West Florida. Nearly twenty thousand slaves were removed by White loyalists during the evacuation of Savannah, Charleston, and St. Augustine and transplanted to the British West Indies.[195]

In the North, following the peace treaty signed in June 1783, the other half of the British army prepared to evacuate. In New York, a large contingent of African Americans reached British lines. Approximately three thousand fugitive men, women, and children crowded aboard military transport ships in New York for resettlement elsewhere in the British empire.[196] The evacuation also strengthened slavery in Canada, as roughly thirteen hundred slaves belonging to Loyalists were brought to Quebec, where White Loyalist settlements had been established.[197] The evacuation of New York resulted in the largest settlement of Blacks, both formerly enslaved and free, in Nova Scotia. According to Sylvia Frey, 1,336 men, 914 women, and 740 children received British certificates of manumission and were granted land allotments in Nova Scotia as a reward for their wartime services.[198] Many of the Black migrants were skilled workers who found employment in Halifax, Shelburne, and other large centers; however, the vast majority were former field hands from the Chesapeake and Lowcountry. Black Loyalists received the poorest land on the barren Atlantic coast and, unaccustomed to the thin soil and severe winters, tended to fare poorly. By 1791, most of the Black settlements were experiencing famine, leading to a second mass exodus from Nova Scotia to West Africa and England.[199]

Mary Perth and her daughter Patience were among those who migrated from Nova Scotia to West Africa and England. Mary had been enslaved by John Willoughby in Princess Anne County, Virginia. She and her daughter were among the eighty-seven people who ran to Lord Dunmore in 1776. In New York, she married Caesar Perth, who had been enslaved by Hardy Waller of Norfolk, Virginia. The couple went to Nova Scotia on board the vessel *L'Abondance* in 1783 with Mary's daughter and two orphans from the Willoughby plantation. The family settled in Birchtown, and in 1792, Mary, Caesar, and their daughter went to Sierra Leone. When Caesar died in 1793, Mary opened a boardinghouse and shop. In 1794, she went to work for the governor, Zachary Macaulay, as housekeeper and teacher, responsible for the many African children living at Macaulay's house. When Macaulay returned to England in 1799, taking twenty-five African children with him, Mary and her ailing daughter went with them. Following the death of Patience in England, Mary returned to Sierra Leone and reopened her boarding-house and shop. She remarried in 1806 and died in 1813.[200]

The passenger lists in the British *Book of Negroes*, which describes those African Americans who were issued certificates of manumission as a reward for their wartime service, contain the histories of African American freedom and bondage: for example, the *Spring*, headed for Saint John's, carried Ann Black, a twenty-five-year-old woman, and Sukey, a five-year-old girl. Twenty-year-old Rose Richards, described as a "healthy young woman," was aboard the *Aurora* traveling to Canada as the former property of a White Philadelphia Loyalist. On the same ship came Barbarry Allen, a "healthy stout wench" of twenty-two who was formerly enslaved by a Virginian, and twenty-four-year-old Elizabeth Black, a free mulatto woman.[201]

***

The American Revolution marked a pivotal turning point in the history of slavery. The Revolution affirmed the idea that freedom was a universal birthright. The outbreak of revolutionary conflict emboldened thousands of enslaved women to declare and claim their freedom. Understanding the circumstances that led fugitive women like Jenny (mentioned earlier; Figure 3.1) to flee bondage provides important insights into how Black women negotiated the threshold between slavery and freedom during the American Revolution. Inspired by natural rights ideology, Black women seized upon every opportunity to undermine the system of slavery through flight. During the Revolution, women not only fled with family members, but also in groups without established kinship relations. Fugitive women had a longitudinal vision of the war and they correctly perceived that their best chances for freedom resided with a British victory and a disruption of the existing social order. With limited exception, the pattern of flight was similar for fugitive women in each region. Enslaved women ran away to find refuge with British forces and also sought safe havens in cities such as New York, Philadelphia, Charleston, and Savannah. At the conclusion of the war, thousands of women and children, the majority of whom were fugitives, departed with the British for Nova Scotia. Although the inner lives of fugitive women have been relegated to historical anonymity, their quest for freedom for themselves and their children allows us to reconsider the terms of agency and power. Runaway slave advertisements expose the power of Black women's flight and recognize their historical visibility. The flight of enslaved women marked a dramatic shift in women's activity in history that had reverberations far beyond individual lives. In the postwar period, their flight and resistance continued.

CHAPTER 4

"A Negro Woman Called Bett"

Overcoming Obstacles to Freedom in Post-Revolutionary America

Ten Hard Dollars Reward. Runaway this morning from the Subscriber, A certain Negroe Woman called Bett, of middle Stature, about 21 years of age: Had on a straw hat, covered with green silk, a long red striped calicoe gown, a brown linsey petticoat, a striped lawn apron; as she took with her a black calimancoe petticoat and many other articles, it is probable she will change her dress; she also took with her a female child, of about three years of age: It is supposed she is either in Philadelphia or gone towards Virginia in the company with two white men. Whoever takes her up, and secures her in any gaol, that her master may have her again, shall have the above reward, and all reasonable charges, if brought home, paid by Jacob Phillips.

Pennsylvania Gazette, July 18, 1781

IN A TYPICAL LATE EIGHTEENTH-CENTURY ADVERTISEMENT, BETT, AN enslaved woman who ran away with her three-year-old daughter in British-occupied Pennsylvania, enters the historical record. Bett's liberatory aspirations provide important insights into the lived experiences of enslaved women seeking freedom through flight. Her resistance to racial oppression and domination by enslavers mirrors that of other enslaved women in Revolutionary America who overcame tremendous obstacles to attain freedom. Like enslaved women everywhere, Bett was not permitted to leave her enslaver's estate without a pass. She broke the rules on where she should be and when she should be there. Like other enslaved women, Bett was enmeshed in a network that included fictive and non-fictive kin relationships, which were central to the Black family. Many women, like Bett, viewed themselves as deeply connected to their communities. Although women considered permanent escape difficult for these reasons, Bett was among thousands of women who absconded before, during, and after the Revolution with family in tow. The advertisement prompted by Bett's escape reveals more than who owned her, what she wore, with whom she ran away, and where she might have gone. It speaks in defiance of the temporal and spatial order of slavery and to fugitive women's defiance of slavery's power dynamic.[1] During the post-Revolutionary period, Bett and other enslaved women developed several strategies for overcoming obstacles to freedom. As daughters, mothers, and wives, they contested oppression and invented solutions that defied their status as enslaved women.

Bett, her child, and the two White men who accompanied her materialize briefly in the runaway advertisement. Their history reveals itself only through the production of the advertisement, from which we can glean the process (their backstory) and conditions (the circumstances of their escape) of their narrative. Only through this overlap can the differential exercise of power that makes some narratives possible while silencing others be elucidated.[2] The involvement of White men in Bett's quest for freedom served to provide the pathway for a successful escape. It is likely that one of the White men involved in Bett's escape sought to portray Bett and her child as his property through subterfuge. Moreover, their presence reduced the likelihood of being stopped by patrols or other inquisitive Whites. The dangers that women anticipated if they thought about escape reveal the many obstacles to freedom: cold, heat, lack of food, unknown directions, the risk of capture, and the certainty of subsequent punishment. These social and logistical difficulties were nearly insurmountable for enslaved women and served to complicate what was possible in freedom's spaces.[3]

Bett's life in Pennsylvania was largely confined to rural spaces in southern parts of the state, where Blacks made up as much as half the workforce in the decades following 1750. Enslavers in Pennsylvania owned at most thirty slaves. In urban areas like Philadelphia they typically owned two to four slaves, though more were owned by a select few. Benjamin Franklin, the owner of the *Pennsylvania Gazette*, in which many runaway slave advertisements were published, owned six slaves, which included Peter, his wife Jemima, and their son Othello, as well as George, John, and King, who served as his personal servants.[4] In his study of colonial Pennsylvania, Gary Nash documents that 521 enslavers in Philadelphia owned one or two slaves in 1767.[5] Enslaved men and women labored as house servants and farm hands, while also working as brickmakers, bakers, carpenters, and shoemakers. Pennsylvania laws began treating slaves differently than servants early in the eighteenth century, and in 1726 the colonial legislature codified laws governing slavery and free Blacks. While these laws were "less rigorous than legislation regulating the activities of slaves in most other colonies," they formalized a caste system on the basis of skin color.[6] Like other enslaved women laboring on small farms, Bett worked the land plowing, hoeing, and harvesting mixed cereals and grains. During the Revolutionary War, partly out of necessity caused by the cutoff of imports, Bett began doing the carding, spinning, and weaving of "homespun" cloth.[7]

As might be expected, Bett's productive functions took precedence over her reproductive ones. However, Bett's pregnancy at the age of eighteen underscored the ways in which enslaved women's bodies were commodified through sexual exploitation. The archive is silent regarding who fathered Bett's daughter. Perhaps one of the two White men who accompanied her was the father. Parallel to Bett's agency and resistance are the ways in which the agency of enslaved women has been gendered and sexualized concerning their sexual relations with White men.[8] Bett's agency is not the residue of her relationship with one of the White men, but is the product of her status as a slave.

Pennsylvania became one of the first battlegrounds of what Sue Peabody has termed the "free soil principle": "the belief among enslaved people and their allies that certain geographies and territorial domains abetted Black freedom."[9] The Pennsylvania General Assembly passed a gradual abolition law in 1780, the first of its kind enacted before the British defeat at Yorktown. The act consigned to twenty-eight years of labor every child born to a slave woman after March 1, 1780, meaning that Pennsylvanians would legally be permitted to have Black slaves in their midst for decades. The average life expectancy of African Americans was thirty-four years.[10] The Abolition Act did not offer freedom to fugitive slaves like Bett. However, eight years after the passage of the Abolition Act, Pennsylvania passed a statute "freeing the slaves of persons who entered the state with an intention to reside there, forbade slaves to be removed out of the state without their consent, punished the sale of slaves out of the state, provided that vessels fitted out in Pennsylvania ports for slave trade would be forfeited to the state, prohibited the separation of wives from husbands and children from parents, and heavily penalized the kidnapping of blacks."[11] Similar acts were passed in Connecticut and Rhode Island in 1784. However, in New York and New Jersey, where Hudson River farmers resisted gradual emancipation, it took until 1799 and 1804 respectively for the gradual abolition bills to be passed. Slavery lingered in both states for several decades. New York's slave population grew by 25 percent in the 1790s and there were nearly twenty thousand enslaved persons in the state in 1800. These numbers declined through the next two decades and, for all practical purposes, slavery ceased to exist in the Northern states by the end of the first quarter of the nineteenth century.[12]

Two factors helped abolition spread in the North, one of which was African Americans' propensity for running away. Fourteen percent of young enslaved men and boys (below age twenty) in the Mid-Atlantic colonies escaped by the 1790s, whereas 9 percent of women and girls from Pennsylvania, Maryland, New Jersey, and Delaware absconded.[13] The vast majority of enslaved men and women advertised in Pennsylvania newspapers escaped from the Mid-Atlantic region: 46 percent ran from Pennsylvania, 10 percent from Delaware, 17 percent from the southern counties of New Jersey, and 19 percent from the northern and eastern areas of Maryland.[14] The economic conditions in the North also helped abolition spread throughout the region: due to the increasing number of inexpensive White laborers entering the country, the Northern economy did not have to rely on slavery. Moreover, as those who did not own slaves resented those who did, and White workers resented having to compete with slave labor, both groups favored abolition.[15] Thus, the humanitarian ideology of the American Revolution was easier to apply to places where slavery was not the foundation of the economy.

Pennsylvania's Abolition Act and the free soil dimensions of the state's borders were shaped by the purposeful actions of African Americans throughout the Mid-Atlantic region. Pennsylvania's free soil identity emerged from both the decision of lawmakers to initiate abolitionist policy and the actions of Black people. After its passage in 1780, both enslaved people and free Blacks began envisioning Pennsylvania as a haven beyond the reach of enslavers and as a place where their broader freedom claims might be heard and validated. African Americans came to view the geography of Pennsylvania in moral terms. For the multitude of Black freedom-seekers, Pennsylvania was, in the words of Black activist James Forten, "almost the only state in the Union wherein the African boasted of rational liberty and the protection of laws."[16]

British occupation of Philadelphia in the late 1770s led to an influx of fugitive slaves to southeastern Pennsylvania. By the early 1780s, many Blacks may not have worried about the details of Pennsylvania state emancipation law, for they interpreted Pennsylvania's borders as a free soil haven. Black freedom-seekers relied on the assistance of the Pennsylvania Abolitionist Society, which had been formed to protect and expand the state's abolition law. By the late 1780s, the pace of Black freedom lawsuits led to the organization enlisting more lawyers and legal aids. According to Richard Newman, three types of cases confronted Pennsylvania abolitionists: "Unlawfully detained African Americans seeking freedom, usually from within the Quaker state, constituted the first grouping; kidnapped free Blacks hoping for restitution of their free status, either from Pennsylvania or surrounding states, formed the second; and fugitive slaves from beyond Pennsylvania hoping to find freedom within the Quaker state formed the third."[17] Each case had some unique characteristics. For example, a runaway slave seeking refuge within Pennsylvania did not receive the same legal protections as a kidnapped free Pennsylvanian. In the case of runaway slaves, national principles of comity and reciprocity applied, while kidnapped free Pennsylvanians were subject to state laws.[18]

The assistance of White reformers was an essential part of defining Pennsylvania as a free soil borderland; however, African Americans often initiated the process. These three types of cases offer strong evidence that African Americans were at the forefront of a movement to envision Pennsylvania as a refuge from enslavers' power. Although it is impossible to determine the overall number of runaway slaves along the Pennsylvania border, available evidence indicates that it was rather sizable over an extended period of time.[19] Pennsylvania's borders came to be viewed as a dividing line between slavery and freedom. Fugitive slaves made freedom moves to Pennsylvania because they believed the state would protect their personal liberty and independence. In fact, free people of color in Pennsylvania viewed their state as a freedom zone following the passage of the Emancipation Act in 1780. Pennsylvania abolitionists were active in litigating the cases of kidnapped free Blacks from the state.[20]

ELIZABETH FREEMAN

In Massachusetts, Elizabeth Freeman did not choose flight to gain her freedom, but instead pursued her freedom through the courts. On the eve of the American Revolution in 1775, Freeman was nearly thirty years old. She spent nearly half of her life enslaved and the second half as a free woman (she died at eighty-five). As a slave in the Ashley household, she was called Bett, a common name given to slave women by their enslavers and short for Elizabeth. She was known for her compassion and expertise as a midwife, and for her skill in helping raise the four children of her enslavers, John and Hannah Ashley, in Sheffield, Massachusetts. As a house slave, Freeman cared for the Ashley children, cleaned, cooked, sewed, worked in the garden, and served guests. She was expected to train and oversee young female slaves. On at least one occasion, she was brutally injured by her enslaver, Hannah Ashley, with a hot shovel. Even though she could not read or write, the tenets of the new Massachusetts State Constitution adopted in 1780 that all men are created equal must have been crystal clear to her. She influenced enslaved and free alike when in 1781 she fought for her freedom in the courts and helped win freedom for all other enslaved women and men in Massachusetts. Elizabeth sued for her freedom at a time when women could not vote, serve on juries, or participate formally in the political process. Talk of freedom and a new nation was everywhere – in churches, at local gathering places like corn-husking and quilting bees, house-raisings, harvest dinners, and of course the Ashley household.[21] Elizabeth was "kind-hearted and quick-witted. She was an incredibly strong woman who, when she put her foot down, kept it down."[22]

Elizabeth Freeman did not have a full name until she was almost forty years old. She lost her husband years earlier after he fought and died in service to the Continental Army during the Revolutionary War, leaving her with one child.[23] When she became free, she chose to call herself Elizabeth Freeman.[24]

Theodore Sedgwick, who helped write the Suffolk Resolves and the Massachusetts State Constitution, represented Freeman in her lawsuit for freedom, despite being rather inconsistent in his opposition to slavery. He owned several slaves, a house servant Caesar, Ann Olds, a cook, a field hand, a young girl, and a woman named Ton whom he purchased in 1777. In keeping with the New England tradition of reading aloud important pronouncements in public places, Elizabeth traveled to the Congregational Church where she heard the Constitution read from atop the building's stone steps in late October 1780. She knew Theodore Sedgwick from his professional relationship with John Ashley, as both men wrote the Suffolk Resolves and Sedgwick was a frequent guest at the Ashley home. Freeman went to Sedgwick's home the day after the Constitution reading. She may have also been propelled by an assault from Hannah Ashley that left a scar on her forehead. According to Catherine Sedgwick, Theodore Sedgwick's daughter, Elizabeth stated, "I heard that paper read yesterday that all men are born equal and that every man has a right to freedom. I am not a dumb critter. Won't the law give me my freedom?"[25]

Sedgwick was considered a leading attorney in Sheffield. He would later serve as the Speaker of the House of Representatives, as a U.S. Senator, and as a justice on the Massachusetts Supreme Court. In 1792, he joined the Abolitionist Society of Pennsylvania, but in 1793, while serving in Congress, he supported the Fugitive Slave Act, which mandated the return of runaway slaves. Despite his inconsistent record, Sedgwick's successful representation of Elizabeth helped build his reputation as an anti-slavery advocate.[26]

No previous case had sought to end slavery on purely constitutional grounds through the Massachusetts courts. Earlier cases involved slaves claiming freedom because they had been abducted, abused, or were previously manumitted. One of the cases that had been brought to the courts in April 1781 by another Ashley slave, Zach Mullen, who claimed abuse, had been postponed several times to allow the Freeman case to proceed. Mullen's case was either dropped or settled by Ashley out of court after Freeman won her lawsuit.[27] One of the first challenges facing Sedgwick and his co-counsel Tapping Reeve was whether any woman – Black or White – could file a suit on her own, and be recognized in a court of law. The two men thus had to ensure their case was not dismissed on procedural grounds. Elizabeth may have suggested a remedy by including a male slave named Brom, owned by John Ashley's son, as co-plaintiff to the suit. Elizabeth and her attorneys may have reasoned that a man and woman acting together would have a better chance of gaining their freedom than a woman filing a lawsuit alone.[28]

The Constitutional Convention of Massachusetts produced a new constitution on March 2, 1780, which became law on October 25, 1780. Specific to Freeman's suit was "A Declaration of the Rights of the Inhabitants of the Commonwealth of Massachusetts. Art. I. – All men are born free and equal and have certain natural, essential, and unalienable rights; among which may be reckoned the right of enjoying and defending their lives and liberties; that of acquiring, possessing, and protecting property; in fine, that of seeking and obtaining their safety and happiness."[29] Freeman and Sedgwick interpreted this declaration as abolishing slavery in the state; however, "the framers of the constitution did not write it for that purpose and did not anticipate that it would be so interpreted."[30] Elizabeth Freeman employed a radical consciousness that challenged the prevailing belief that enslaved women could not bring a lawsuit in a court of law to gain their freedom.

The suit began with a writ of replevin, filed by Sedgwick in the Berkshire County Court of Common Pleas on May 28, 1781. This writ, an action for a recovery of property, was instituted on the grounds that Elizabeth and Brom were not the legitimate property of the Ashleys. The writ demanded the Ashleys release the pair, but they refused, claiming they had a "right of servitude in the persons of the said Brom and Bett."[31] The case *Brom & Bett vs. J. Ashley* moved forward to trial. There is no record of the trial, only of the jury's verdict. On August 21, 1781, the jury ruled that "Brom & Bett are not and were not at the time of the purchase of original writ the legal Negro servants of the said John Ashley during their life," and demanded that Ashley pay thirty shillings in damages to each of them in addition to covering the court costs.[32] Ashley did appeal the verdict, but dropped it in the fall and accepted the ruling, perhaps discouraged by the ruling in the *Quok Walker vs. Jennison* case, a freedom lawsuit filed in Barre, Massachusetts, also in 1781. The enslaver in that case, Nathaniel Jennison, lost his appeal of an earlier trial decision that freed his runaway slave Walker.

Brom and Elizabeth's case was a clear victory. After the verdict or perhaps even earlier, Elizabeth left the Ashley home and went to work for the Sedgwick household, where she remained until 1807. The jury freed Brom and Elizabeth because they accepted the arguments that slavery had never been legal in Massachusetts and, therefore, Ashley and his son could not own them.[33] Ashley's decision to accept judgment marked the formal recognition of the abolition of slavery in Massachusetts. This inspired other enslaved women to file suits against their enslavers. In 1783, Belinda petitioned the Massachusetts state legislature demanding back pay for her labor as a slave. Belinda complained that her enslaver denied her "one morsel" of his "immense wealth, a part whereof hath been accumulated by her own industry."[34] The legislature agreed with Belinda and awarded her an annual pension drawn from the funds acquired by her former enslaver by renting out his home.[35]

Elizabeth Freeman died in 1829 in Stockbridge, Massachusetts. She was an extraordinary woman who lived an ordinary life. She "raised her daughter, saved her money, enjoyed spending time with her friends and neighbors, bought a home for herself, and had a passion for collecting jewelry and fine clothing."[36] When she was in her sixties, Susan Sedgwick, Theodore's daughter-in-law, painted her portrait, the only known likeness of her (Figure 4.1). Elizabeth sat for the portrait in a "pale robin's egg-blue dress, ivory colored head scarf, and her favorite necklace with golden beads." As she aged, Bett became a beloved "elder stateswoman" in her community.[37] For Elizabeth and African Americans throughout the nation, the debate on slavery in the North and South set the stage for a national discussion on race and freedom that would take place at the Constitutional Convention in Philadelphia as Northern and Southern state leaders compromised on slavery to preserve national unity.[38]

***

4.1 Elizabeth Freeman at 70 years of age in 1811. Portrait by Susan Ridley Sedgwick. Courtesy of Massachusetts Historical Society.

HANNAH

On June 25, 1785, thirty-five-year-old Hannah escaped from her enslaver Isaac Horner in Gloucester County, New Jersey. Located south of Philadelphia, the county topography was characterized by low-lying rivers and coastal plains. Hannah, who had been transported to the Waterford Township from Guinea, would use these natural resources to her advantage to reach Philadelphia. She would not be traveling alone. Hannah's husband, "Big Bill," a free Black man in Gloucester County, whom her enslaver believed was harboring her, would join her on her journey.[39]

New Jersey's slave port Perth Amboy had received thousands of Africans and seasoned West Indian slaves between 1700 and 1774. With a population of over 13,000, Blacks constituted over 10 percent of the inhabitants of East Jersey.[40] Hannah worked as a domestic while her husband Bill was a laborer. Hannah's escape underscores the fact that the end of the American Revolution did not diminish the thirst for freedom from bondage of fugitive slaves. Hannah had watched her husband navigate the interstices of slavery and freedom in Waterford where free Blacks were treated as second-class citizens. Blacks in northern rural districts, with little chance of obtaining land and true economic independence, quickly experienced the bite of rural poverty. It is thus not surprising that Bill and other free Blacks would move toward greater economic opportunities offered in northern coastal cities like Philadelphia, Boston, and New York. African American populations in Boston, New York, and Philadelphia soared with the ending of the war. New York's population of free Blacks lagged behind that of the other two cities because of the continuing existence of a large slave population in the area. Philadelphia attracted newly freed Blacks and runaways from Maryland and Virginia, as well as New Jersey. From 1780 to 1800, while the city's White population doubled, its African American population increased six-fold.[41]

Although urban cities provided limited opportunities for true economic advancement, African Americans were still able to sustain themselves, even if it was on a low level. More African American women, like Hannah, moved to the cities than men because jobs as domestics were plentiful, if not lucrative. At the same time, skilled urban Black men began losing their positions, finding discrimination in apprenticeships once open to them as slaves, and realizing that Whites would now hire free Blacks for only the most menial labor.[42] Among those arriving in Philadelphia was Richard Allen, a former slave and successful preacher who moved to the city in 1786 and became a leader of prayer meetings for fellow African Americans. Allen attended and sometimes preached at St. George Methodist Church until White officials spoke of segregating Blacks who came to hear Allen's message. In 1792, after a church leader interrupted Allen and several companions in prayer, pulling one from his knees and sending the rest to the rear gallery to assume their "proper" place to pray, Allen led his followers elsewhere. He would go on to establish Bethel A.M.E. Church in Philadelphia in 1794.[43] Allen, and other free African Americans, had to work to combat the racial prejudice of Whites, which increased during the Revolutionary Era. Black almanac author and surveyor Benjamin Banneker, for instance, publicly challenged Thomas Jefferson's contention in *Notes on the State of Virginia* that Blacks were inherently inferior.[44]

In Philadelphia, Hannah and Bill would have entered a free African American community where ministers like Richard Allen and Absalom Jones were the focus of activity. "They preached on Sundays, led social and religious gatherings organized on weeknights through the Free African Society (FAS) formed in 1787, and served as school masters" during the day. Their churches grew rapidly, becoming the heart of the free Black community. As the community's leaders, the ministers used their institutional bases to guide the long evolution of independent African American churches through the nineteenth century.[45] At the center of this process of molding a self-identity stood the Free African Society of Philadelphia, which had gathered several dozen members and had instituted a visiting committee to inspect the conduct of fellow city-dwellers. The FAS worked with the Pennsylvania Abolition Society to improve the living conditions of free Blacks.[46] By 1791, the FAS, led by Absalom Jones, had forged crucial connections in the White community, which led to plans for building a Black church. The African Episcopal Church of St. Thomas was formed in 1794 with Absalom Jones as minister.[47]

Developments in Philadelphia from 1787 to 1794 were crucial to Bill and Hannah's future as husband and wife. In 1787, the first Constitutional Convention was held in Philadelphia, attended by the representatives tasked with agreeing on a Constitution that would ensure a stronger union. As Northern states began to dismantle slavery, some of their delegates thought abolition should be a gradually instituted outcome of the Revolution. However, delegates from the Lower South refused to join a union that would not guarantee the interests of slaveholders.[48] The Constitution that the delegates created rested on compromise between slaveholders and non-slaveholders. Delegates from South Carolina and Georgia asserted their opposition to any government that might restrict their ability to import Africans or exclude human property from the population considered in determining representation in Congress. Southerners were wary of new arrangements that might endanger one-third of all privately held wealth in the region. Delegates from New England and the Mid-Atlantic therefore had to assure the planter class that their property would be safe in the new nation. The unsettling language of slavery was omitted from the content, but there is no doubt that slaveholders gained special treatment in the document. Paul Finkleman has argued that multiple features of the Constitution helped protect the institution: the three-fifths clause gave additional power to slave states in the House of Representatives and the Electoral College and limited taxation in the South (Article I sec. 2); the slave trade clause prohibited Congress from interfering for almost three decades, and any amendments were forbidden during the same time period (Article I sec. 9); Congress's power to suppress insurrection included slave revolts (Article I sec. 8); proscriptions on import and export taxes favored slave states; and the onerous amendment procedure gave representatives of slave states the veto power.[49] Delegates came to terms more easily on a clause requiring states to return fugitive slaves in Article IV sec. 2. It is noteworthy that twenty-six of the Convention's fifty-five delegates were slaveholders.[50]

The Constitution did not have to sanction slavery or even refer to it explicitly to solidify the institution in American society. It was a document that guaranteed individual rights to property above all else and accommodated slavery. By providing a tacit recognition of slavery, the Constitution left to the individual states the authority to determine the institution's fate. It also provided the power to the federal government to enforce the law and keep order. Hence, it strengthened the hold slaveholders had on enslaved people and made possible the steady expansion of slavery across newly opened southern and western lands.[51] In sum, despite the rhetoric of the Revolution, the United States developed as a slave nation. The Constitutional Convention gave the Southern states bonus representation in the House of Representatives and the electoral college, ensuring their domination in national politics. "Even as northern states dismantled slavery, white southerners called on federal troops to put down slave insurrections. The nation divided into free and slave sections, and by the middle of the nineteenth century, the issue of slavery in a democratic republic came to dominate national politics."[52] James Madison, who was a leading voice in the Constitutional Convention, had long wondered whether emancipation "would certainly be more consonant to the principles of liberty," and though the Madison family depended on slave labor, he hoped "to depend as little as possible on the labour of slaves." When one of his bondmen who accompanied him to Congress in Philadelphia in 1783 refused to return with Madison to Virginia, Madison apprenticed him to a Philadelphia Quaker, since he "cannot think of punishing him ... merely for coveting the liberty for which we have paid the price of so much blood, and have proclaimed so often to the right, & worthy pursuit, of every human being."[53] For Hannah and countless other fugitive women, the Constitution endorsed the slave system by providing for their return to enslavers. The Fugitive Slave Act of 1793 created the legal mechanism for capturing and reclaiming fugitives like Hannah. According to this act, "a slave owner or his agent could legally seize a runaway and force the apprehended slave to appear in front of a judge or magistrate in the locality where he or she was captured. After written or oral 'proof of ownership' was presented by the slaveholder, a judge could order the return of the alleged fugitive."[54]

Although it was difficult for young Black women like Hannah to obtain work, it proved practically impossible for elderly Black women. In 1790, Philadelphia widow Isabella Robins, "believing that freedom is just and right of all mankind," set free her seventy-seven-year-old mulatto slave Phillis.[55] This was not an isolated case, however, for slaveholders routinely relieved themselves of the burdens attached to caring for aging slaves. Phillis's old age placed her in a precarious position, since the majority of the labor available to Black urban women at the turn of the century involved arduous manual work, such as carrying large loads of laundry and hauling heaps of trash from the streets. Without having skills such as sewing, she would most likely become a member of the desperately poor.[56]

Specific rules and limitations were usually imposed on manumissions. In several cases, enslavers drafted documents that granted freedom only if the ex-slave followed certain provisions. William McMurtrie agreed to set free his "Negro woman named Teeny" in 1786. The agreement was standard except for one provision, stipulating "that she shall have no more children [and] on failure of those considerations this agreement [will] be void."[57] Teeny's manumission depended on her ability to avoid pregnancy. McMurtrie's restriction on her reproductive future was a way to keep Teeny unmarried and available to work for him, without the burdens and responsibilities of marriage and family. The fate of her living children supports this interpretation. Two months after being freed, Teeny's children were bound out to different enslavers. Two-year-old Scipio was indentured for a period of twenty-eight years and four-year-old Ishmael would be set free on his twenty-eighth birthday.[58]

SOUTHERN FREEDOM

The retrenchment of slavery in the South following the Constitutional Convention served as further impetus for flight by enslaved people. On January 13, 1789, Austin Brockenbrough of Westmoreland, Virginia, advertised the flight of Romeo in September 1788. According to Brockenbrough, "he is fond of prescribing and administering to sick negroes ... he reads, writes, and knows something of figures, and for some time before his departure had exercised his talents in giving passes and certificates of freedom to runaway slaves." Of this Romeo "it is believed that a small Black girl named Juliet (belonging to Benoni Williams of Spotsylvania) is with him .... It is likely he may steer his course towards Amelia, as he has several very near relations ... in that county."[59]

Three groups of runaways symbolized the courage that women displayed in seeking to flee bondage. An advertisement dated August 11, 1785 shows Charles H. Simmons of Charlestown announcing the flight of three women – an elderly woman Jenny, her daughter Dido, "about 35 years of age, middle stature, and Tissey, her granddaughter with a young child at her breast."[60] Thomas Johnston, administrator of the estate of Benjamin Wilson of Savannah, Georgia, announced that six adult slaves fled Wilson's plantation early in May 1790. Four of these were men, and two were women, one of whom was described as "Sue about 35 years old and quite short. She is now and has been for a long time lame with rheumatism even to her finger ends."[61] Nevertheless, it was Sue who had "carried her three children with her – Juno a girl of 10 years; Sarah, 7 years; and Dolly 3 ½ years old."[62] James Cochran of Savannah announced that five of his slaves (four of them women) had fled in mid-March 1788. The women – Sarah, Hannah, Nancy, and Grace – were in their twenties. One was missing a finger on her right hand; another,

Nancy, fled despite "an iron put on her leg" for previous attempts to run away.[63]

Reports indicate that the disappearance of those enslaved could be either spontaneous or well planned. Henry Gibbs of Georgetown, South Carolina, announced that four of his slaves had fled in January 1790; they were all men and Gibbs suggested that two were fleeing to areas where they had wives. The advertisement announced that the "subscriber has some reason to suspect that there are despicable characters in the city who harbor and encourage the desertion of Negroes from their owners, and by furnishing them with tickets in their master's name, render their recovery extremely difficult."[64] In other cases, women fled with their partner or to be with their partner. In the Baltimore newspaper *Maryland Journal and Advertiser*, Raphael Boarman advertised for the capture of "a [T]awney woman, about 20 years old of middle size, long, curly hair who it was thought had been led astray by a white man who has been very intimate with her for some years."[65] Similarly, George Troup advertised in the *Savannah Gazette of the State of Georgia* that five of his slaves, including one woman (the wife of one of the escapees) of forty years, had recently fled from his plantation.[66]

Black women initiated their own liberation amid disparate circumstances. Mothers who fled took extreme risks by taking with them young children in the middle of the night and walking for days until they reached places of refuge. Some mothers were so desperate to leave that they abandoned their children in the most vulnerable circumstances. Maria, who was "hardly discernible from a white woman," fled in men's clothing wearing a "red and white jacket, white ticken breeches, white stockings, old men's shoes, and an old beaver hat." She left behind her three young children in New Jersey. According to her enslaver, Maria was headed for New York or Philadelphia.[67] This case represents atypical behavior on the part of an enslaved mother, for available runaway and truancy data indicate that mothers cared dearly for their children and often escaped with them in tow. According to her enslaver, Maria was determined to reunite with a married White man who was fighting with the Continental Army in New York.[68] While we may never know why Maria felt compelled to leave her children, like countless enslaved women, she was desperate to escape a life of violence and abuse.[69]

Flight was a major factor in the battle against bondage. Enslaved women fled wherever havens of liberation appeared. In *The Kidnapped and the Ransomed: Being the Recollections of Peter Still and His Wife Vina after Forty Years of Slavery* (1856), author Kate E.R. Pickard recounts the experience of Sydney, Peter Still's mother who, unable to escape with her four children in tow, fled Maryland's Eastern Shore with her two daughters, leaving behind her sons Peter and Levin.[70] This was Sydney's second attempt to flee slavery. During her first attempt, she escaped with her four children and her husband Levin, who had purchased his freedom from his enslaver. The family found refuge in Greenwich, New Jersey, but were later captured by slave catchers. Determined to escape again, Sydney made the heart-wrenching decision to leave her two boys and flee with her daughters. They escaped to Burlington County, New Jersey, where her husband had been living. Her journey was long and difficult. She was forced to leave one of her daughters on the road and once she reached New Jersey, she sent her husband to bring their daughter home. Their sons Peter and Levin, aged six and eight respectively, were sold to slavers in Alabama as retribution against Sydney. Levin died enslaved in Alabama. Sydney changed her name to Charity and began her life in freedom.[71] She gave birth to another son in freedom, William Still, who became a leading Black abolitionist.

The forces of the American Revolution that reverberated after the Constitutional Convention altered the circumstances surrounding slave escape. Increasing rebelliousness among African Americans emboldened persons in slavery to take flight in greater numbers than prior to the Revolution as evidenced by newspaper advertisements for escaped slaves. Enslaved women and men were influenced by the news of the blow to slavery struck by Blacks on Saint-Domingue, led by Toussaint L'Overture in the 1790s, and the message of equality preached by evangelicals traveling in the South.[72] After the war, the resettlement of planters with their slaves "into the newly opening backcountries of several southern states, followed by the massive movement of African Americans into the cotton-producing lands of the Mississippi Territory, broadened the enslaved motives for escape," but for some made escape more difficult.[73] Rumors of abolition in the North and selective emancipation in the South also affected African Americans' inclination to escape following the Revolution.

Virginia occupied a prominent place during the Revolutionary Era. It was home to several leaders of the Revolutionary War and drafters of the Declaration of Independence and the Constitution, including George Washington, Thomas Jefferson, and James Madison. The language in Thomas Jefferson's first draft of the Declaration of Independence, which attacked the slave trade as a "cruel war against human nature itself," was replaced by a new, milder admonition of "domestic insurrections among us" incited by King George.[74] As Vermont, Pennsylvania, New Hampshire, Connecticut, and Rhode Island pursued policies to abolish slavery between 1777 and 1787, there was a belief among some that slavery might also be abolished in Virginia. Yet, despite pressure from Virginia Quakers to emancipate all slaves, "general emancipation" was not endorsed by those in power. Instead, "legislators made small legal changes that made it easier to free individual slaves. These changes had unexpected consequences, both in terms of the claims enslaved people brought, and in the political shifts they set in motion."[75]

African American women who petitioned Southern legislatures to recognize their freedom often times referred to their own political allegiance when they presented their grievances for legislatures. In June 1777, newly freed Rachel of Virginia submitted a manumission petition in which she complained that the brother of her late enslaver threatened to kidnap her and her infant daughter and sell them into slavery "in foreign parts," despite the fact that his deceased brother had freed them both by will a year earlier. Rachel's enslaver, however, failed to obtain the license he needed to manumit his slaves officially, an omission she attributed to the political situation in 1776, when "Earl Dunmore instead of exercising any legal acts of Government and Country, was in open arms against the same."[76] Rachel, by citing Dunmore as the chief obstacle to her emancipation, astutely reminded the legislators that she had not participated in the recent attempt to subvert Virginia's social order. More emphatically, Grace Davis of North Carolina petitioned jointly with her son Richard in 1791 and connected her legal claim to freedom to her son's willingness to fight in the Revolution. Grace requested confirmation of her own emancipation and that of her children by informing the legislators that Richard's status as a free man inspired him to volunteer to fight "in defence of his Country & . . . in the cause of Liberty."[77]

The expansion of freedom after the Revolutionary War was caused by an expansion of the legal landscape and was driven by both ideological change and greater pressure from African Americans. In Virginia, the Manumission Act of 1782 provided for private manumission as well as gave the enslaved the right to sue for freedom. Through the Manumission Act, enslaved people could bring freedom claims in the newly established courts. By 1802, a network of eighteen district chancery courts that heard cases from multiple counties was established. Through these courts, a slave seeking freedom could bring her case, and was made aware that "she might also petition the legislature for her freedom, or to remain in the commonwealth after emancipation."[78]

The Manumission Act of 1782 emanated from four years of debate in the Virginia House of Delegates that began with a petition for freedom from an enslaved man named George. George had petitioned the legislature in 1778 to enforce his deceased enslaver's promise of freedom. Rather than pass an individual bill to free George, the House of Delegates instructed a committee to broaden its consideration to a general manumission law. The 1782 Act eased manumission by dispensing with the requirement of legislative approval and allowing freed slaves to remain in Virginia. The Act resulted in creating a community of free people of color larger than had ever existed in Virginia, which numbered 12,866 by 1790.[79]

The Manumission Act was not accepted by some slaveholders, who advocated for its immediate repeal. In their petitions to the state legislature, they focused on the problems resulting from individual manumissions and the risk of freed and escaped slaves running to the lines of the British Army. One such petition by sixty-two residents of Accomack County urged the delegates to vote against the passage of the Act. The petitioners expressed that they were "much alarmed" at several Quakers' applications to manumit all of their slaves, "however desirable an object that of universal Liberty in this country may be" and "however religious or upright the intentions of their owners, large scale emancipation would be undesirable because free people of color would harbor runaway slaves sympathetic to the British, or they would become charges of the state."[80]

The number of manumissions by deed and will increased by tenfold in Accomack County, Virginia, in the 1780s. Enslavers who freed their slaves expressed religious anti-slavery motivations. In 1787, for example, Charles Stockly emancipated thirty-one enslaved men, women, and children by deed, expressing his belief in equal rights and personal liberty. Similarly, Levin Teackle freed twenty-six enslaved persons, citing his belief that God "originally distributed equally to the Human Race the unalienable right to the Enjoyment of Personal Liberty." Manumissions were included in 295 wills written in Accomack after 1782.[81]

More important to the expansion of freedom in Virginia were the direct efforts of enslaved women. By the early 1790s, the number of self-purchase agreements surpassed recorded manumissions by deed and by will. Eady Cary, for instance, made an agreement to pay Rebecca Brown, a free Black woman, for her freedom. In her freedom suit, the judge recognized that Cary had paid her full purchase money to Rebecca Brown and that she had been "going at large probably" for some years. At some point, Brown sold Cary to Stith Burton, who believed he had a right to her. According to witnesses at the hearing, Brown agreed to transfer the bill of sale to Eady when she paid her thirty dollars. Eady declared at the hearing that she paid the thirty dollars "long ago" whereas Rebecca Brown claimed that she had not. The judge ruled that Rebecca Brown could not recover Eady's freedom.[82]

In the Deep South states of the Carolinas and Georgia, challenging slavery was nearly impossible in the postwar period. Although for a brief period in the 1780s the number of manumissions in South Carolina increased to 198 persons gaining their freedom, 96 of whom were women and girls,[83] by 1800, opportunities for freedom through manumission became increasingly difficult. In 1800, a further stipulation was added, whereby an examination of the slave by a magistrate and five freeholders was required before a manumission could be legally valid, although this seems to have been aimed at preventing the emancipation of aged and infirm slaves. However, in 1820, South Carolina forbade emancipation without the approval of the legislature. Similarly, Georgia's 1798 constitution prohibited the legislature from emancipating the enslaved without consent of the owners, which served as an effective ban on abolition. In 1801, the Georgia legislature also forbade individual emancipation without the permission of the state legislature. North Carolina state "lawmakers went even further by requiring in an

1801 statute a prohibitively high £100 maintenance bond for individual emancipation."[84]

The Deep South's commitment to slavery was also evident in the states' involvement in the Atlantic slave trade after the Revolution. Importation was permitted in Georgia, except from the West Indies and Florida, until 1798. South Carolina banned the slave trade from Africa in 1787 due to its postwar indebtedness. In 1803, it reopened the high seas slave trade because of economic self-interest. Although modern estimates vary widely as to the number of slaves imported into the United States after the Revolution, tens of thousands were brought to the region between 1803 and 1807. As South Carolina legislators had anticipated denunciations following trade resumption, they did not attempt to defend the morality of this practice, instead they argued for its necessity. The legal and moral implications of the trade did not matter. By 1810, "southern laws provided that Blacks illegally imported were to be disposed of, not by being handed over to federal authorities for transportation back to the point of origin, but rather by being sold into slavery, with the proceeds accruing to the benefit of the state."[85]

The rapid growth of the free Black population in the Upper South provides an indication of the extent of anti-slavery sentiment in the region. Maryland's free Black population, which was 1,817 in 1755, reached 8,000 by 1790 and nearly 20,000 by the turn of the century. In Virginia, the free Black population increased from 1,800 in 1782 to 13,000 by 1800. Delaware's free Black population similarly swelled from 3,899 in 1790 to 8,268 in 1800.[86] These trends underscore the fact that, even in the absence of a gradual emancipation law in the Upper South, thousands of slaveholders were disentangling themselves from coerced labor. Throughout most of the country, the idea that slavery was incompatible with the principles of the Revolution and could not be reconciled with Christian morality, and was unsatisfactory for the economy of the new nation, served to reinforce abolitionism during the postwar period.[87] Yet, as Eva Sheppard Wolf argues, the second wave of manumissions in the 1790s were also motivated by self-interest rather than revolutionary idealism as enslavers freed less valuable slaves.

These diverse pressures on slavery – its manifest opposition to the ideals of the Revolution, as well as the growth of the free Black population brought on by manumissions, self-purchase, and self-emancipation – weakened its institutional power in the states north of South Carolina; however, it did not slow the growth of the slave population. In 1760, there were 325,000 slaves in the British mainland colonies. By 1790, according to the first U.S. Census, their number had increased to 698,000, while 60,000 Blacks were registered as free persons. Based on these figures, the slave population in the new nation roughly doubled during the Revolutionary and Confederation periods, indicating that the anti-slavery sentiment and actions of the Revolution did not stem "the growth of the American slave population, which was due to importations and natural increase."[88]

Enslaved women relied on manumission, self-purchase, and self-emancipation to gain freedom during and after the debate on gradual emancipation. The Fugitive Slave Act of 1793, which sought to alleviate Southern fears that Northern states would become sanctuaries for freedom-seeking Blacks, did not deter enslaved women from seeking to escape bondage.[89] Ona Judge, the enslaved domestic servant of George and Martha Washington, escaped bondage in 1796 after learning that she would be given as a wedding present to Eliza Custis, Martha Washington's granddaughter. The offspring of an enslaved seamstress named Betty who labored for the Washington family and a White indentured servant from Leeds, England, Ona became a domestic in 1784 at the age of ten at Washington's Mount Vernon plantation. At the age of sixteen, Ona traveled to Philadelphia, the nation's capital, with the Washingtons, who stayed in Philadelphia intermittently up to six months at a time, always bringing the enslaved who traveled with them back to Virginia to prevent them from claiming their freedom under Pennsylvania's manumission law, which emancipated slaves who resided in the state for at least six months. Ona fled the executive mansion on May 21, 1796, just before the Washingtons were to return to Mount Vernon for summer recess in 1796.[90] Ona gave the following account of her escape: "Whilst they were packing up to go to Virginia, I was packing to go, I didn't know where; for I knew that if I went back to Virginia, I should never get my liberty. I had friends among the colored people of Philadelphia, had my things carried there beforehand, and left Washington's house while they were eating dinner."[91]

Ona boarded a ship bound for Portsmouth, New Hampshire, commanded by Captain John Bolles. In relating her flight, she added, "I never told his name till after he died, a few years since, lest they should punish him for bringing me away."[92] Ona settled in Portsmouth, New Hampshire, where the Washingtons were able to track her down. Like other fugitives, Ona Judge lived a life in the shadows, as her enslavers, George and Martha Washington, relentlessly pursued her capture and return. Washington made two attempts to recover her. First, he sent his nephew Burrell Bassett to persuade her to return, without success. Bassett told her they would set her free when she arrived at Mount Vernon, to which she replied, "I am free now and choose to remain so."[93] Washington's agent in Portsmouth also reported in September 1796 that "popular opinion here is in favor of universal freedom," which made it difficult for him to seize and shackle Ona without public outcry.[94]

Two years later, the Washington family was still trying to capture Ona by surreptitiously sending Bassett after her, this time instructing him to bring her by force. Knowing that Senator John Langdon of Portsmouth, the former Governor of New Hampshire, was opposed to slavery, Bassett informed him of the plan. Langdon, in turn, advised Ona Judge to leave town before twelve o'clock at night, which she did, thereby escaping Bassett's clutches. It was only upon Washington's death in 1799 that Ona could finally feel a measure of safety, declaring "they never troubled me any more after he was gone."[95] Washington stipulated in his will that his slaves be freed upon the death of his widow. After he died, Martha prudently decided not to make the slaves' freedom contingent upon her death and freed them immediately.[96] Ona was a dower slave and belonged to the estate of Martha Washington, who died on May 22, 1802. However, as Martha's will mandated that all of her slaves were to be divided among her grandchildren, Ona's freedom was still not legally secure. Ona married "Jack Staines, had a baby, and put down roots in New Hampshire where she lived out her life, poor but free."[97]

Ona Judge was among very few eighteenth-century slaves who shared their stories about their flight from bondage. At the end of her life, she granted interviews to two reporters for abolitionist newspapers, the first of which appeared in the *Granite Freeman* in May 1845, almost forty-nine years to the day after her escape. Judge's second and final interview was published in 1847 on New Year's Day in the *Liberator*.[98] According to historian Erica Armstrong Dunbar, Ona's "interviews are quite possibly the only existing recorded narratives of an eighteenth century Virginia fugitive. On February 25, 1848, Ona Maria Staines was carried away, not by slave catchers, but by her God."[99]

Fugitive women like Ona Judge often found it difficult to support themselves and their families with their meager earnings. As a result, many African American women experienced poverty once they attained freedom. While they were no longer bound laborers, the paltry wages received from their employers did not sustain them. Black women continued to find ways in which to resist and rebel within the workplace as they toiled long hours in physically demanding jobs. In one of her diary entries, wealthy Philadelphian Deborah Norris Logan noted how difficult it was to find "good servants." She recounted the dismissal of one of her servants, stating "I have had some domestic disquiets as of late with my servants and there seems a propriety in discharging Maggy Jones a coloured woman who has lived with us near three years. She has been of late (as the Irish say) too warm in her place and very impertinent in her remarks."[100]

SPACES OF FREEDOM

Freedom, while full of possibilities, also brought many problems for fugitive women. As Black women moved from slavery to freedom, many found themselves trapped as unskilled domestics working in the homes of White families. For instance, approximately half of the 1,897 free Blacks who lived in Philadelphia in 1790 lived and worked in White households, and the majority of those live-in workers were women. "Black women who did not perform live-in services for white city residents found very little in the way of diverse employment."[101] In 1795, the Philadelphia City Directory listed 105 Black residents, and 22 of these were women listed as head of household. Although the majority of free Black women were listed as "washers," there were a few exceptions. Tinee Crenshaw was listed as a "Dealer in Fruit" and Minia Brummage was listed as a "Cake Seller." Polly Haine was listed as a "Pepper Pot Maker" selling soup to Black and White Philadelphians, as one of the avenues for Black female entrepreneurship. Phoebe Anderson and Phoebe Seymour were listed as "Hucksters," selling fruits and vegetables on the streets of Philadelphia. "Typically, poor women of both races worked in two or more forms of employment throughout the year. African American women who worked as street sellers turned to work as laundresses and seamstresses in cold weather."[102] As Eric Armstrong Dunbar argues, employment and freedom were always fragile for Black women.

Although many enslaved women escaped to northern cities, an untold number of fugitive women never migrated out of the slaveholding South. Fugitive women sought to remain invisible before the eyes of authorities. Consequently, analyzing their lives and characteristics in any capacity is no easy task. Although these fugitives have not gone completely unnoticed by leading scholars in the field, they have rarely been the focus of historical inquiry.[103] Employing Damian Pargas's conceptualization of various "spaces of freedom" on the North American continent, "slave flight within the South reveals how runaway slaves sought and navigated spaces of informal freedom, where freedom from slavery was constructed in a clandestine manner that had no legal basis."[104] Such spaces of freedom complicate our understanding of what freedom meant to enslaved people. Freedom was temporally and spatially changing, and was dependent on the interplay of a variety of processes. Thus, spaces of freedom were not always confined to areas where slavery had been abolished.[105]

Fugitive women gravitated to Southern cities like Richmond, Baltimore, Charleston, Savannah, and New Orleans because of the possibility of obtaining anonymity there. The proximity of the Upper South to Northern free soil in particular might suggest that most fugitives from states like Virginia and Maryland would attempt to leave the slaveholding South altogether. As their ads would indicate, enslavers often feared that their runaway slaves would make their way north. However, in many cases, factors such as "family ties, employment prospects, a lack of contacts or networks in the northern states, or simply physical proximity, made flight to a nearby urban city within the South a more promising endeavor."[106] Fugitives Mary, Haebe, and Haebe's twelve-month-old daughter ran away to Charleston according to their enslaver. In 1790, Charleston was home to 586 free Blacks.[107] By 1800, its free Black population reached 1,024 and included émigrés from the revolution occurring on Saint-Domingue (Haiti).[108] In Charleston, Black women could find a wide array of jobs, such as fruit vendor, baker, seamstress, and washerwoman. Forty-seven-year-old Becky Jackson came to Charleston with her eight children from Cheraw, South Carolina. She found employment as a washerwoman and rented a house on Alexander Street. She and other Black women came to Charleston, as they did to other cities, to gain access to churches, schools, and social activities, and to take advantage of the protections and opportunities available in a large Black community.[109] Similarly, Hannah, Venus, and Venus's fourteen-year-old daughter escaped from the Carolina countryside in 1784 and were believed to be employed in the city of Charleston.[110] By the 1780s, family units constituted 12 percent of all runaways in South Carolina, with 118 slaves absconding in family units.[111] The vast majority of female runaways in South Carolina were field slaves, house slaves, tradeswomen, and market women. From 1732 to 1779, forty-six house slaves, ten trades-women, and six market women fled slavery.[112] In Charleston and other urban centers, Black women recognized that, if not legally attained, freedom could be *exhibited* through dress, language, and employment skills.[113]

Greater economic opportunities in urban centers led some women to head to cities like Baltimore. The free Black population in Maryland continued to increase in the late eighteenth century and in the early decades of the nineteenth century despite the efforts of enslavers who saw free Blacks as an incitement to slave disorder and made their elim-ination a priority by passing legislation that restricted manumission and mandated that newly freed Blacks leave the state. With 5,671 free Blacks, in 1790, Baltimore had the largest free Black population in the Upper South.[114] Occupational and social opportunities led fugitives and free Blacks alike to the city as did the fact that runaways could easily blend into the large free Black community and avoid detection by their enslavers.[115] According to Seth Rockman, "hiring fugitive slaves was a fairly common practice in Baltimore, either because runaways would accept lower wages in exchange for cover or because employers could always collect the reward if the worker proved unsatisfactory."[116] In 1805, the enslaver of a runaway named Chloe was sure that she had hired herself out in the city. Similarly, Thomas Owen warned other Baltimore householders against employing his servant Ann, a twenty-three-year-old woman who had run away and who was "reportedly lurking about town."[117]

Southern cities were sites of informal freedom for women who escaped slavery. Fugitive women were permanent freedom seekers who made illegal yet quite earnest attempts to rebuild their lives in what Damian Pargas terms informal freedom – "a freedom that did not exist on paper but that allowed them to escape bondage" – rather than bolt for geographic spaces of formal freedom in the North where slavery was abolished.[118] Whatever distances they traveled, fugitives who remained in the South were in constant danger of being discovered and sent back to their enslavers. Due to the need to effectively conceal their identities to outsiders upon arrival, they depended on others to aid and assist them. "Slave families and communities in rural districts provided fugitives with the social networks necessary to sustain themselves for long periods of time without being caught. Fugitive women who remained in the countryside were almost always partly or wholly 'harbored' by loved ones, sometimes within slave households, but also often in the forests that bordered the plantations or farms."[119] The experience of one formerly enslaved woman in the 1800s might also speak to the experience of enslaved women in the late 1700s:

> One night I was fast asleep an' heard a rap-bump, bump-on my do'. I answered, Who's dat? De answer was, Hush, don' say nothin', but let me in! Dat 'oman was out a breath, wisperin', Can I stay here all night? I told her she could, so dare de 'oman done Slept right dar 'hin' me in my bed all night . . . . I took an' heard de horses an' talk' in de woods. Dog barkin' . . . . I peeped out de window an' saw dem white folks go by an' ain' never dreamed of 'em lookin' fer de 'oman whar was over 'hind me. Next morning she stole out from dar, and' I Baby, ain' never seen her no more. You see we never told on each other.[120]

For fugitive women, passing for a free person meant looking and acting free. As Damian Pargas argues, "visibility was everything and erasing all markers of their slave identity was the key to navigating urban spaces undetected."[121] To this end, some light-skinned runaways attempted to pass as White, as was the case of Sal, who her enslaver declared "sometimes says she is white."[122] For most fugitives in southern cities, assuming free identities entailed looking and acting like local free Blacks. Upon arrival in urban areas, runaways' first order of business was often to procure the more fanciful attire of the free Black population to replace the clothing that gave them away as slaves. In this regard, free Blacks helped cloak the true identities of fugitive women by harboring them in their homes or arranging safe hiding places. Julia Johnson from Staunton, Virginia, ran away to Richmond, where Issac Adams, a free Black man, was suspected of arranging a hiding place for her.[123] Molly, who disappeared in the city of Alexandria, Virginia, was believed to be "connected with some evil-disposed free negroes, and secreted by them."[124]

The ability of fugitive women to abscond to and successfully earn a living in urban areas by passing as free Blacks produced a great deal of anxiety among enslavers, who demanded that cities tighten supervision of African Americans' economic activities in public spaces. During the early 1800s, city councils throughout the South passed laws designed to restrict the activities of free Blacks.[125] In Maryland, free African Americans were prohibited from selling agricultural produce without a special permit, while they were banned from becoming riverboat captains and pilots in Virginia and Georgia. In addition, Virginia, Georgia, and South Carolina legislation levied special taxes on free persons of African descent. In all slave states, urban free Blacks were required to re-register each year, and in Florida, Georgia, and several other states, they had to have White guardians. "Vagrancy laws became standard devices for extorting free Black labor, and when those were insufficient, states began to find ways to 'bind out' free Blacks between the ages of eight and twenty-one."[126] As noted by Ira Berlin in *Slaves Without Masters*, by the beginning of the nineteenth century, "At any time, any White could demand proof of a free Negro's status; even if [her] papers were in order, an unemployed free Negro could be jailed and enslaved and [her] children bound out to strangers."[127]

Fears generated by the Haitian Revolution, which began in 1791 and ultimately overthrew the brutal French slave regime and established the first Black republic in the Americas, and by the widespread unrest of Gabriel Prosser's insurrection in 1800, further eroded free Black rights and privileges. In Maryland, for instance, African Americans were required to license their guns and dogs, whereas "Delaware barred Blacks from town on election day; and in various places free Blacks were fined or whipped for entertaining slaves, meeting in groups of more than seven, attending school, or holding church meetings."[128] Free African Americans in the South faced life's challenges soberly and sought to make their existence as good as it could be.[129]

The rewards offered for fugitives varied according to the valuation placed on them by their owner, but due to currency fluctuations, the real amount of the reward was rarely constant. In 1783, a South Carolina enslaver promised an eight-dollar reward for the return of Jenny. An additional eight dollars was offered to "any person who will inform of her being harboured [sic] by a white person, and four dollars if harboured [sic] by a negroe [sic]."[130] In contrast, when thirty-year-old Luce ran away from her enslaver, a reward of fifteen dollars was offered for her return.[131] The rewards offered for male and female fugitives were, however, fairly similar, amounting in some cases to five guineas. This was the case for nineteen-year-old Franck, who ran away in December 1783 from South Carolina.[132] Similarly, when forty-year-old Hagar ran away with her daughter Mary, a reward of five guineas was offered for their capture. Enslavers placed a premium on information that would support fugitives being assisted or harbored by a White person. In the case of Mary and Hagar, the advertisement stated that an additional five-guinea reward would be given to those who provided information on a White person harboring them.[133] On the other hand, some rewards were trivial and seemed to indicate a waning in the value of Black labor or the inability of the enslaver to pay more for the recovery of his property. This was the case for Billy and his wife Sarah, who ran away in November 1783 in Charleston, South Carolina. Their enslaver, Thomas Waring, only offered "one guinea for each" to those that captured and returned the pair.[134] The reward offered for the return of fugitive women differed markedly from their appraised value. Historian Daina Ramey Berry has determined that between 1771 and 1865, the average appraised value for women and men ages twenty-three to thirty-nine were, respectively, $528 and $747.[135]

Before the end of the eighteenth century, the domestic slave trade was well developed in Maryland, Virginia, and South Carolina.

According to Allan Kulikoff, the great migration of slaves that began after the Revolution "was one of the most significant events in the history of Black society in the United States."[136] Between 1790 and 1820, enslavers took nearly a quarter million enslaved people from their families and friends to cultivate tobacco or cotton on frontier plantations. In the decades following the American Revolution, many enslaved women were subjected to forced interregional trade. Their forced migration across the South had enormous human consequences, for they left behind their loved ones, departed from familiar surroundings, often changed enslavers, and were forced to live among strangers when they reached their destinations.[137] In directing sales, "planters and traders assessed monetary values of the enslaved based on sex, age, skill, health, beauty, temperament, and reproductive ability among other criteria."[138] Women's bodies in particular were catalysts of nineteenth-century economic development. It thus stands to reason that women would seek ways to challenge the institution that threatened their families with sale and subverted their bodies through breeding. Advertisements for sales of enslaved women frequently touted "good breeders" or "very prolific in her generating qualities." In interviews, a number of former slaves recalled living in circumstances akin to "stud farms." According to Richard Sutch, slave owners "systematically bred slaves for sale ... . They held disproportionately large numbers of women in the child bearing age groups. They fostered polygyny and promiscuity among their slaves ... so that the profits ... could be maximized."[139] Women like Hagar (discussed earlier) who fled with their daughters were keenly aware that they were saving them from a life of sexual exploitation.

***

Freedom for African American women did not come with ease. Women such as Bett, Elizabeth Freeman, and Hannah overcame tremendous obstacles to attain their freedom. They had watched the Revolution birth a new nation that resulted in freedom for many African Americans. Enslaved women who escaped bondage were able to achieve varying degrees of liberty and self-determination. There are a substantial number of cases of women fleeing bondage in the post-Revolutionary period that are anecdotal, singular in nature, poorly documented, randomly scattered throughout dissimilar sources, and spread among multiple contexts. These cases represent powerful accounts of women's resolute pursuit of freedom and demonstrate that enslaved women often absconded while managing family relationships in complex and unconventional ways. Their struggles enhance our understanding of both the lived experiences of fugitive women and the ways in which enslaved women negotiated and resisted their bondage. Enslaved women pursued freedom through the courts; they fled with and to family members, or reunited with relatives once freedom was attained. When possible, women escaped within groups or relied on networks. As opportunities for self-purchase were presented, they purchased their freedom. Women who escaped treaded the middle ground between slavery and freedom, literally and metaphorically. Freedom through flight allowed women to control their own ideas about freedom.

CHAPTER 5

Confronting the Power Structures

Marronage and Black Women's Fugitivity

> A number of runaway Negroes (supposed to be upwards of 100) having sheltered themselves on Belleisle Island, about 17 or 18 miles up Savannah River, and for some time past committed robberies on the neighboring Planters, it was found necessary to attempt to dislodge them.
>
> *Charleston Morning Post,* October 26, 1788

AFTER THE REVOLUTIONARY WAR, CAPTAIN LEWIS AND CAPTAIN Sharper (also known as Captain Cudjoe) led a band of maroons to an encampment near the Savannah River. The group included several women who were either wives of the men or who fled alone seeking refuge from slavery. Among the women were Juliet and Peggy, who would later testify at the trial of Captain Lewis. The group supported itself by growing its own foodstuffs and raiding outlying plantations. It is likely that the band formed during the Revolutionary War, when Georgia and South Carolina were still under full British control and runaways gathered on Tybee Island (in the mouth of the Savannah River) by the hundreds. Given the chaotic situation in the Lowcountry after the departure of the British, with tens of thousands of displaced enslaved women and men and numerous disputes over ownership, it is not surprising that rather than return to slavery, some women and men chose to take advantage of the situation and make their homes in the Savannah River swamps. The Revolutionary War not only prompted an increase in the number of runaways, but also provided the impetus for marronage.[1] In this context, freedom has been equated with marronage, or escape from slavery, by scholar Neil Roberts.[2] "Freedom as marronage" provides a lens through which to view the actions of fugitive women in maroon societies.

The term "maroon" is an English corruption of the word *cimarron* which means "wild, not tame," and was "originally applied to livestock that had escaped from farms to roam free in the woods."[3] The English adapted the term "maroon" and used it, along with the French and Dutch, to refer to fugitive slaves. Maroons were fugitives from slavery who established independent communities in swamps, deep woods, mountains, isolated islands, and other wilderness sanctuaries. They defended their territory from enslavers, built villages, produced crops, raised children, and from time to time staged raids into slavery country to free persons still held in bondage. From the sixteenth to the nineteenth century, such communities were widespread in the West Indies and Latin America, where enslaved Africans sought refuge in the interior mountainous regions of Hispaniola, Haiti, and Jamaica, and the heavily forested areas of Cuba, Panama, Suriname, and Brazil.[4]

The most renowned Caribbean spaces were the maroon communities of Jamaica in the late seventeenth and early eighteenth century. The Jamaican maroons became widely known during two wars with British colonial troops that were detailed in reports. The First Maroon War, which began in 1728, ended with treaties signed by Captain Cudjoe of the Leeward maroons and Queen Nanny of the Windward maroons in 1739 and 1740, respectively. These treaties established maroon land claims in the western and eastern Jamaican highlands and facilitated a peace between the maroons and British colonial officials. This tenuous peace ended in 1795 with the onset of the Second Maroon War. This war, which lasted for one year, resulted in forced deportation of the residents of Cudjoe Town (known as Trelawny Town) and coincided with early nineteenth-century reports of marronage in the French, Spanish, and Dutch Caribbean.[5] The maroon state of Palmares in Brazil numbered tens of thousands and defeated several Portuguese and slaveholder armies. The maroons of Suriname numbered in the thousands and maintained political autonomy. In Central America, there were the maroons of Panama, and the Haitian Revolution was initiated by maroons.[6]

While maroon societies in Suriname, Haiti, Brazil, and Jamaica were sizable, sustainable, and isolated enough to serve as destinations for runaway slaves, those in North America were amorphous and less populous, and therefore may have served more as intermediate, liminal spaces where enslaved people worked and subsisted before attempting to reach safer, more sustainable communities elsewhere. Although runaways formed maroon communities, many more slaves fled from bondage than ever became maroons. Small groups of enslaved people engaged in *petit marronage* by fleeing oppressive slave societies in the short term, without intending to remain indefinitely in flight or to escape permanently from the region in which they lived. The largest maroon camps reflected *grand marronage*, communities that penetrated the foundations of plantation systems throughout the Atlantic world.[7] Fugitive women's active engagement with maroon societies in the Great Dismal Swamp and in South Carolina, Georgia, Louisiana, and Florida illustrates their tenacity and staunch pursuit of freedom.

THE DISMAL SWAMP

The Great Dismal Swamp located between Virginia and North Carolina acted as a strong magnet for runaway slaves. The Dismal Swamp included the Virginia counties of Princess Anne, Norfolk, Nansemond, and to a limited extent the Isle of Wight. In North Carolina, the counties of Currituck, Camden, Pasquotank, Perquimans, Chowan, and to a lesser extent Gates, comprised the areas that included the Dismal Swamp.[8] This area consisted of deserted swamp that was relatively close to the plantation regions of Virginia, which made it easy for enslaved men and women to disappear into its dense forests. In 1728, Virginia Governor William Byrd came across "a family of mullatoes" in the swamp when surveying the border between the two colonies. Byrd stated that "it is certain many slaves shelter themselves in this obscure part of the world, nor will any of their righteous neighbours discover them."[9] Traveling through North Carolina, the German Johann Schoepf reported in 1783 that, in the Great Dismal Swamp, "small spots are to be found here and there which are always dry, and these have often been used as places of safety by runaway slaves … these Negro fugitives lived in security and plenty, building themselves cabins, planting corn, raising hogs and fowls which they stole from their neighbours, and naturally the hunting was free where they were."[10]

In 1784, John Smyth agreed that "Run-away Negroes have resided in these places for twelve, twenty, or thirty years and upwards, subsisting themselves in the swamp upon corn, hogs, and fowls, that they raised on some of the spots not perpetually under water, nor subject to be flooded, as forty-nine parts of fifty of it are; and on such spots they have erected habitations, and cleared small fields around them; yet these have always been perfectly impenetrable to any of the inhabitants of the country around, even to those nearest to and best acquainted with the swamps."[11] Consequently, runaways "in these horrible swamps are perfectly safe, and with the greatest facility elude the most diligent of their pursuers."[12] It is difficult to estimate the number of women that lived in the Great Dismal Swamp; however, some historians have suggested that, from the eighteenth to the nineteenth century, the swamp may have been home to several hundred and maybe even a thousand escaped slaves. The invisibility of fugitive women in studies of maroon societies in North America reflects the violence of archival silence, a problem of historical methodology that has limited comprehensive narration of the histories of enslaved women.

The area of the Great Dismal Swamp covered roughly 200–300 square miles. As it was a freshwater swamp, it was habitable. Located near the ocean, the swamp contained islands where settlements could be built and crops grown. The place also teemed with game for hunting. The inner swamp was inaccessible to outsiders, due to deep mud, pools, and wild vegetation. "Only those who knew the routes or were guided could enter and live. It was a jungle."[13] The Dismal Swamp comprised four overlapping regions: the deep interior; the outer portions, closer to the edge; the edge; and the outside areas of open countryside nearest to the Swamp edge. During the mid-eighteenth century, swamp planters sought to drain the swampland to create fertile soil for rice farming. To accomplish this, twelve men formed the Dismal Swamp Company (DSC) in 1763 and secured a 40,000-acre tract of the Dismal Swamp in Virginia, which included Lake Drummond, the second largest lake in Virginia.[14]

George Washington was among the DSC shareholders and he resided temporarily at Dismal Plantation, a slave labor camp located in the swamp which existed from 1765 to the early 1780s. The DSC officials established Dismal Town, a 402-acre tract of land located six miles south of Suffolk and centered in a swamp field known as White Marsh. The DSC managed the workforce of fifty-four enslaved people: forty-three men, nine women, one boy, and one girl.[15] The enslaved laborers cleared trees, dug irrigation ditches, and shaved cedar trees into 10,018 one-inch shingles, which became an important natural resource that provided the early profits for the DSC. Enslaved labor also excavated the Washington Ditch (named after George Washington) between 1763 and 1769, which served as the main artery for transporting goods out of the swamp until Jericho Ditch was completed in 1812.[16]

Seeking to bolster the labor force and believing that increasing the number of women in the camp would reduce the propensity of men to run away, the partners voted to send more women to the camp. By 1765, the Dismal Plantation had sixty-six enslaved people, including twelve more women.[17] This increase in the population did not deter enslaved women and men from "running about" at night. In June 1768, John Augustine Washington, the brother of George Washington, advertised that "a new negro man named Tom" had fled "the proprietors of the Dismal Swamp" in April 1767. Tom stood about five feet, six inches tall and bore "his country marks," four on each cheek. Washington offered a three pounds sterling reward for Tom's return. Another ad for Tom was placed by DSC proprietor John Mayo in October 1768, where Tom was described as "about 6 feet high," with a "roguish look"; he also had "lost part of one of his ears [an indication of recidivism]." Tom had been seen "in Nansemond and Norfolk counties" but "is supposed to be about the Dismal Swamp." Tom remained a fugitive in the Dismal Swamp for nearly twenty years until he was captured in December 1784.[18]

Tom's example may also convey the plight of women in the Great Dismal Swamp. In his initial proposal to drain the Dismal Swamp, Governor Byrd suggested the purchase of ten "seasoned negroes" of both sexes. In providing an estimate of expenses, Byrd envisioned acquiring approximately 170 more enslaved laborers over the course of the following seven years, who when combined with their expected progeny would total nearly three hundred.[19] Although the slave population in the Dismal Swamp in the eighteenth century did not reach Byrd's vision of three hundred, it is clear that women were desired by proprietors to naturally increase the population. In addition to their reproductive value, women were also valued for their ability to raise crops, cook meals, and cut shingles for the DSC. Crops such as corn and rice were grown on Dismal Plantation and, as was the case in the Lowcountry, enslaved women performed much of the labor required to produce the rice crop successfully. Rice was valued as both a dietary staple and an export crop, although Dismal Plantation did not produce rice on the same scale as the Lowcountry.[20] By 1775, enslaved laborers produced seven tons of rice, "equal in quality to that of South Carolina," which was shipped to Antigua.[21] Dismal Plantation, however, remained an unhealthy environment for enslaved people. Although more enslaved labor was brought to the swamp, "their numbers were considerably lessened by deaths."[22]

The deleterious conditions at Dismal Plantation and a desire for freedom led enslaved women to escape. In 1771, Nathaniel Burwell reported that Jack and Venus both fled the morass of the Dismal Swamp. Venus, who was "thirty-two years old, five Feet four Inches high, stout made, [and] very smooth tongued," worked in the Dismal Swamp for two years and both she and Jack "carried with them several different Kinds of Apparel."[23] Jack, also known as Jack Dismal, remained on the run as late as 1773, when his enslaver, Robert Burrell, placed an additional ad for his return. The pair was at large in July 1778, when Mary Burwell placed an ad for their capture and return, along with two other women, Zeny and her daughter Nelly.[24] They were reportedly seen in the Isle of Wight, near the swamp. Sylviane Diouf has noted that the Dismal's maroon communities were unique in that they were established in two distinctive zones, the interior hinterland and the borderlands along the edges. The Dismal's shingle getters comprised one key population of potential maroons, although they are documented in limited primary sources. Enslaved people who fled local farms and plantations comprised a second population. Dismal swamp maroons gradually became confined to "shrinking geographic spaces into the Dismal's deepest reaches."[25]

Petit marronage was accepted by many enslavers as a part of the slave system. Some enslaved women often ran away with temporary goals in mind. This was the case with Moses Grandy's mother, who lived near the swamp in Camden, North Carolina. According to Grandy, his mother hid his four sisters and four brothers in the woods "to prevent master from selling us. When we wanted water, she sought for it in any hole or puddle formed by falling trees or otherwise . . . . For food, she gathered berries in the woods, got potatoes, raw corn . . . . After a time, the master would send word to her to come in, promising he would not sell us."[26]

While living in the Dismal Swamp, African Americans produced rice and other grains, as well as engaged in informal economies of exchange. Two Norfolk merchants who worked with the DSC, William Atchison and James Parker, wrote in their account ledger in the 1780s or 1790s that an African American man "ran away from his Master & lived by himself in the [Great Dismal Swamp] about 13 years & came out 2 years ago." The man raised "Rice & other grain & made Chairs Tables & musical instruments."[27] Although the merchants did not mention the market for which the maroon produced his wares, their description provides evidence that an informal exchange economy existed in the Great Dismal Swamp among maroons.

The swamp life was difficult. Wild animals remained a threat and the difficulties of traveling through the terrain constituted a danger to life and limb. Greater exposure to the elements and the ever-present damp were injurious to health. However, the swamp was unaffected by decay, as luxuriant vegetation constantly dying and falling into the water and wet ground turned into peat, due to the bacteria-free water of the Dismal Swamp. "This water of high acid content (and black in color) was self-purifying. The maroons had the purest, safest drinking water," which may have also had medicinal properties.[28] "The swamp also teemed with game animals, and the maroon livelihood was above all that of a hunter." Opossum and racoon, venison, wild pig, wild goat, duck, partridges and pheasant, and fish were available to maroons. For vegetables, women kept small kitchen gardens on the elevated drier land of their settlements. "An ever-present flower, the lupine, contained grains which made a palatable cereal dish, even eaten dry." Bread was made from a type of Dismal Swamp reed, which was "a fair substitute for wheat."[29]

A description of a Dismal Swamp maroon community in the deeper Swamp is described in Albert R. Ledoux's *Princess Anne: A Story of the Dismal Swamp and Other Sketches* (1896). According to Ledoux, the dry land on which the community was built rose gently from the surrounding swamp. "The houses were not scattered but close enough to constitute a village. They were built of logs and stood on sturdy stilts, to discourage insect or animal invaders. The houses were furnished with benches and chairs hewn from logs and effectively carpentered. Beds were in the form of wooden shelves, piled high with blankets stuffed with moss and sewed up."[30] Ledoux's description of maroon furnishings is consistent with the account given by an unnamed maroon who came out of the swamp, claiming that he raised "Rice & other grain & made Chairs Tables & musical instruments."[31]

During the American Revolution, *petit marronage* in the Dismal Swamp was common. In 1777, traveler and writer Elkanah Watson rode from Suffolk to Edenton, North Carolina, along the western edge of the swamp. He recalled, "We travelled near the North border of the great Dismal Swamp, which at this time, was infested by concealed royalists, and runaway negroes, who could not be approached with safety. They often attacked travelers, and had recently murdered a Mr. Williams."[32] Many of the DSC slaves saw wartime confusion as an opportunity to run away. Six of the company's slaves fled to the British and many "more ran away only to be captured and held as war prizes by neighboring enslavers. Others simply disappeared."[33] During the war, the DSC's company partners did not regularly meet since many of the partners, including George Washington, were directly engaged in the war effort. There is limited information about Dismal Plantation during these years; however, the records do indicate that the plantation's "enslaved people became marooned in the swamp under limited oversight. The plantation fell into significant disrepair during the war and operations subsequently did not restart easily, with slave flight remaining a problem."[34]

The Revolutionary War halted shingle production in the swamp as enslaved workers escaped to the British lines. In August of 1780, John Driver reported that "the Remnant of Negroes left is by no means sufficient to keep the place in order," due to which "the ditches were in disrepair, and rising water levels ruined what corn crop remained."[35] From July 21 to 22, 1781, British soldiers destroyed much of Dismal Plantation, damaging buildings and confiscating animals and provisions. According to Jacob Collee, the company's new agent and overseer, "all the slaves" left with the British, except the aged and infirm. The escapees included twenty-two enslaved men, five children, and seven enslaved women.[36] Eighteen Black men enslaved by the DSC enlisted in Dunmore's Regiment. The DSC recorded the names and descriptions of each fugitive. Davy was "Black and lusty," Ned was "yellow and middle sized," while Jamie was "Black with scars ab[out] his neck."[37] The risk of flight was so great that, when Dismal Swamp Company partner Samuel Gist, who resided in London, directed his Virginia representative and son-in-law William Anderson to purchase more men, Anderson declined due to the lack of money and the risk that "another Dunmore should appear on the Coast."[38] In December 1782, Collee reported more problems with fugitives in the Dismal Swamp stating "We have had a Very Dry summer and have been much plagued with the Runaway Negroes. I have had my barns robed of Corn and Rice."[39] When the British evacuated in 1783, fugitives from Dismal Plantation made their way out of slavery in the United States. The roll of "Negro emigrants" included a number of people with the surname "Dismal," an indication that they chose to identify with the place where they labored, loved, and which they finally abandoned.[40]

The DSC purchased additional slave labor after the war, though not enough to compensate for the loss of women and men during the war. Lacking tools for ditching, draining, and making shingles, Dismal Plantation focused on cultivating rice and corn, which barely covered expenses and taxes on the plantation. A difficult winter in 1784 brought harsh conditions to Dismal Plantation, exacerbated by reports of the company's hogs being killed by "runaway Negroes from other plantations."[41] Because of "a lack of hands," women and girls were said to be plowing the fields instead of men. By June 1788, the plantation suffered from a lack of provisions of all kinds, forcing enslaved men and women to supplement their diets with hunting, fishing, and trading. During the 1790s, Dismal Plantation remained a haphazard operation with agents and overseers unable to compel enslaved laborers to perform routine maintenance tasks or to prevent slaves from fleeing.[42] As a result, the company began transitioning to hiring enslaved workers from nearby plantations instead of purchasing them. However, this became difficult as Jacob Collee, the overseer, reported that "no person inclines to hire their

Negroes to work at the Swamp."[43] This reluctance could have been due to the potential for escape. At the 1804 Dismal Swamp Company meeting, the managers had resolved to sell all remaining enslaved men, women, and children owned by the company, which officially ended the plan of a self-sustaining farming plantation. Workers in the swamp were now mostly leased enslaved men or hired free Black men.[44]

The economic decline of Dismal Plantation coincided with the outbreak of slave conspiracies and rebellion in Virginia and North Carolina. The Dismal Swamp region played an important role in the conspiracies that unfolded from 1792 to 1802. Maroons conspired with participants and leaders of the planned revolts to subvert the slave system. In the summer of 1792, plans for insurrection commenced, involving enslaved women and men in Norfolk, Portsmouth, Hampton, and Northampton counties. According to a letter dated May 17, 1792, the planned revolt involved about 900 slaves "assembled in different parts, armed with muskets, spears, clubs & [who] committed several outrages upon the inhabitants."[45] Celeb, "the property of Mr. Simkins was to command the banditti." Celeb had been a favorite servant of his enslaver and had also held the position of overseer. "The group engaged in talks with slave communities across the Dismal Swamp and Norfolk side of the Chesapeake Bay. Their plan was to cross over at night, join with other slaves of the mainland, and blow up the arsenal at Norfolk" and massacre the inhabitants.[46] The authorities confiscated several weapons that were made by an enslaved Blacksmith on Virginia's Eastern shore, which included spears, guns, musket balls, powder, and provisions. A large number of slaves were captured and hanged.[47] Rumors of slave conspiracies and revolts emanated from the outbreak of the Haitian Revolution on the island of Saint-Domingue in 1791. Servants listened intently to the dinner conversations of their enslavers, and Black sailors carried word of the insurrection to cities such as Norfolk. Throughout the 1790s and early 1800s, planters and government officials remained on edge and were growing increasingly fearful that enslaved women and men would take up arms against them.[48]

Fear of conspiracies and slave flight was not limited to the slave South. In Albany, New York, two women and one man were executed in 1794 for setting fires, which caused damage totaling $250,000. Another arson scare involving slaves occurred in New York and New Jersey in 1796. The number of enslaved people who ran away from their enslavers reached a peak in the decade before New York enacted its gradual manumission law in 1799. Nearly one-third of the 1,232 self-emancipated people of color took flight between 1796 and 1800.[49] The 1790s also witnessed the arrival of emigrants and their slaves from Saint-Domingue into New York and New Jersey. Although the bulk of refugees from the revolution settled in Charleston, hundreds more came north to New York and East Jersey. Haitian slaves came mostly from Angola and from a society characterized by marronage and rebellion. Their struggle strongly affected the French abolition of slavery in its colonies, which occurred on February 4, 1794, and freed more than 700,000 people in the West Indies, although Napoleon revoked the decree abolishing slavery in 1802. Saint-Domingue slaves were quick to run away and many participated in the arson scare of 1796. For some Haitian Blacks, however, the transfer to a new slave society was too traumatic and they committed suicide.[50]

The American Revolution and the revolution in Saint-Domingue also inspired Gabriel Prosser's rebellion in 1800. Born in 1776, Gabriel Prosser lived on Brookfield plantation, a tobacco and wheat estate six miles north of Richmond. In 1796, Gabriel married Nanny, an enslaved woman working on a nearby plantation. Very little is known about Nanny and whether she bore children with Gabriel. She was likely a few years younger than Gabriel, since enslaved women typically married and bore children young and had settled into permanent relationships by the age of twenty. The age of revolution had impressed upon enslaved people like Gabriel and Nanny that the "tree of liberty must be refreshed from time to time with the blood of patriots and tyrants," as Thomas Jefferson observed.[51] The men Gabriel assembled had been "raised amidst the heady talk of liberty and freedom and lived in a region awash with refugees from Saint-Domingue."[52] Service in the American Revolution had played a role in the later actions of Dominguan rebels Henri Christophe and André Riguad, and word of victory in Saint-Domingue emboldened American slaves who hoped to make the American republic live up to its stated ideals.[53]

By the spring of 1800, the conspiracy was well formed. Fears of an insurrection alarmed Governor James Monroe, who wrote to Thomas

Jefferson in April of his concerns that a "negro insurrection" could occur. Nanny, Gabriel, and his lieutenants had assembled crude swords, bayonets, and five hundred bullets. Each Sunday, Gabriel entered Richmond, impressing the city's features upon his mind and paying particular attention to the location of arms and ammunition. He also used these visits to spread word of his plans and to recruit followers. The rebellion was set to take place on August 30, on which day 150 slaves, "some mounted, armed with clubs, scythes, home-made bayonets, and a few guns," appeared at a rendezvous point six miles outside of Richmond.[54] The attack did not occur because a torrential thunderstorm that evening destroyed the bridge across which the slaves would pass. Over the course of several days, scores of slaves were arrested across the state of Virginia. Gabriel attempted to escape aboard the schooner *Mary*, but when the vessel reached Norfolk, he was recognized and betrayed by two slaves, and was subsequently captured and brought back in chains to Richmond. Governor James Monroe personally interviewed him and reported that Gabriel had "made up his mind to die." Nanny was likely among those who were captured, although her fate remains unknown. At least thirty-five of the rebels were hanged.[55]

Gabriel fled to Norfolk and his planned insurrection reached areas far from Richmond. Norfolk served as a communication center where Black people had the opportunity to receive news of slave revolts and to discuss the prospect of general freedom. The presence of Dismal Swamp maroons in these regional and interregional insurrections and conspiracies is evident in the events that took place between 1801 and 1802. During these two years, maroons launched frequent guerilla raids on surrounding plantations from both North Carolina and Virginia. The maroon Tom Cooper led a settlement in the Dismal Swamp behind Elizabeth City, North Carolina, and his band inflicted so much terror in the region that a bounty was placed on his head in Virginia. Captain Jeremiah led a maroon settlement in Virginia's Dismal Swamp. Jeremiah and his band of maroons were captured by authorities in what became a massive round-up of slaves believed to be conspiring to revolt. Jeremiah, along with several other slaves, was executed. Fear of insurrections was pervasive in the months and years following Gabriel's conspiracy.[56]

Freedom was achievable for enslaved people at Dismal Town, who faced myriad challenges during and after the Revolution. Enslaved men and women escaped with the British or fled to spaces within the swamp, where they remained for months or years. The construction of waterways during the 1800s to "maximize exploitation of the swamp's lumber resources had the secondary effect of increasing the capability for fugitives to pass through the swamp landscape along ditches and canals, through the central point of Lake Drummond, and along the Dismal Swamp Canal north to the port of Norfolk" and for ships to reach northern ports and Canada.[57]

BELLEISLE AND BEAR CREEK

Most maroons did not look for freedom in remote areas. Instead, they settled in the borderlands of farms and plantations. Sylviane Diouf refers to this group as "borderland maroons." Borderland maroons proved effective at disrupting the plantation regimen. In North Carolina, smaller maroon bands resided in various swamps, at different times plundering plantations and causing widespread panic. In 1767, the Wilmington militia was dispatched to deal with "upwards of Twenty runaway slaves in a body arm'd," and in 1788 a captured runaway slave was summarily executed from "a gang of runaways who infested the said Town & neighborhood," much to the disgust of the enslaver.[58] Efforts to deter maroons from rebelling through executions were not effective, as demonstrated by another band of maroons located near Wilmington in 1795 who "in the daytime secrete[d] themselves in the swamps and woods [but] at night committed various depredations on the neighboring plantations."[59] The group was led by a "chieftain who styled himself The General of the Swamps," but after he and others were killed by the militia, local White authorities were hopeful that they had broken up "this nest of miscreants."[60]

The Revolutionary War inspired fugitive women and men to remain at large in maroon camps after the war. Fatima and Hannah, along with several others, joined a maroon colony on Belleisle Island in Lowcountry, Georgia, after being transported to Florida to labor on plantations and subsequently sold to South Carolina planter Godin Guerard in 1785.

Sixteen people escaped on May 1, 1785 from Guerard's plantation, including seven women and three children ranging in age from eighteen months to eight years. Earlier, Guerard had purchased a "considerable number of Negroes from St. Augustine," whereby at least five from this group – Frank, Sechem, Dembo, Cook, and his wife Peggy – ran away to join the maroon community. The leaders of this corps of runaways had been trained by the British during the siege of Savannah and called themselves the King of England's soldiers. They included Captain Sharper, also known as Captain Cudjoe, and Captain Lewis.[61] After the war, these maroons, consisting of one hundred, established themselves on Belleisle Island near the Savannah River, where they grew rice and corn. Among them were Jimmy, Nancy, and Patience, who emancipated themselves from Philip Ulmer's plantation in Chatham County, Georgia. According to the *Charleston Morning Post*, the men and women "committed robberies on the neighboring Planters" with such frequency that in October 1786 the militia was called to attack their encampment.[62]

The Grand Jury of Savannah-Chatham County in early October 1786 denounced the fact that "large gangs of runaway Negroes are allowed to remain quietly within a short distance of this town" and blamed the militia officers for their inaction.[63] The Grand Jury's admonition had immediate effect. On Wednesday, October 11, men from the Chatham artillery militia, which had formed six days prior, were sent to pursue the maroons, who referred to themselves as the "King of England's soldiers." The militia located and attacked the settlement on Belleisle Island, located seventeen miles north of Savannah. The maroons "came down in such numbers that it was judged advisable" for the militia to return to their boats.[64] The militia, led by James Jackson, a hero of the Revolution and future U.S. senator and Georgia governor, came back prepared and "burnt a number of their houses and huts and destroyed about four acres of green rice." The loss of the maroons' provisions was expected to disperse them, which would aid in their capture.[65] When Jackson arrived, however, he found the settlement empty. "The maroons had either fled on foot deeper into the island carrying with them their most precious belongings, or they had other boats at their disposal and left the area altogether."[66] The militia had confiscated fourteen canoes owned by the maroons.

Following the destruction of the camp on Belleisle Island, Jackson informed the governor of South Carolina, Thomas Pinckney, that the "daring banditti of slaves, who some weeks since, attacked two of my detachments, & were at last with difficulty dislodged from their camp," were his problem too.[67] Jackson discovered that the "banditti" were at or near Hartstone's Swamp in South Carolina, where one hundred had been seen in the area. The swamp was located twenty miles north of Savannah and the maroons were making frequent incursions into Georgia. Despite losing their canoes, the maroons were still mobile. They needed food and were determined to get it on both sides of the Savannah River, aggravating citizens in Georgia and South Carolina from October 1786 through March 1787.[68]

Pinckney and other legislators called on the militia and authorized the recruitment of twenty Catawba Native Americans to capture or kill the maroons. On March 23, 1787, the governor issued a proclamation offering ten pounds for each maroon, "dead or alive." Pinckney then informed the governor of Georgia, George Matthews, of the upcoming assault and asked for cooperation, stating, "As the Citizens of both States are interested in the reduction of these [people,] I have no doubt that your honor will see the expediency of a joint exertion."[69]

From Hartstone Swamp, the maroons headed to Bear Creek in Georgia, where they built another encampment. They constructed twenty-one houses on Bear Creek and fortified their encampment with logs and canes four feet high. The breastwork had a small opening that admitted only one person at a time. The maroons placed a sentinel 150 yards from the encampment to give warning of an attack. In the end, all of the defensive work the maroons constructed proved futile. On May 6, 1787, the militia killed the sentry and they were able to reach the settlement and enter it despite the fortification. Captain Cudjoe followed a classic maroon strategy. He ordered the women to flee and his men fired a few shots to slow the militia's progress.[70] Six maroons were killed and their possessions – seven boats and provisions – were taken by the assailants. The militia attacked the encampment, "burnt their houses and destroyed their crops." The next day, the militia and the Catawbas killed two maroons while Captain John Martin Dasher, who led a small militia company from Effingham County, Georgia, came across eighteen men, women, and children. The group was planning to reach the "Indian nation" in Florida, according to Dasher. The assault lasted four days and led to the death and capture of several maroons who fought the militia vigorously.[71] Captain Cudjoe and his wife Nancy managed to escape and made their way to St. Augustine, Florida, according to historian Jane Landers.[72] Among those who were captured were Juliet and Peggy, who acknowledged that "they were among the runaway negroes in Abercorn swamp," which served as an appellation for Belleisle Island.[73]

Captain Lewis, the other maroon leader, had escaped; however, he was captured in South Carolina sometime during the week commencing May 14, 1787. He was brought to Savannah and placed on trial for the murder of John Casper Herman and the robbery of Philip Ulmer, John Lowerman of Georgia, and Col. Bourqin of South Carolina. In addition to Lewis, two other maroons – Juliet and Peggy – testified. The trial was held in front of four justices of the peace and seven jurors. Lewis, who had no legal representation, tried to exonerate himself of the murder charge and sought to portray himself as helpful to three planters to diminish the robbery charges. Lewis denied killing Herman and instead pointed the finger at fellow maroon Sechem.[74] "Juliet, whose husband Pope was killed, testified that Lewis was present when Sechem murdered Herman and threw him into the pond." However, she also conceded that her testimony was based on hearsay since she was not present during the events she described. Juliet added that Lewis was part of the group that had robbed Lowerman and that he was in the camp and armed when the militia arrived. Peggy, who also lost her husband Cook in the assault, implicated Lewis in not only the plunder at Philip Ulmer's place, but also the bloody incident at Bourquin's, and two other incidents: the expedition to planter Guerard's home; and the shootout with enslaver Jacob [Winkler]. Peggy also confirmed that Lewis was present when Herman was killed.[75] While both women concurred that Lewis did not kill Herman, he was found guilty by the jury. Lewis was condemned to death by hanging on the South common of Savannah, "After which his head to be Cut of and Stuck upon a pole to be sett up on the Island of Marsh opposite the Glebe land in Savannah River." Lewis was hung on Saturday June 9, 1787. The jury and justices appraised his worth at thirty pounds sterling.[76]

The fate of Juliet and Peggy remains unclear; however, other survivors of Bear Creek returned to their enslavers. On May 17, 1787, the press reported that "some of them are coming in daily to their owners." Still, others might have found refuge in Florida as Captain Cudjoe and Nancy had done, or may have settled as borderland maroons in familiar territory. About two months after the destruction of the Bear Creek settlement, maroon activity increased on the Stono River, roughly eighty miles east. The sentiment among enslavers and their allies, however, was that a calamity had been narrowly avoided.[77]

LOWER MISSISSIPPI VALLEY MAROONS

Borderland maroons lived in non-kin groups that coalesced around shared experiences of oppression and flight. In July 1771, a group of six fugitive women and men were arrested in the fields of Attakapas County, Louisiana. Their interrogation records shed light on the longevity of their marronage and how they survived. One of its members, Mariana, was looking for food when she was caught in the dairy of Mr. de Saint Denis. Mariana escaped slavery in New Orleans and had been away for eight months in the company of another woman, a man, and a young child.[78] "She stayed briefly on Louis Harang's plantation before meeting Louis, a maroon of two years, who took her and the other woman to the woods. Joining them were Charlot, who had run away from New Orleans and was absent for fourteen or fifteen months; Gil, also from New Orleans and a fugitive for two years, and Miguel, who had left the city three months earlier and spent most of his time in the woods. Jean-Baptiste Raoul had been away from New Orleans for seven months and had lived in various places together with other maroons."[79] The group, formerly held by different enslavers over 130 miles away, "had gathered at different times and pooled their resources together in order to survive."[80]

In St. Charles Parish, Louisiana, a group of twelve fugitives was arrested by the slave patrol in October 1805. The group included women and men born in Africa, Louisiana, and the Caribbean. Among them was forty-year-old Celeste, who was born in the Congo and lived in New Orleans before she fled with her husband James, a Creole. Other members of the group included Marie, Charles, Lucie, Senegaux, and Eitienne, as well as mulattos Augustine Kernion and John. The group lived in the cypress swamp near the Labarre Plantation, but decided to split up when they saw one of their enslavers searching for his runaways. Eight of the fugitives hid near Ms. Pain's place while four stayed at Labarre. "Celeste revealed that she and three others lived for two weeks with other maroons, whose leader was a man named Francois from New Orleans," and that she was aware of another group "hiding in the swamps along the shore of Lake Ponchartrain."[81]

Throughout Louisiana, enslaved women and men fled into the swamps and bayous bordering plantations on the Mississippi River. Three fugitive women – Maria Juana, Margarita, and Nancy – were part of a maroon camp established in the borderlands of Mr. Raguet's plantation at Cane's Bayou in 1781. The maroon camp consisted of twenty-one persons from fifteen plantations, and women represented a quarter of the community. Maria, Margarita, and Nancy were arrested by an expedition led by the captain of the New Orleans militia, Juan Bautista Bienvenu, but managed to join another group of maroons headed to Terre Gaillarde. "Terre Gaillarde was not a village but a territory on which a settlement had been erected."[82] Louisiana was under Spanish control at the time, and the Spaniards "acknowledged the reality of marronage and either named settlements or called them by their maroon names in official correspondence."[83] Terre Gaillarde was located far enough from settled areas to provide safety and was hard to reach due to its unknown and inaccessible paths. According to Governor Esteban Miró, to get there one had to wade through reeds in chest-high water. The zone the land abutted was scarcely populated and the land could not be cultivated beyond the banks due to the presence of marshes. "Terre Gaillard was thus ideally located amid wild land and, as an added safety feature, it could only be entered through small waterways from Lake Borgne."[84]

In the late 1770s and 1780s, Maria, Margarita, and Nancy became a part of the St. Malo maroons located in permanent settlements such as Ville Gaillarde and Chef Menteur. The group menaced nearby plantations by "stealing what they wanted."[85] The maroons also received assistance from enslaved men and women working on those plantations who provided them with food and shelter. The maroons established villages in the cypress swamps of Bas du Fleuve in St. Bernard Parish and forged an economic relationship with local sawmill owners, who paid the maroons for cutting and supplying cypress logs. The St. Malo maroons were targeted by Spanish authorities, who launched a military expedition to destroy the villages. The testimony of the maroons captured during the March 1, 1783 raid reveals the strength of family ties. Ville Gaillarde was a haven for wives and children. Goton, a fugitive woman, testified that she had run away because her enslaver repeatedly punished her. She left with her husband Huberto, her sons Bautista and Cupidon, her daughter Catiche, and Cupidon's wife Theresa. They hid behind their enslaver's plantation for two months, eating rice that they carried with them and meat supplied by other fugitives in the woods. After leaving the bayou, the group traveled to Ville Gaillarde and met other fugitives along the way. La Violette, a male with a feminine name, was one of the maroons Goton met. He was killed by a gunshot when Ville Gaillarde was attacked.[86] The dozens of maroon women and men who were attacked at Ville Gaillarde led to the surrender of women such as Theresa who "gave herself up" when she thought her husband Cupidon was about to be killed by Whites.[87] Goton's daughter, Catiche, was captured at Ville Gaillarde and later testified that she had run away because her mother and stepfather were fleeing.

The raid on the Ville Gaillarde was a serious blow to the leader St. Malo and the maroons of Bas du Fleuve. Authorities sought to follow up on the raid by capturing St. Malo and his band of maroons. St. Malo's band consisted of thirty-eight maroons, which included twelve women. Only two of the maroons were listed as wives. On July 1, 1784, Spanish authorities reported the capture of 103 maroons, which included those caught in the raid on Ville Gaillarde on March 1, 1783. The expedition succeeded in capturing the maroon leadership, including St. Malo and his wife Cecilia Canuet, a free Black woman who was charged with being his "inseparable companion in all his exploits."[88] Fifteen women in all were captured. While St. Malo was executed by hanging, his wife Cecilia was spared because she claimed to be pregnant, which was likely untrue because on October 25, 1784, "her execution was suspended when she claimed again to be in the early stages of pregnancy."[89] Her ultimate fate remains unknown. Six women were condemned "to wear a halter around their necks and were to be flogged two hundred times at the foot of the gallows." The women were also branded with an "m" for maroon on the right cheek.[90]

PROSPECT BLUFF

Compared with women who ran away in groups, isolated women faced even greater challenges. To take care of themselves and their children in the woods, "women needed to build shelters, fish, hunt, and trap. They had to learn how to do these things as they went along, and some never did."[91] A young North Carolina woman whose husband "deserted her" was not good at hunting and fishing. "She fed her children frogs, terrapins, snakes, and mice" to sustain them, and when she was no longer able to feed her family after seven years, she surrendered.[92] Mothers who took their children to the woods and swamps were able to spare them from the brutality and oppression of slavery, but their lives were nonetheless dangerous, restrictive, and stressful. "Although nominally free, they were virtual prisoners as their movement was restricted to a small perimeter mostly accessible at night and condemned to a life of whispers. The children of a mother from North Carolina experienced severe constraints . . . by the strictest discipline, she prevented them ever crying aloud, she compelled them to stifle their little cries and complaints . . . [and] prohibited them from speaking louder than a whisper."[93] Sally, a Georgia fugitive woman, and her "two mulatto children" escaped in May 1764 a few days after they were bought. Their former enslaver had died, and they had been auctioned off to Alexander Wylly, a justice of the peace in Christ Church Parish in Savannah. According to Wylly, the family had "run away into the woods," and he was so anxious to get them back that he placed twenty-two ads for their return. Ten months after they had escaped, Sally and her two children were still at large and were believed to have gone to Florida.[94]

After the American Revolution, Spain recovered Florida but only exercised nominal control over the territory. Although the Spanish policy of offering freedom officially ended in 1790, enslaved women and men from Georgia and South Carolina continued to find safe haven in Florida and gradually formed maroon communities with minimal interference from the Spanish. The case of Prospect Bluff in western Florida illustrated the extent to which women desired their freedom. In the second decade of the nineteenth century, a large and well-organized maroon community emerged at Prospect Bluff during the War of 1812, when British Colonel Edward Nicolls was ordered to raise an army of slaves and Indians in the Southeast as part of the larger British plan to capture New Orleans. Nicolls viewed his mission as an opportunity to execute an anti-slavery plan by granting former slaves full political and legal equality with other members of the British Empire. As a result of his plan, hundreds of former slaves were convinced that they were full British subjects in charge of a British-built fort at Prospect Bluff and its immense store of supplies and hardware. At its peak, the community's population numbered hundreds of men, women, and children originating from numerous societies across the African diaspora, including Pensacola, Mobile, and adjacent areas. They lived in and around a formidable British-built fort in well-constructed houses, cultivated their fields, participated in an exchange economy, enjoyed flourishing cultural lives, served in an organized militia, and developed a political system. Fugitive women found in Prospect Bluff an opportunity to escape their bondage and join a maroon community with little fear of being persecuted. Women stayed at Prospect Bluff because they believed that the community offered a realistic opportunity for permanent freedom and safety.[95] This was the case for Sally and her three children, who fled their enslaver and found refuge there.[96]

What distinguished Prospect Bluff from other successful maroon settlements in the Western Hemisphere was its relationship with the British, as well as its brief status (for the duration of fifteen months) as a fully independent community once the British departed in May 1815. The maroons produced a consistent supply of food for themselves and established several plantations "on the fertile banks of the Appalachicola which would have yielded them every article of sustenance."[97] A British soldier described the plantations as consisting of "green corn, melons," and the Creek informant William McGirt saw "several houses inside the fort filled with everything plenty corn and Rice a side; no scarcity."[98] In addition to corn, melon, and rice, marine life and wild game provided sustenance. Fish, alligators, deer, and wild turkey regularly drew hunters deep into the woods. This may have contributed to the demise of Prospect Bluff, as the fort's defenders were out hunting and fishing when the American military launched its assault on the compound.[99]

In July 1816, hundreds of American and Creek soldiers destroyed the fort at Prospect Bluff after a ten-day siege.[100] According to Herbert Aptheker, 270 men, women, and children were killed, but 40 souls survived. Among those captured was Dolly and her five children. Dolly worked at a store on the Apalachicola River and refused to leave when the invasion occurred. She and her children were moved east to Pensacola, where they remained enslaved. Other women captured by Americans entering the fort met a gruesome fate. The wife of Garçon, the captain at Prospect Bluff, was killed when the troops "hewed her head with their Swords until they killed her."[101] Similar acts of destruction occurred in other maroon settlements. In March 1811, a runaway community in a swamp in Cabarrus County, North Carolina, was wiped out by authorities. These maroons were defiant against any force and were "resolved to stand their ground." In the attack, two fugitive women were captured, two fugitive men killed and another was wounded. Likewise, the *Norfolk Herald* reported the capture of a leader and "an old woman" member of the outlaws in June 1818 who, along with thirty other runaways, damaged property in Princess Anne County, Virginia.[102]

***

Black women's marronage throughout the South reveals much about slave resistance during the Age of Revolution, which inspired profound and rapid intellectual, social, and political change across the Western Hemisphere. Enslaved and free people of color played a pivotal role in this early period of abolitionism. They shared in the collective stream of hope at the profound change that was occurring, and they orchestrated an unprecedented series of escapes that resulted in the first large-scale rebellion (through flight) of enslaved women and men in the mainland colonies and states. Although their desire for freedom did not originate with the American Revolution, the Revolution intensified it. Despite facing tremendous challenges during and after the Revolution, fugitive women in maroon societies made freedom moves into spaces of their own. Their own interests and concerns for their families prompted a declaration of independence in the swamps and woods of Virginia, North Carolina, Louisiana, South Carolina, Georgia, and Florida. A sense of self-identity, forged in the Colonial period and strengthened by the Revolutionary War, imbued them with a sense of community and cooperative effort. Enslaved women who escaped to join maroon communities unabashedly claimed the liberty denied to them and fundamentally transformed their lived experience.

Conclusion

O N NOVEMBER 14, 1776 ENSLAVER FRANCIS PERKINS PLACED
an advertisement in Boston's *Continental Journal* for Nane,
a twenty-seven-year-old enslaved woman who ran away twelve months
earlier. Nane, who wore a "blue Callimanco Gown" and who took
"other Wearing Apparel," told Perkins that she was going on a visit,
perhaps to see friends. She never returned.[1] For Nane and countless
other enslaved women, the era of the American Revolution was as critical
as it was for Black men and for White Americans who gained their
independence from Great Britain.

Black women's various efforts to escape bondage have been viewed as
ancillary in studies of slavery. However, Black women's freedom was inter-
twined with the movement for American independence, and African
American women followed the military conflict and were powerfully influenced by its outcome. Thousands became free and gave new voice to
a growing abolitionist movement. Black women, in fact, played an integral
role in the expansion of abolitionism during the American Revolution.
Abolition in the U.S. occurred in two waves. The American Revolution
triggered the first wave and led to the abolition of slavery in the North.
The second "radical" wave began with the development of immediate
abolitionism enunciated by William Lloyd Garrison in 1831 and lasted
until the end of the Civil War. Instead of viewing Black women as at the
margins of the American Revolution and abolitionism, it is imperative to
see Black women as visible participants and self-determined figures who
put their lives on the line for freedom. Black women have placed their lives
on the line throughout history as evidenced by escapes from slavery,

petitions to courts for freedom, written testimonies of racial violence, and organized protests.

The American Revolution brought into sharp focus the paradox of slavery and freedom. African American women contributed mightily to the story of American Independence. They believed in the independence of the individual. They valued in the most fundamental way what Thomas Jefferson and others would identify as the inalienable rights of life, liberty, and the pursuit of happiness. For African American women, the tyranny of slavery was not simply a metaphor for Anglo-American relations but a real daily lived experience. Their pursuit of liberty broadened the ideology of the American Revolution to include Black women. While the vast majority remained enslaved in a new nation whose 1787 Constitution endorsed the slave system by providing for the return of runaway slaves, the quest for freedom through flight remained one of the most enduring occurrences throughout the era of slavery.

How enslaved women ran is just as informative and intriguing as why and where they ran. They did not run haphazardly into the woods, but established creative and subversive escape strategies. Enslaved women disguised themselves as waiting boys and men, faked physical and mental illness, impersonated White women, posed as Black male soldiers, served as spies, and boarded ships headed to northern cities. Historian Michael Gomez argues that enslaved women's fierceness of spirit can be traced to West Africa, where women had a sense of body autonomy and took risks to protect themselves and their children. Enslaved Igbo women, for example, "featured large as runaways in America" because their "sense of independence" in West Africa was exhibited in multiple arenas – home, marketplace, commerce, and government.[2]

The escape of ordinary Black women is essential to understanding how women built a culture and a politics of resistance to slavery. Through ingenuity, countless enslaved women chose to abscond, providing evidence of their internal fortitude to think critically under pressure in the midst of gendered, racialized, and vulnerable moments in history. Under the daily threat of bodily harm, they imagined the possibility of freedom and transformed that possibility into a lived reality. In doing so, they outsmarted those who sought to subjugate and belittle them. Fugitivity was a political act that changes what we know about Black women's resistance. Black women risked their lives in creative and subversive ways because they believed they had a right "to own your own body," as one former slave stated.[3] The resistance strategies of enslaved Black women are an important lens through which to view their challenges to the structure and power of slavery and their enslavers. The individual stories of escape are historical traces of enormously important acts that shifted the course of human history.

Black women's resistance increased as the nation expanded. The Fugitive Slave Law of 1793 was not just aimed at returning male fugitives, but also aimed to ensure the return of fugitive women, whose productive and reproductive labor were highly valued by enslavers. Fugitivity facilitated a persistent labor problem in the slave economy after the Revolution. Black women voiced their desire for freedom not only through flight, but through freedom suits and petitions for freedom. The freedom claims of women such as Elizabeth Freeman, Grace Davis, and Eady Cary underscore the ways in which women subverted the power dynamic in pursuit of their freedom dreams. In Virginia, the 1795 Freedom Suit Act allowed claimants to submit a petition stating that they had a right to freedom and to sue *in forma pauperis*, as a pauper. In the 1806 case of *Hudgins vs. Wright*, Hannah sued for her freedom based on the Indian ancestry of her mother, Butterwood Nan, who was enslaved. The question of whether Nan was an Indian or just reputed to be one or whether she was legally or illegally enslaved was not proven at the trial. Hannah's enslavers argued that she was legally enslaved whether Black or Indian. Virginia's Supreme Court ruled that Hannah "enjoyed a legal presumption of freedom" because of her Indian ancestry.[4] Using the courts to gain freedom proved to be a propitious strategy for enslaved women who did not see flight as a viable option. Regardless of how they obtained their freedom, Black women played vital roles in their communities by becoming the backbone of mutual aid and benevolent societies, Black churches, and schools, which were established within Black churches or in the homes of African Americans.

The continuing emergence of African American culture and politics in the postwar period and the centrality of Black women in this process is an important part of the larger struggle against slavery and legal inequality. Black women helped lay the foundation of Black institutional life in the North and South and became the conscience of the nation. Free Black women became more politically active as the desire for citizenship and equal rights became central to women's activism in the nineteenth century. Women such as Charlotte Forten and Sarah Douglass worked in the anti-slavery movement to the benefit of not only their communities, but the nation at large. This organic link between the circumstances of Black women's lives and their political thought and action underscores the agency of Black women. In seeking to hold the post-Revolutionary generation to its founding principles, Black women pressed the nation toward its highest possibilities and toward a more perfect union.

The intersection of a number of developments conspired against the egalitarianism of the Revolution and dramatically altered North American slavery. The emergence of cotton as a profitable plantation crop gave slavery a new lease on life. White southerners rapidly moved into the interior of South Carolina, Georgia, Alabama, Mississippi, and Louisiana, taking their slaves with them, and transformed the area into a vibrant and profitable slave society. In the nineteenth century, slavery was central to the Southern economy due to the profitability of cotton and the emergence of the sugar industry in Louisiana and along the Gulf Coast. Thus, ample labor could be acquired through the expanding and highly lucrative internal slave trade fueled by the persistence of plantation slavery in the Chesapeake and Lowcountry. Moreover, the 1791 Haitian Revolution provided a vivid example of what could happen when enslaved people and people of color claimed the inheritance of the Age of Revolution as their own. It emboldened slaves and terrified White enslavers, who became more suspicious of the behavior of the enslaved, which led to a major upsurge in resistance that lasted well into the nineteenth century. White anxiety and Black hope were further heightened by Gabriel's Rebellion in 1800 (Gabriel's wife Nanny was involved in the planning) and the Charles Deslondes revolt of 1811, both of which were viewed through the lens of the Haitian Revolution.

Like the American Revolution, the Haitian Revolution constituted a major conflict in the long war against slavery and in the history of abolitionism. Black abolitionism was exemplified in the words and deeds of the Haitian rebels and they inspired the imagination of abolitionists. The Haitian Revolution facilitated President Thomas Jefferson's acquisition of the Louisiana Territory by ending Napoleon's hope of establishing a French empire in the Western Hemisphere. The acquisition of the Louisiana Territory led to the expansion of slavery in Missouri and Arkansas and implementation of a policy of economic isolation toward Haiti, which lasted until the presidency of Abraham Lincoln. The cross-current of slave revolts across the Atlantic which were inspired by the Haitian Revolution bestowed a legacy of self-determination and activism that reached enslaved and free Black women. In Baltimore, free women of color of Haitian descent founded the Oblate Sisters of Providence, the first Black order of nuns, which played a pivotal role in educating Black children.

The War of 1812 expanded opportunities for Black abolitionism through fugitivity. Enslaved women and men ran away to the lines of the British and played a role in shaping military strategy. Thousands of fugitive slaves supplied information, labor, and military service to the British, and multiple slave conspiracies were uncovered in Maryland, North Carolina, and Virginia. In the Chesapeake, Admiral Alexander Cochrane deliberately planned to encourage slaves to flee to demoralize their enslavers. Cochrane's proclamation of 1814 reprised Lord Dunmore's offer of freedom to slaves and included their families. Over three thousand slaves defected to the British, and some fought as uniformed Colonial Marines. Following the destruction of the Negro Fort at Prospect Bluff in 1816, fugitives in Florida joined with Indian allies to wage war against the United States in Spanish Florida. The First Seminole War was a result of Andrew Jackson's determination to root out Black and Indian resistance, which served as a beacon to runaway slaves from the Carolinas, Georgia, and Alabama.

Freedom-seeking women were inspired to run away both during the Revolutionary War and as the nation expanded. Phillis, an eighteen-year-old fugitive woman, marshaled the strength to escape with her two daughters, eight-year-old Clarry and five-year-old Patience, at the start of the War of 1812. They had been on the run for a month when their enslaver placed an advertisement for their return in Raleigh, North Carolina's *The Star* newspaper.[5] Perhaps his delay in placing an advertisement for their return was based on his belief that Phillis and her children would return on their own. Large numbers of enslaved women escaped or *attempted* to escape bondage, often at great cost to themselves and others. As historians recognize and analyze the depth of this reality, the profundity of the moral, legal, social, and psychological effects of such resistance cannot be ignored, as Cheryl Janifer LaRoche has argued. Runaway newspaper advertisements provide valuable insight into slavery and fugitive women, who are under-represented in other primary sources. As sites of memory, fugitive adver-tisements convey the experiences of enslaved women.

Given the large number of Black women in bondage and their impor-tance to enslavers, one cannot accurately represent the institution with-out considering gender as a focal variable. The centrality of Black women to our understanding of experience and identity has taught scholars much about the deep and complex connections between the personal and the political. Diverse types of evidence beyond the historical narra-tive – including enslaved women's consciousness, culture, and value systems – are equally crucial to the understanding of their struggles. By highlighting the varied strategies and conditions of escape that freedom-seeking women encountered during the Revolutionary Era, it becomes evident that enslaved Black women used their resourcefulness to expand the boundaries of freedom.

Bringing to life the stories of the faceless and nameless individuals that are typically the subject of historical discussions on Black runaways dur-ing the Revolution underscores the ways in which enslaved women struggled to gain their freedom. One-third of Revolutionary War run-aways were women, and more than half fled in groups rather than alone. Roughly 25 percent of the ads sought slaves who had fled in family groups consisting of husbands, wives, and young children. These fugitives con-sidered the possibility of creating a new life outside of slavery far more realistic during the chaos of the Revolution and wanted to take that chance with their entire families. The evidence presented refutes the misconception that enslaved women did not flee or *attempt* to flee slavery. Women and girls of highly diverse circumstances escaped both individu-ally and collectively before, during, and after the American Revolution.

When Black women's fugitivity and resistance is mapped throughout the American Revolution it becomes evident that it was more widespread and multifaceted than previously thought. Fugitive women did not con-stitute a monolithic population. They made the decision to escape for a variety of reasons and they established diverse social and economic strategies. They were willing to take drastic measures to secure their freedom and dared to invent alternatives to what enslavers delineated as their position and status within a slave society. To the extent that fugitive women's actions can be gleaned from the scanty historical record, their efforts contribute to our understanding of a critical transformation in the locus of slave resistance.

Telling the stories of fugitive women is a necessary act of recovery for understanding the ethical and racial foundations of the nation. It has been 245 years since Thomas Jefferson issued the Declaration of Independence, proclaiming that all men are created equal and have a right to life, liberty, and the pursuit of happiness. Yet, America is still struggling to live up to the ideals enshrined in that document. Both successful and attempted escapes of enslaved women matter to the present-day discourse on freedom and equality, as evidenced by the Black Lives Matter movement, which was started by three Black women – Alicia Garza, Patrisse Cullors, and Opal Tometi – to fight for freedom, liberation, and justice. Black women's resistance matters in the historical discourse on slave resistance since women did much of the work in sustaining family and kinship networks and anchoring slave communities.

Indeed, the experiences of fugitive women have occupied a peripheral position in studies of fugitivity. Many historians have simply incorporated women's experiences into those of men rather than recognizing enslaved women's stories of escape as unique sources of historical evidence. The stories of the women discussed in this study reflect a resolute form of resistance in the face of the nation's reliance on their reproductive capacity to perpetuate and sustain its economic development. In their roles as wives, mothers, and family and community members, women developed several gendered strategies of escape, persisting to overcome myriad disadvantages. Although their histories represent unresolvable narratives in that, for a majority of the cases, we do not know their ultimate fate, their flight is a testament of their resistance to the subjugation and commodification of their bodies. The movement of Black bodies, objects, and information *away* from plantations and enslavers' spaces through flight established a "rival geography" that allowed Black women to enter into the historical record through runaway newspaper advertisements as ideologues and contributors to America's first freedom war. Fugitive Black women were producers of knowledge who carefully thought about their actions and carefully devised strategies and tactics. Recognizing their contribution requires broadening our perspectives to recognize how the actions, ideas, and the political vision of enslaved Black women were an integral part of this social movement.

Enslaved women were neither passive participants to their oppression nor victimized women who waited passively for God to deliver them. They often acted on their own behalf by using a variety of resistance strategies, some subtle and silent such as feigning illness, others more dramatic, which included self-mutilation and suicide. When an enslaved woman hanged herself in 1829, a Georgia planter expressed shock and dismay, asserting that he could see no reason why she would want to take her own life. The violence that was an everyday feature of Black women's lived experience and the experience of their children often motivated Black women to escape bondage in any way possible. Clarry (mentioned earlier), Phillis's eight-year-old daughter, had been burned on one of her sides, which could have motivated Phillis to flee with her children. Other women with young children took similar actions. Sooky fled with her four-year-old daughter Olive two days after she was purchased by Henry Potter at a Wake County, North Carolina sheriff's sale. Peggy escaped with her three children ranging in age from two months to six years from New Hanover County, North Carolina and seventeen-year-old Poll fled with her fourteen-month-old son Hardy from Jones County, North Carolina.[6]

As Black women escaped, they transformed the wilderness into spaces where creative imagination could flourish and subversive action could begin. In the maroon communities established in Virginia, North Carolina, South Carolina, Georgia, Florida, and Louisiana Black women helped to establish subsistence economies, they contributed to an exchange economy, and they nurtured their families in an environment of anxiety and struggle. The woods and swamps were home to a range of people who would rather "die in the woods [or] live in a cave ... rather than remain a slave."[7] For Hannah, a habitual runaway from Virginia, who escaped to the woods with two of her children, living in the woods proved deadly. One of her children died and the other became ill from exposure. She was captured but ran away again pregnant with her third child. She remained in the woods for nearly a year and lost her child to exposure.[8] Despite the dangers of their inhospitable environments, maroons made the most of the opportunities to live away from plantations and endeavored to carve out spaces and create communities that offered self-determination and freedom.

As the nineteenth century unfolded, it became apparent that revolutions that go forward can also go backward as Patrick Rael has stated. The counter-revolution that occurred was characterized by the consolidation of power by the slavocracy and a massive expansion of the plantation system. There would be 698,000 Black people enslaved at the end of the Revolution, nearly double the pre-Revolutionary slave population. Even as the nation wrapped itself in the cloak of equality, new ideologies fueled by scientific racism emerged that excluded Black people from democracy's promise. As free Blacks began the process of building their communities, they found themselves excluded from all but the most menial employment, barred from White established churches, denied equal access to education, and deprived of the many rights of citizenship. Yet, as historian Martha Jones demonstrates, free African Americans were able to "perform citizenship" by doing some things that citizens did and thus normalizing their presence and the exercise of their rights in a free society.

Embedded in larger narratives of escape are loss, trauma, and resilience. Hannah (mentioned earlier), who lost two children, experienced a historical fracturing of her identity as a result of the loss of her children and the trauma of recapture and then escape again. Her enslaver, Mary Bowie, whose guardian R.L.T. Beall acted on her behalf, petitioned the court of Westmoreland County, Virginia to have her sold because of her recidivism. According to the petition "it was useless to attempt to hire her out" and that "Hannah [should] be sold and that the money arising from her sale, either loaned out, or invested again in negroes."[9] Hannah's story is one of loss, but also perseverance and persistence. Fugitive women's stories are a necessary act of recovery from the trauma in the archive of Black women's experiences. Their stories speak to aspects of a collective past that hold present-day meaning for the continuous and changing present of slavery's unresolvable past.

Fugitive Women Émigrés to Nova Scotia and Sierra Leone

SARAH

Sarah, who had been enslaved by Harry Smith of Charleston, South Carolina fled to the British Army in 1775. She married Isaac Anderson in 1776, who also left Charleston with the royal governor, Lord William Campbell. Both were evacuated to Nova Scotia in 1783. In Nova Scotia, Sarah and Isaac lived in Birchtown, where Isaac worked as a carpenter.

HANNAH

Hannah was a free widow in South Carolina. Hannah married Samuel Burke in New York, who served as a recruiter for Bahamas governor Brigadier Montfort Browne's Loyalist regiment in New York. Both Hannah and Samuel were at the British capture of Charleston in 1780. After being wounded at Hanging Rock, Samuel and Hannah were evacuated to England.

PHYLLIS

Phyllis evacuated from Charleston with her husband David George and their children. Settling in Halifax, Nova Scotia, David established Baptist churches at Shelburne, Preston, and St. Johns, New Brunswick. The couple migrated to Sierra Leone, where Phyllis gave birth to four additional children, adding to the six the couple shared. David took nearly all of his Baptist congregation with him to Sierra Leone.

MINEY

A runaway from Philadelphia, Miney arrived in New York and married Ralph Henry, who joined Lord Dunmore's Ethiopian Regiment in 1776. Henry was enslaved by Patrick Henry, the first governor of Virginia. Miney evacuated with Ralph to Nova Scotia in 1783 and settled at Preston. The couple and their child left for Sierra Leone in 1792.

PEGGY

Peggy ran away from Norfolk, Virginia with her husband and two children. They were taken to New York by the British and evacuated to Nova Scotia in 1783. In 1791, Peggy and her family went to Sierra Leone. Her husband James Jackson was identified as a leader of a riot against officials of the Sierra Leone Company and he was sent to England to be tried for insurrection, leaving Peggy and their children in Sierra Leone.

MARGARET

Margaret and her children were smuggled out of Yorktown to New York. Margaret was married to Thomas Johnson, a free man from Charleston, South Carolina. Margaret and her family were evacuated with the British Legion to Nova Scotia, where they settled at Guysborough. In 1784, Margaret and Thomas went to England and were living at the workhouse in the parish of St. Marylebone, where their third child, Elizabeth, was baptized. In 1787, they were listed among the families receiving weekly payments from the Committee for the Relief of the Black Poor.

RACHEL

Rachel, her husband Luke Jordan, and their four children ran away from the plantation of Solomon Slaughter in Nasemond County, Virginia in 1779. They were taken to New York by a British warship and were evacuated to Nova Scotia in 1783. Rachel and her family lived at Birchtown. In 1792, the family, which now consisted of ten children, migrated to Sierra Leone. The family left Freetown to establish a separate settlement at Pirates Bay in 1796.

VIOLET

Violet fled her enslaver Colonel Young of Wilmington, North Carolina and arrived in New York. She married Boston King, a fugitive from South Carolina who ran away after the siege of Charleston in 1780. Violet and Boston were evacuated to Nova Scotia and lived at Birchtown, where they became converts of "Daddy Moses." Violet and Boston migrated to Sierra Leone in 1792; however, soon after their arrival, Violet died.

SALLY

Sally and her husband Thomas Peters and daughter Clairy ran away from their enslaver William Campbell in Wilmington, North Carolina in March 1776. William served as a sergeant in the Black Pioneers throughout the war. The family was evacuated to Nova Scotia in 1783 and settled near Digby, but when they did not receive the promised land grant, they moved to St. John, New Brunswick. In 1791, Thomas went to England to petition the government, and upon his return organized nearly 1,200 people to relocate to Sierra Leone in 1792. Sally, who had borne six additional children with Thomas, became a widow in 1792 upon the death of Thomas from malaria.

VIOLET SNOWBALL

Violet and her son Nathaniel were enslaved by Richard Murray of Princess Anne County, Virginia. Her husband Nathaniel Snowball was enslaved to Mrs. Shrewstin of Norfolk, Virginia. The family ran away to join Lord Dunmore in 1776. Nathaniel's brother Timothy also went with them. The family was taken to New York and evacuated to Nova Scotia. They lived in Birchtown, where they were members of Daddy Moses's congregation. They left for Sierra Leone in 1792, where Nathaniel was an outspoken critic of the Sierra Leone Company. Nathaniel and Luke

Jordan led an exodus to a new settlement at Pirates Bay, where he was elected governor in 1797.

CHLOE

Chloe came to New York with General Matthews in 1779. She married Nathaniel Wansey, who had run away to the British when they occupied Philadelphia in 1778. Nathaniel went with the British to New York, where he married Chloe. The couple were evacuated to Nova Scotia in 1783 and went to Sierra Leone in 1792.

Source: Cassandra Pybus, *Epic Journeys of Freedom: Runaway Slaves of the American Revolution and Their Global Quest for Liberty* (Boston: Beacon Press, 2006).

Acknowledgments

This book was made possible by a sabbatical from the Department of History and Government at Bowie State University and a grant from the Office of Research and Sponsored Programs at Bowie State University. I thank my dean, George Acquaah, and my department chair, Diarra Robertson, for their support. Since graduate school, the faculty in the History Department at Howard University has shaped my understanding of slavery and women's experiences under the institution. I am indebted to Edna Green Medford, Joseph Reidy, Daryl Michael Scott, Arnold Taylor, Olive Taylor, and Emory Tolbert for modeling the work that historians do in their seminars and classes to inspire and mold my thinking on critical issues in the field. I carry with me each day the desire to make a significant contribution to the field of slavery and women's history and it is my hope that in some small way, I have realized that aspiration with this study.

To my colleagues at Bowie State University who created a collegial environment for me to think through ideas and the intellectual space to work, I am especially thankful. The support and encouragement received from M. Sammye Miller, Mario Fenyo, and William B. Lewis made challenges and road blocks easier to navigate. The librarians for the University System of Maryland at Bowie State University, the University of Maryland, College Park, the University of Maryland Baltimore County, and Morgan State University were instrumental in providing hard to reach sources for this study. My editor, Dr. Natasha, met deadlines and aided in improving the flow of my ideas. I am also indebted to Dr. Peter Breaux, Dr. Edward Baptist, and Dr. Anne Bailey for reading the manuscript and providing helpful comments for improvement, as well as anonymous readers of this manuscript.

I am also grateful to the editors at Cambridge University Press, who were enthusiastic about this project and who enhanced the book's clarity. Cecelia Cancellaro and Rachel Blaifeder at Cambridge shepherded this project along and provided needed support. Although no longer at Cambridge, Deborah Gershenowitz was an early supporter of this project and I am grateful for her insights on this study. I also want to thank the editors at the *Journal of Women's History* who read a chapter of this manuscript and provided helpful feedback to improve the clarity of my arguments. Walter Biggins, formerly of the University of Georgia Press, also read the manuscript and supported its publication. This study was inspired by the work of a multitude of women scholars whose work on Black women and resistance informed my research and writing including Cheryl Janifer LaRoche, Marissa Fuentes, Sylviane A. Diouf, Erica Armstrong Dunbar, Deborah Gray White, Darlene Clark Hine, the late Stephanie M.H. Camp, Thavolia Glymph, Jennifer Morgan, Daina Ramey Berry, and Kali Gross.

I am also indebted to the input of scholars such as Vanessa Holden, who read a chapter of the manuscript in its early stages and provided helpful comments at the Association for the Study of African American Life and History (ASALH) conference. J.T. Roane as Editor of *Black Perspectives*, the blog of the African American Intellectual History Society, also read an abbreviated version of an article published in *Black Perspectives* on Black women and fugitivity. I had the privilege of speaking to Erica Armstrong Dunbar about this study at the ASALH Conference in October 2019 when, in search of an open seat at the Emmanuel Nine Luncheon, she sat next to me. Her study of Ona Judge and African American women in Philadelphia has inspired me in countless ways.

This book builds on ideas presented in my previous publications on enslaved women's resistance during times of war. Most notable are the following: *Claiming Freedom: Race, Kinship, and Land in Nineteenth Century Georgia* (2018); "Self-Emancipating Women, Civil War, and the Union Army in Southern Louisiana and Low Country Georgia, 1861–1865," *Journal of African American History*, Vol. 101, Nos. 2–3 (Winter–Spring 2016), 1–22; "Black Women's Fugitivity in Colonial America," *Black Perspectives*, African American Intellectual History Society, www .aaihs.org/Black-womens-fugitivity-in-colonial-america/, May 14, 2019;

"Black Women, Agency, and the Civil War," *Black Perspectives*, African American Intellectual History Society, www.aaihs.org/Black-women-agency-and-the-civil-war/ Sept. 22, 2017.

My family has been my greatest supporters and inspiration. To Clarence, Kiara, Chris, and Clarence Jr, thank you for your love, support, and encouragement.

Notes

INTRODUCTION

1. *Pennsylvania Gazette*, September 27, 1770; Lottie M. Bausman, *The General Position of Lancaster County in Negro Slavery* (Lancaster County Historical Society, 1911); Franklin Ellis and Samuel Evans, *History of Lancaster County Pennsylvania with Biographical Sketches of Many of its Pioneers and Prominent Men* (Philadelphia: Everts and Peck, 1883), 913; www.eldersweather.com, accessed March 18, 2019.

2. *Pennsylvania Gazette*, September 27, 1770; Don N. Hagist, *Wives, Slaves, and Servant Girls: Advertisements for Female Runaways in American Newspapers, 1770–1783* (Yardley, Pa.: Westholme Publishing, 2016), 10.

3. Ellis and Evans, *History of Lancaster County*, 916, 923. The slave population of Lancaster County was 348 in 1790.

4. Susan E. O'Donovan, Comments presented at the American Historical Association Conference, New Orleans, Louisiana, January 6, 2013.

5. Marisa J. Fuentes, *Dispossessed Lives: Enslaved Women, Violence, and the Archive* (Philadelphia: University of Pennsylvania Press, 2016), 17.

6. *South Carolina Gazette*, July 21, 1733; Slave Trade Database, Speaker, VIN 76714, accessed March 16, 2019; Sylviane A. Diouf, *Slavery's Exiles: The Story of the American Maroons* (New York: New York University Press, 2014), 46.

7. *Georgia Gazette*, 1766.

8. Matthew Spooner, "Freedom, Reenslavement, and Movement in the Revolutionary South," in Whitney Stewart et al. eds., *Race and Nation in the Age of Emancipation* (Athens: University of Georgia Press, 2018), 16. See also Michael Zuckerman and Patrick Spero eds., *The American Revolution Reborn: New Perspectives for the Twenty-First Century* (Philadelphia: University of Pennsylvania Press, 2016).

9. Ibid.; Stephanie Camp, *Closer to Freedom: Enslaved Women and Everyday Resistance in the Plantation South* (Chapel Hill: University of North Carolina Press, 2004), xxix.

10. Camp, *Closer to Freedom*, 21–22, 31, 43.

11. See for example, Marcus Rediker et al. eds., *Runaways: Workers, Mobility, and Capitalism, 1600–1850* (Oakland: University of California Press, 2019), 15–18.

12. Camp, *Closer to Freedom*, 28.

13. *Virginia Gazette*, November 14, 1771.

14. *Virginia Gazette*, July 19, 1770; Hagist, *Wives, Slaves, and Servant Girls*, 7.

15. Manisha Sinha, *The Slave's Cause: A History of Abolitionism* (New Haven, Conn.: Yale University Press, 2016); Graham Russell Gao Hodges, "Black Self-Emancipation, Gradual Emancipation, and the Underground Railroad in the Northern Colonies and States, 1763–1804," in Damian Alan Pargas ed., *Fugitive Slaves and Spaces of Freedom in North America* (Gainesville: University Press of Florida, 2018), 23; C.L. R. James, "The Atlantic Slave Trade and Slavery," in John R. Williams and Charles Harris eds., *Amistad I* (New York: Random House, 1971), 142.

16. Herbert Aptheker, *American Negro Slave Revolts* (6th ed., New York: International Publishers, 1993), 21.

17. Benjamin Quarles, *The Negro in the American Revolution* (Chapel Hill: University of North Carolina Press, 1996).

18. Benjamin Quarles, "The Revolutionary War as a Black Declaration of Independence," in Ira Berlin and Ronald Hoffman eds., *Slavery and Freedom in the Age of the American Revolution* (Charlottesville: University of Virginia Press, 1983), 284; Gerald Mullin, *Flight and Rebellion: Slave Resistance in Eighteenth Century Virginia* (New York: Oxford University Press, 1972), 16, 40; Philip Morgan, *Slave Counterpoint: Black Culture in the Eighteenth Century Chesapeake and Lowcountry* (Chapel Hill: University of North Carolina Press, 1998), 57–78, 89.

19. Ira Berlin and Ronald Hoffman eds., *Slavery and Freedom in the Age of the American Revolution* (Charlottesville: University of Virginia Press, 1983); David Brion Davis, *The Problem of Slavery in the Age of Revolution, 1770–1823* (2nd ed., New York: Oxford University Press, 1999); Sylvia Frey, *Water from the Rock: Black Resistance in a Revolutionary Age* (Princeton, N.J.: Princeton University Press, 1991); Woody Holton, *Forced Founders: Indians, Debtors, Slaves and the Making of the American Revolution in Virginia* (Chapel Hill: University of North Carolina Press, 1999); Gary B. Nash, *The Forgotten Fifth: African Americans in the Age of Revolution* (Cambridge: Harvard University Press, 2006); Simon Schama, *Rough Crossings: Britain, the Slaves, and the American Revolution* (New York: Harper Collins, 2007); Cassandra Pybus, *Epic Journeys of Freedom: Runaway Slaves of the American Revolution and Their Global Quest for Liberty* (Boston: Beacon Press, 2006); Gerald Horne, *The Counter Revolution of 1776: Slave Resistance and the Origins of the United States of America* (New York: New York University Press, 2014). See also Alan Gilbert, *Black Patriots and Loyalists: Fighting for Emancipation in the War for Independence* (Chicago: University of Chicago Press, 2012); Edward Countryman, *Enjoy the Same Liberty: Black Americans and the Revolutionary Era* (Lanham, Md.: Rowman & Littlefield, 2012); Douglas R. Egerton, *Death or Liberty: African Americans and Revolutionary America* (New York: Oxford University Press, 2009).

20. Walter Johnson, "On Agency," *The Journal of Social History* (Fall 2003): 113–24. The New Social History emphasizes the experiences of the enslaved and their agency. Enslaved agency (or lack thereof) often determined divergent experiences of autonomy and liberation from bondage. Studies that have been groundbreaking in emphasizing the agency of slaves include W.E.B. DuBois, *Black Reconstruction in America, 1860–1880* (1935); John Blassingame, *The Slave Community: Plantation Life in the Antebellum South* (1972); Herbert Gutman, *The Black Family in Slavery and Freedom, 1750–1925* (1976); Deborah Gray White, *Ar'n't I a Woman? Female Slaves in the Plantation South* (1st ed., 1985); Nell Irvin Painter, *Sojourner Truth: A Life, A Symbol* (1996).

21. Marisa Fuentes, "Power and Historical Figuring: Rachael Pringle Polgreen's Troubled Archives," *Gender and History* Vol. 22 No. 3 (November 2010): 577.

22. Dale W. Tomich, *Slavery in the Circuit of Sugar: Martinique and the World Economy, 1830–1848* (Baltimore: Johns Hopkins University Press, 1990), 1.

23. Barbara Bush, "Towards Emancipation: Slave Women and Resistance to Coercive Labor Regimes in the British West Indian Colonies, 1790–1916," in David Richardson, ed., *Abolition and Its Aftermath: The Historical Context, 1790–1916* (London, 1985), 27–54.

24. Barbara Bush, *Slave Women in Caribbean Society, 1650–1838* (Bloomington: Indiana University Press, 1990), 63–64; Gad Heuman ed., *Out of the House of Bondage: Runaways, Resistance, and Marronage in Africa and the New World* (London, 1986).

25. Barbara Bush, *Slave Women*, 65.

26. Ibid.; Arlette Gautier, "Les Esclaves femmes aux Antilles françaises, 1635–1848," *Reflexions Historiques* Vol. 10 No. 3 (Fall 1983): 409–35.

27. www.slavevoyages.org; see also Philip Curtin, *The Atlantic Slave Trade: A Census* (Madison: University of Wisconsin Press, 1969), 137.

28. *Virginia Gazette*, April 5, 1770; Hilary Beckles, *Afro-Caribbean Women and Resistance to Slavery in Barbados* (London: Karnak House, 1988), 5.

29. Nash, *The Forgotten Fifth*, 27; Lathan Windley, *Runaway Slave Advertisements: A Documentary History from the 1730s to 1790*, Vols. I–IV (Westport, Conn.: Greenwood Press, 1983); Graham Russell Gao Hodges and Alan Edward Brown, *"Pretends to Be Free": Runaway Slave Advertisements from Colonial and Revolutionary New York and New Jersey* (New York: Fordham University Press, 2019); Billy G. Smith and Richard Wojtowicz, *Blacks Who Stole Themselves: Advertisements for Runaways in the Pennsylvania Gazette, 1728–1790* (Philadelphia: University of Pennsylvania Press, 1989); Antonio Bly ed., *Escaping Bondage: A Documentary History of Runaway Slaves in Eighteenth-Century New England, 1700–1789* (Lanham, Md.: Lexington Books, 2012).

30. *New York Journal*, February 15, 1770; *New York Gazette*, March 7, 1770; *Virginia Gazette*, July 12, 1770.

31. Diouf, *Slavery's Exiles*, 43.

32. Ibid., 44.

33. Damian Alan Pargas ed., *Fugitive Slaves and Spaces of Freedom in North America* (Gainesville: University Press of Florida, 2018), 4.

34. Jefferson to William Gordon, 16 Jul 1788, in Julian P. Boyd ed., *Papers of Thomas Jefferson*, 34 vols. (Princeton, N.J., 1950–), Vol. XIII, 364; Johann von Ewald, *Diary of the American War: A Hessian Journal*, trans. and ed. Joseph P. Tustin (New Haven, Conn.: Yale University Press, 1979), 305; Gregory J.W. Urwin, "When Freedom Wore a Red coat: How Lord Cornwallis' 1781 Campaign Threatened the Revolution in Virginia," *Army History*, No. 68 (Summer 2008): 14.

35. William Duane and Thomas Balch trans. and eds., *The Journal of Claude Blanchard: Eyewitness Accounts of the American Revolution* (1876; reprint ed. New York, 1969), 162; St. George Tucker to Fanny Tucker, 11 Jul 1781, in Charles Washington Coleman Jr., "The Southern Campaign, 1781, from Guilford Court House to the Siege of York Narrated by St. George Tucker in Letters to His Wife, Part II, The Peninsula Campaign," *Magazine of American History*

7 (September 1881): 207; Lafayette to Jefferson, 28 May 1781, in Boyd, *Papers of Thomas Jefferson*, Vol. VI, 26; Urwin, "When Freedom Wore a Red Coat," 15.

36. Edmund Randolph, *History of Virginia*, ed. Arthur H. Shaffer (Charlottesville, Va., 1970), 285. This fear was an American military weakness throughout the Revolution. As historian David K. Wilson observed, "The threat of a slave insurrection (and/or Indian attacks in the case of frontier counties) usually kept half of a Southern county's militia at home." See David K. Wilson, *The Southern Strategy: Britain's Conquest of South Carolina and Georgia, 1775–1780* (Columbia, S.C., 2005), 3; Urwin, "When Freedom Wore a Red coat," 16.

37. Windley, *Runaway Slave Advertisements*, Vols. I–IV; Herbert Aptheker, "We Will Be Free: Advertisements for Runaways and the Reality of American Slavery," Occasional Paper No. 1, Ethnic Studies Program, University of Santa Clara, 1984, 11.

38. *Virginia Gazette* (Purdie), July 10, 1778; Windley, *Runaway Slave Advertisements*, Vol. I, 274; Mary Beth Norton, *Liberty's Daughters: The Revolutionary Experience of American Women, 1750–1800* (Ithaca: Cornell University Press, 1996), 209–10; Norman Fuss, "Prelude to Rebellion: Dunmore's Raid on the Williamsburg Magazine, *Journal of the American Revolution*, April 2, 2015, https://allthingsliberty.com/2015/04/prelude-to-rebellion-dunmores-raid-on-the-williamsburg-magazine-april-21–1775/, accessed June 28, 2019.

39. Frey, *Water from the Rock*, 49–50; L.H. Butterfield ed., *Diary and Autobiography of John Adams*, 4 vols. (Cambridge, Mass.: Harvard University Press, 1962), 2:183; Julius Scott, *The Common Wind: Afro-American Currents in the Age of the Haitian Revolution* (New York: Verso Books, 2018).

40. *Royal Georgia Gazette* (Savannah), September 7, 1780; Windley, *Runaway Slave Advertisements*, Vol. IV, 79.

41. Karen Cook Bell, *Claiming Freedom: Race, Kinship, and Land in Nineteenth Century Georgia* (Columbia: University of South Carolina Press, 2018), 24.

42. Joan R. Gunderson, *To Be Useful to the World: Women in Revolutionary America, 1740–1790* (Chapel Hill: University of North Carolina Press, 2006), 41; Carol Berkin, *Revolutionary Mothers: Women in the Struggle for American Independence* (New York: Alfred A. Knopf, 2005), 124; http://blackloyalist.com/cdc/index.htm, accessed November 3, 2019. Twenty-two-year-old Kitty had two children, Sarah and Lucy, within British lines.

43. Frey, *Water from the Rock*, 51; Gunderson, *To Be Useful to the World*, 41; *Royal Georgia Gazette* (Savannah), September 7, 1780; Windley, *Runaway Slave Advertisements*, Vol. IV, 79.

44. Jacqueline Jones, "Race, Sex, and Self-Evident Truths: The Status of Slave Women during the Era of the American Revolution," in Ronald Hoffman and Peter J. Albert eds., *Women in the Age of the American Revolution* (Charlottesville: University Press of Virginia, 1989), 322–23.

45. Ibid.

46. Ibid.

47. Ibid.

48. Frey, *Water from the Rock*, 211.

49. Tom Costa, "What Can We Learn from a Digital Database of Runaway Slave Advertisements," *International Social Science Review* Vol. 76 No. 1/2 (2001): 40.

50. Ibid., 42.

51. Diouf, *Slavery's Exiles*, 13.

52. Lathan Windley, *Runaway Slave Advertisements*; Aptheker, "We Will Be Free."

53. Ibid.

54. Ibid.

55. Erica Armstrong Dunbar, *Never Caught: The Washingtons' Relentless Pursuit of their Runaway Slave Ona Judge* (New York: Atria, 2017), xvii.

1 "A NEGRO WENCH NAMED LUCIA"

1. *Royal Georgia Gazette* (Savannah), November 19, 1766; Georgia Writers Project, Rosanna Williams, Tatemville and Ophelia Baker, Sandfly, Ga. in *Drums and Shadows: Survival Stories among the Georgia Coastal Negroes* (Athens, GA., reprint 1986), 71, 91.

2. Ira Berlin, *Many Thousands Gone: The First Two Centuries of Slavery in North America* (Cambridge, Mass.: Harvard University Press, 1998), 8; Peter Wood, *Black Majority: Negroes in Colonial South Carolina* (New York: Alfred A. Knopf, 1974), 152; Emily West, *Enslaved Women in America: From Colonial Times to Emancipation* (Lanham, Md.: Rowman and Littlefield, 2014), 35–36. For a study of slavery in the heartland see M. Scott Heerman, *The Alchemy of Slavery: Human Bondage and Emancipation in the Illinois Country, 1730–1865* (Philadelphia: University of Pennsylvania Press, 2018), which examines the long history of slavery in the interior of North America and traces its connections out to the larger and changing empires that controlled the region.

3. Donald R. Wright, *African Americans in the Colonial Era: From African Origins through the American Revolution* (Wheeling, Ill.: Harlan Davidson Press, 2000), 66.

4. Ibid., 79; Philip Morgan, *Slave Counterpoint: Black Culture in the Eighteenth Century Chesapeake and Lowcountry* (Chapel Hill: University of North Carolina Press, 1998), 61; Gerald Mullin, *Flight and Rebellion: Slave Resistance in Eighteenth Century Virginia* (New York: Oxford University Press, 1972), 43.

5. Winthrop Jordan, *White Over Black: American Attitudes Toward the Negro, 1550–1812* (Chapel Hill: University of North Carolina Press, 2012), 20; Zakiyyah Iman Jackson, *Becoming Human: Matter and Meaning in an Anti-Black World* (New York: New York University Press, 2020); Jennifer Morgan, *Laboring Women: Reproduction and Gender in New World Slavery* (Philadelphia: University of Pennsylvania Press, 2004), 27, 40; Amani N. Marshall, "Enslaved Women Runaways in South Carolina, 1820–1864" (Ph.D. Diss. Indiana University, 2007), 28. See also Sharon Block, *Colonial Complexions: Race and Bodies in Eighteenth Century America* (Philadelphia: University of Pennsylvania Press, 2018).

6. Morgan, *Laboring Women*, 36, 49.

7. Marshall, "Enslaved Women Runaways," 28; Kathleen M. Brown, *Good Wives, Nasty Wenches, and Anxious Patriarchs: Gender, Race, and Power in Colonial Virginia* (Chapel Hill: University of North Carolina Press, 1996), 31, 110. See also Stephanie Camp, "Early European Views of African Bodies," in Daina Ramey Berry and Leslie Harris eds., *Sexuality and Slavery: Reclaiming Intimate Histories in the Americas* (Athens: University of Georgia Press, 2018).

8. Brown, *Good Wives*, 115–16; Marshall, "Enslaved Women Runaways," 28–29.

9. Marshall, "Enslaved Women Runaways," 29.

10. Cynthia M. Kennedy, *Braided Relations, Entwined Lives: The Women of Charleston's Urban Slave Society* (Bloomington: Indiana University Press, 2005), 130; Brown, *Good Wives*, 115–19, 128, 369–70; Marshall, "Enslaved Women Runaways," 29.

11. Betty Wood, *Gender, Race and Rank in a Revolutionary Age: The Georgia Lowcountry, 1750–1820* (Athens: University of Georgia Press, 2000), 55; Marshall, "Enslaved Women Runaways," 29.

12. Wood, *Gender, Race and Rank*, 55; Marshall, "Enslaved Women Runaways," 29–30.

13. A. Leon Higginbotham, *In the Matter of Color: Race and the American Legal Process, The Colonial Period* (New York: Oxford University Press, 1978); West, *Enslaved Women in America*, 37–38.

14. Marshall, "Enslaved Women Runaways," 29.

15. Ibid.; Brown, *Good Wives*, 135; Marli Weiner, *Mistresses and Slaves: Plantation Women in South Carolina, 1830–1880* (Urbana: University of Illinois Press, 1998), 57, 61–62. For a discussion of White women as enslavers during the antebellum period see Stephanie Jones-Rogers, *They Were Her Property: White Women as Slave Owners in the American South* (New Haven: Yale University Press, 2020).

16. West, *Enslaved Women in America*, 39–40.

17. Ibid.

18. Daina Ramey Berry, *Swing the Sickle, For the Harvest is Ripe: Gender and Slavery in Antebellum Georgia* (Urbana: University of Illinois Press, 2007), 13–17; Marshall, "Enslaved Women Runaways," 32; Weiner, *Mistresses and Slaves*, 7, 12.

19. Berry, *Swing the Sickle*, 17; Betty Wood, *Women's Work, Men's Work: The Informal Slave Economies of Lowcountry Georgia* (Athens: University of Georgia Press, 1995), 17.

20. Berry, *Swing the Sickle*, 13–17; West, *Enslaved Women in America*, 41.

21. Berry, *Swing the Sickle*, 13–17; West, *Enslaved Women in America*, 41.

22. West, *Enslaved Women in America*, 41; Karen Cook Bell, *Claiming Freedom: Race, Kinship, and Land in Nineteenth Century Georgia* (Columbia: University of South Carolina Press, 2018), 13–14.

23. Bell, *Claiming Freedom*, 14.

24. Herbert Aptheker, "We Will Be Free: Advertisements for Runaways and the Reality of American Slavery," Occasional Paper No. 1, Ethnic Studies Program, University of Santa Clara, 1984, 9–10.

25. Deborah Gray White, *Ar'n't I a Woman? Female Slaves in the Plantation South* (New York: W.W. Norton, 1999), 24–25; Bell, *Claiming Freedom*, 15.

26. Stephen Hahn, *A Nation Under Our Feet: The Political Struggles of Rural Blacks from Slavery to the Great Migration* (Cambridge, Mass.: Harvard University Press, 2003), 38–39.

27. West, *Enslaved Women in America*, 41; Morgan, *Slave Counterpoint*, 187–92.

28. Damian Alan Pargas, *The Quarters and the Fields: Slave Families in the Non-Cotton South* (Gainesville: University Press of Florida, 2010), 40–41.

29. Ibid.

30. Marshall, "Enslaved Women Runaways," 31; White, *Ar'n't I a Woman?*, 94–95, 121, 128–32, 138–41; Jacqueline Jones, *Labor of Love, Labor of Sorrow: Black Women, Work, and the Family from Slavery to the Present* (New York: Basic Books, 2010), 18, 42–43.

31. Brenda Stevenson, *Life in Black and White: Family and Community in the Slave South* (New York: Oxford University Press, 1996), 236.

32. West, *Enslaved Women in America*, 42; Wright, *African Americans in the Colonial Era*, 65–66; White, *Ar'n't I a Woman?*, 69–70.

33. Berlin, *Many Thousands Gone*, 127.

34. Ibid. See also James Roberts, *The Narrative of James Roberts: A Soldier under Gen. Washington in the Revolutionary War and under Jackson at the Battle of New Orleans, in the War of 1812...* (Chicago: James Roberts, 1858), 26, which discusses how enslavers bred enslaved women by making fifty to sixty women available for breeding with White men in Louisiana. Accessible at https://docsouth.unc.edu/neh/roberts/roberts.html.

35. West, *Enslaved Women in America*, 43–44.

36. Ibid.

37. Ibid., 46; John K. Thornton, "African Dimensions of the Stono Rebellion," *American Historical Review* Vol. 96 No. 4 (October 1991): 1101–1113; Mark M. Smith, "Remembering Mary, Shaping Revolt: Reconsidering the Stono Rebellion," *Journal of Southern History* Vol. 67 No. 3 (August 2001): 513; Peter C. Hoffer, *Cry Liberty: The Great Stono Rebellion of 1739* (New York: New York University Press, 2010); Perry Kyles, "Resistance and Collaboration: Political Strategies Within the Afro-Carolinian Slave Community, 1700–1750," *Journal of African American History* Vol. 93 No. 4 (Fall 2008): 497–508.

38. Wood, *Black Majority*, 325.

39. West, *Enslaved Women in America*, 46–47.

40. Ibid.

41. Ibid.; Sharla Fett, *Working Cures: Healing, Health, and Power on Southern Slave Plantations* (Chapel Hill: University of North Carolina Press, 2002).

42. West, *Enslaved Women in America*, 46–47.

43. Ibid.

44. Ira Berlin, *Generations of Captivity: A History of African American Slaves* (Cambridge, Mass.: Harvard University Press, 2003), 44.

45. *South Carolina Gazette*, June 3, 1760; West, *Enslaved Women in America*, 47–48.

46. *South Carolina Gazette*, June 3, 1760.

47. *South Carolina Gazette and Country Journal*, July 8, 1772.

48. *South Carolina Gazette*, April 1, 1767.

49. West, *Enslaved Women in America*, 47.

50. Ibid.; White, *Ar'n't I a Woman?*, 70.

51. Aptheker, "We Will Be Free," 9.

52. Daniel Meaders, "South Carolina Fugitives as Viewed Through Colonial Newspapers with Emphasis on Runaway Notices, 1732–1801," *Journal of Negro History* Vol. 60 No. 2 (1975): 291.

53. Ibid.

54. See Betty Wood, "Some Aspects of Female Resistance to Chattel Slavery in Low Country Georgia, 1763–1815," *The Historical Journal* Vol. 30 No. 3 (September 1987): 607–608; White, *Ar'n't I a Woman?*, 75–76; Camp, *Closer to Freedom*, 28–30; Leslie Ann Schwalm, *A Hard Fight for We: Women's Transition from Slavery to Freedom in South Carolina* (Urbana: University of Illinois Press, 1997), 32, 45.

55. Marshall, "Enslaved Women Runaways," 37; Amani Marshall, "'They Will Endeavor to Pass for Free': Enslaved Runaways' Performances of Freedom in Antebellum South Carolina," *Slavery & Abolition* Vol. 31 No. 2 (June 2010): 161–80.

56. Wood, "Some Aspects of Female Resistance," 607–08.

57. Marshall, "Enslaved Women Runaways," 38; Schwalm, *A Hard Fight for We*, 31; Camp, *Closer to Freedom*, 28, 31.

58. Marshall, "Enslaved Women Runaways," 38.

59. Ibid.

60. Ibid.; *Augusta Chronicle*, May 20, June 21, September 23, 1826; June 16, 1827.

61. Amrita Chakrabarti Myers, *Forging Freedom: Black Women and the Pursuit of Liberty in Antebellum Charleston* (Chapel Hill: University of North Carolina Press, 2011), 10–14; Damian Alan Pargas, *The Quarters and the Fields: Slave Families in the Non-Cotton South* (Gainesville: University Press of Florida, 2010), 97–104; Marshall, "Enslaved Women Runaways," 38–39.

62. Marshall, "Enslaved Women Runaways," 38–39; Marshall, "They Will Endeavor to Pass for Free," 161–80; Schwalm, *A Hard Fight for We*, 31; Wood, *Women's Work, Men's Work*, 81, 84, 88–91, Kennedy, *Braided Relations*, 138–39.

63. Marshall, "Enslaved Women Runaways," 39.

64. Information about Sarah Washington is in the *Charleston Mercury*, August 28, 1862; Marshall, "Enslaved Women Runaways," 39.

65. White, *Ar'n't I a Woman?*, 62–90.

66. No Author. "Recollections of Slavery by a Runaway Slave," 1838, Documenting the American South. University Library, The University of North Carolina at Chapel Hill, http://docsouth.unc.edu/neh/runaway/runaway.html.

67. *South Carolina Gazette* March 2, 1734; January 1, 1739.

68. White, *Ar'n't I a Woman?*, 10.

69. Marshall, "Enslaved Women Runaways," 44.

70. White, *Ar'n't I a Woman?*, 10.

71. Thomas Foster, *Rethinking Rufus: Sexual Violations of Enslaved Men* (Athens: University of Georgia Press, 2019), 31–45.

72. Karen Robbins, "Power Among the Powerless: Domestic Resistance By Free and Slave Women in the McHenry Family of the New Republic," *Journal of the Early Republic* Vol. 23 No.1 (Spring 2003): 47–69; Marshall, "Enslaved Women Runaways," 44.

73. Ibid.; Weiner, *Mistresses and Slaves*, 12–13; Schwalm, *A Hard Fight for We*, 51–52.

74. John Andrew Jackson, *The Experience of a Slave in South Carolina* (Chapel Hill: University of North Carolina Press, 2011), 22.

75. White, *Ar'n't I a Woman?*, 32–33.

76. John Hope Franklin and Loren Schweninger, *Runaway Slaves: Rebels on the Plantation* (New York: Oxford University Press, 1999), 211.

77. White, *Ar'n't I a Woman?*, 76–84; Daina Ramey Berry and Kali Nicole Gross, *A Black Women's History of the United States* (Boston: Beacon Press, 2020), 40–63; Marshall, "Enslaved Women Runaways," 45.

78. George Rawick, *The American Slave*, Vol. IV (Westport, Conn.: Greenwood Publishing, 1972), 25.

79. Berry and Gross, *A Black Women's History*, 40–63; *South Carolina Gazette*, November 3, 1758.

80. Jennifer Fleischner, *Mastering Slavery: Memory, Family, and Identity in Women's Slave Narratives* (New York: New York University Press, 1996), 4, 29.

81. White, *Ar'n't I a Woman?*, 119–41.

82. Schwalm, *A Hard Fight for We*, 68–69; White, *Ar'n't I a Woman?*, 95–96.

83. Berry and Gross, *A Black Women's History*, 46–47.

84. White, *Ar'n't I a Woman?*, 70–71; Wood, "Some Aspects of Female Resistance," 622; Camp, *Closer to Freedom*, 37; Wilma King, "Suffer with Them Till Death: Slave Women and Their Children in Nineteenth Century America," in David Barry Gasper and Darlene Clark Hine eds., *More Than Chattel: Black Women and Slavery in the Americas* (Bloomington, Ind.: Indiana University Press, 1996), 161; Marshall, "Enslaved Women Runaways," 53.

85. West, *Enslaved Women in America*, 48–49; Wright, *African Americans in the Colonial Era*, 87.

86. Catherine Adams and Elizabeth Pleck, *Love of Freedom: Black Women in Colonial and Revolutionary New England* (New York: Oxford University Press, 2010), 12–14.

87. Ibid.

88. Ibid., 47–48; Berlin, *Generations of Captivity*, 82; Felicia Y. Thomas, "Entangled with the Yoke of Bondage: Black Women in Massachusetts, 1700–1783" (Ph.D. diss., Rutgers University, 2014), 66; Wright, *African Americans in the Colonial Era*, 87–88. For a discussion on the impact of Black men on the sailing and shipping industry see W. Jeffrey Bolster, *Black Jacks: African American Seamen in the Age of Sail* (Cambridge: Harvard University Press, 1997).

89. Jared Ross Hardesty, *Unfreedom: Slavery and Dependence in Eighteenth Century Boston* (New York: New York University Press, 2016), 113; Berlin, *Many Thousands Gone*, 182. See also Wendy Warren, *New England Bound: Slavery and Colonization in Early America* (New York: Liveright, 2016).

90. Erica Armstrong Dunbar, *A Fragile Freedom: African American Women and Emancipation in the Antebellum City* (New Haven, Conn.: Yale University Press, 2008), 15–17.

91. Camp, *Closer to Freedom*, 20, 31–32, 52–53.

92. Ibid, 24; Herbert Aptheker, *American Negro Slave Revolts* (6th ed., New York: Columbia University Press, 1993), 173.

93. *New York Gazette*, March 5, 1763; Graham Russell Gao Hodges and Alan Edward Brown, *"Pretends to Be Free": Runaway Slave Advertisements from Colonial and Revolutionary New York and New Jersey* (New York: Fordham University Press, 2019), 101.

94. West, *Enslaved Women in America*, 48. See also Ellen Newell, *Brethren by Nature: New England Indians, Colonists, and the Origins of American Slavery* (Ithaca: Cornell University Press, 2015); Christopher Cameron, *To Plead Our Own Cause: African*

Americans in Massachusetts and the Making of the Antislavery Movement (Kent, Ohio: Kent State University Press, 2014).

95. Berlin, *Many Thousands Gone*, 187.

96. Ibid.

97. Ibid.

98. Ibid.

99. Michael Gomez, *Exchanging Our Country Marks: The Transformation of African Identities in the Colonial and Antebellum South* (Chapel Hill: University of North Carolina Press, 1998), 27; William D. Pierson, *Black Yankees: The Development of the Afro-American Subculture of New England* (Amherst: University of Massachusetts Press, 1988); Adams and Pleck, *Love of Freedom*, 39–40.

100. Adams and Pleck, *Love of Freedom*, 39–40.

101. Ibid., 43.

102. Ibid.

103. Ibid.

104. Ibid., 45–46.

105. Ibid.

106. Ibid.

107. John Noble, "The Case of Maria in the Court of Assistants in 1681," *Publications of the Colonial Society of Massachusetts* 6 (1904): 323–26; Abner Cheney Goodell Jr., "The Trial and Execution, for Petit Treason, of Mark and Phillis Slaves of Captain John Codman, Who Murdered their Master at Charlestown, Mass., in 1755; for which the Man was Hanged and Gibbeted, and the Woman was Burned to Death, Including, also, Some Account of Other Punishments by Burning in Massachusetts," *Proceeding of the Massachusetts Historical Society* (1882): 122–49; Adams and Pleck, *Love of Freedom*, 46.

108. Adams and Pleck, *Love of Freedom*, 47.

109. Rex vs. Jenny Chapman, Superior Court, Newport, Rhode Island, March 1767, E: 324, Rhode Island Supreme Court Judicial Records Center; John Wood Sweet, *Bodies Politic: Negotiating Race in the American North, 1730–1830* (Baltimore: Johns Hopkins University Press, 2003), 156; Adams and Pleck, *Love of Freedom*, 47.

110. Nicholas Lechmere, New London County Superior Court Record, Files, Box 12, File of 1751; Adams and Pleck, *Love of Freedom*, 48.

111. Antonio T. Bly ed., *Escaping Bondage: A Documentary History of Runaway Slaves in Eighteenth-Century New England, 1700–1789* (Lanham, Md.: Lexington Books, 2012), 7. This percentage is based on an examination of published advertisements in Bly's *Escaping Bondage*. Fifty-six advertisements for fugitive women and girls were published between 1700 and 1789 out of a total of 800 notices.

112. Berlin, *Many Thousands Gone*, 111; White, *Ar'n't I a Woman?*, 64–65. See also Ryan A. Quintana, *Making a Slave State: Political Development in Early South Carolina* (Chapel Hill: University of North Carolina Press, 2018).

113. White, *Ar'n't I a Woman?*, 64–65.

114. Mullin, *Flight and Rebellion*, 34.

115. William Waller Hening ed., *The Statutes At Large: Being a Collection of All the Laws of Virginia from the First Session of the Legislature in the Year 1619*, 13 vols. (Philadelphia: Bartow, 1823), 447–63.

116. William L. Saunders ed., *The Colonial Records of North Carolina, 1734–1752*, 4 vols. (Raleigh: Hale, 1886).

117. Camp, *Closer to Freedom*, 27.

118. Ibid., 28.

119. Thomas Cooper, ed., *The Statutes at Large of South Carolina, 1682–1716* (Columbia: A.S. Johnson, 1837), 2:13; David J. McCord, ed., *The Statutes at Large of South Carolina* (Columbia: A.S. Johnson, 1840), 7:343–47; Sylviane A. Diouf, *Slavery's Exiles: The Story of the American Maroons* (New York: New York University Press, 2014), 27.

120. An Act for the Better Ordering of Slaves, Records of the General Assembly, March 2–16, 1696, South Carolina Department of Archives and History; William Wiecek, "The Statutory Law of Slavery and Race in the Thirteen Mainland Colonies of British America," *William and Mary Quarterly* Vol. 34 No. 2 (April 1977): 270; Diouf, *Slavery's Exiles*, 27.

121. Diouf, *Slavery's Exiles*, 27.

122. Ibid., 28–29.

123. Camp, *Closer to Freedom*, 29–30.

124. Ibid., 31.

125. Mullin, *Flight and Rebellion*, 43.

126. *South Carolina Gazette* (Timothy), January 29, 1753; Lathan Windley, *Runaway Slave Advertisements: A Documentary History from the 1730s to 1790* (Westport, Conn.: Greenwood Press, 1983), Vol. III, 117.

127. Hugo Prosper Leaming, *Hidden Americans: Maroons of Virginia and the Carolinas* (New York: Garland Publishing, 1995), 395; Mullin, *Flight and Rebellion*, 43.

128. *Royal Georgia Gazette* (Savannah), December 7, 1774; Sylvia Frey, *Water from the Rock: Black Resistance in a Revolutionary Age* (Princeton, N.J.: Princeton University Press, 1991), 54.

129. Betty Wood, *Slavery in Colonial Georgia, 1619–1776* (Lanham, Md.: Rowman & Littlefield, 2005), 65.

130. Edward Baptist, *The Half Has Never Been Told: Slavery and the Making of American Capitalism* (New York: Basic Books, 2014), 4–5; Calvin Schermerhorn, *Unrequited Toil: A History of United States Slavery* (New York: Cambridge University Press, 2018), 1.

131. Schermerhorn, *Unrequited Toil*, 1; Baptist, *The Half Has Never Been Told*, 4–5.

132. Schermerhorn, *Unrequited Toil*, 1.

133. West, *Enslaved Women in America*, 50–51; Marshall, "Enslaved Women Runaways," 54.

2 "A MULATTO WOMAN NAMED MARGARET"

1. *Virginia Gazette*, April 5, 1770; Don N. Hagist, *Wives, Slaves, and Servant Girls: Advertisements for Female Runaways in American Newspapers, 1770–1783* (Yardley, Pa.: Westholme Publishing, 2016), 3–4. The prospect of enslaved women changing into men's clothing

as they escaped was also revealed by enslavers in New England. See, for example, *New England Weekly Journal,* October 24, 1738; Lorenzo Greene, "The New England Negro as Seen in Advertisements for Runaway Slaves," *Journal of Negro History* Vol. 10 (April 1944): 141.

2. Virginia Gazette, April 5, 1770; *Maryland Gazette,* May 13, 1773; Hagist, *Wives, Slaves, and Servant Girls,* 37.

3. Stephanie Camp, *Closer to Freedom: Enslaved Women and Everyday Resistance in the Plantation South* (Chapel Hill: University of North Carolina Press, 2004), xxix.

4. Herbert Aptheker, *The Negro in the American Revolution* (New York: International Publishers, 1940), 7–8.

5. Anthony Benezet, *A Short Account of That Part of Africa Inhabited by the Negroes . . .* (2nd ed. Philadelphia: W. Dunlap, 1762), 30–32; William W. Wiecek, *The Sources of Anti-Slavery Constitutionalism in America, 1760–1848* (Ithaca: Cornell University Press, 1977), 41.

6. Thomas Paine, *Writing of Thomas Paine: A Collection of Pamphlets from America's Most Radical Founding Father* (St. Petersburg, Fla.: Red and Black Publishers, 2010).

7. Lester J. Cappon ed., *The Adams–Jefferson Letters: The Complete Correspondence between Thomas Jefferson and Abigail and John Adams* (Chapel Hill: University of North Carolina Press, 2012); Aptheker, *The Negro in the American Revolution,* 8.

8. Aptheker, *The Negro in the American Revolution,* 9; Herbert Aptheker ed., *A Documentary History of the Negro People in the United States,* Vol. I (New York: The Citadel Press, 1968), 5–16.

9. Peter Wilson Coldham, *The Complete Book of Emigrants in Bondage, 1614–1775* (Baltimore, Md.: Genealogical Publishing Company, 2002), 146.

10. John Thomas Scharf, *History of Maryland,* Vol. I (Baltimore: John B. Piet, 1879), 14.

11. Ibid., 2, 58.

12. Ibid., 37–38. For a discussion of the denial of rights in Maryland see Martha S. Jones, *Birthright Citizens: A History of Race and Rights in Antebellum America* (New York: Cambridge University Press, 2018).

13. Redemptioners were German immigrants whose passage was paid by family members or patrons in America; Aaron S. Fogelman, "From Slaves, Convicts, and Servants to Free Passengers: The Transformation of Immigration in the Era of the American Revolution," *Journal of American History* Vol. 85 (June 1998): 51.

14. Scharf, *History of Maryland,* 38; Gwenda Morgan and Peter Rushton, "Running Away and Returning Home: the Fate of English Convicts in the American Colonies," *Crime, History, and Societies* Vol. 7 No. 2 (2003): 62; Fogelman, "From Slaves, Convicts, and Servants to Free Passengers," 44.

15. Scharf, *History of Maryland,* 5, 17, 41.

16. Ibid., 42.

17. Winthrop Jordan, *White over Black: American Attitudes Toward the Negro, 1550–1812* (Chapel Hill: University of North Carolina Press, 2012), 106; Jennifer Morgan, *Laboring Women: Reproduction and Gender in New World Slavery* (Philadelphia: University of Pennsylvania Press, 2004), 167.

18. Morgan, *Laboring Women,* 170.

19. Daina Ramey Berry, *The Price for Their Pound of Flesh: The Price of the Enslaved, from Womb to Grave, in the Building of a Nation* (Boston: Beacon Press, 2017). Morgan and Rushton, "Running Away and Returning Home," 61–80.

20. Ibid., 64–66.

21. Ibid., 66, 70.

22. Morgan, *Laboring Women*, 179–81.

23. Ibid., 181.

24. Ibid.

25. Ibid., 180–83.

26. Edwin Olson, "Some Aspects of Slave Life in New York," *Journal of Negro History* Vol. 26: 66–77.

27. *Maryland Gazette*, May 13, 1773; Hagist, *Wives, Slaves, and Servant Girls*, 37.

28. *Pennsylvania Gazette*, September 27, 1770; Hagist, *Wives, Slaves, and Servant Girls*, 10.

29. *Virginia Gazette*, March 22, 1770; *New York Journal*, February 15, 1770; Hagist, *Wives, Slaves, and Servant Girls*, 3.

30. *Virginia Gazette*, July 12, 1770; *New York Gazette*, May 7, 1770; Hagist, *Wives, Slaves, and Servant Girls*, 6–7.

31. *Daily Advertiser*, September 14, 1795; Shane White, "A Question of Style: Blacks in and around New York City in the Late Eighteenth Century," *Journal of American Folklore* Vol. 102 No. 403 (January–March 1989), 30.

32. *Maryland Gazette*, August 16, 1777; Shane White and Graham White, "Slave Clothing and African-American Culture in the Eighteenth and Nineteenth Centuries," *Past and Present* No. 148 (August 1995): 156.

33. Ibid.

34. *Daily Advertiser*, December 22, 1794; White, "A Question of Style," 32.

35. Charles Joyner, *Down by the Riverside: A South Carolina Slave Community* (Urbana: University of Illinois Press, 1984), 113; White, "A Question of Style," 32.

36. *Daily Advertiser*, June 23, 1801; *New York Evening Post*, December 20, 1804; White, "A Question of Style," 32.

37. *Daily Advertiser*, July 26, 1799; *Daily Advertiser*, March 3, 1800; White, "A Question of Style," 32.

38. Wood, *Black Majority*, 232; White and White, "Slave Clothing and African-American Culture," 159.

39. Wood, *Black Majority*, 232; White, "A Question of Style," 32; *Maryland Gazette*, January 9, 1783; *Royal Georgia Gazette* (Savannah), August 1, 1765; White and White, "Slave Clothing and African-American Culture," 159.

40. White and White, "Slave Clothing and African-American Culture," 159.

41. Ibid.

42. Ibid.

43. Ibid.; Joyce E. Chaplin, "Slavery and the Principle of Humanity: A Modern Idea in the Early Lower South," *Journal of Social History* Vol. 24 (1990–91), 309; Philip D. Morgan, "Task and Gang Systems: The Organization of Labor on New World Plantations," in

Stephen Innes ed., *Work and Labor in Early America* (Chapel Hill: University of North Carolina Press, 1988), 189–220.

44. *Maryland Gazette,* July 15, 1784; September 3, 1782; *Maryland Journal and Baltimore Advertiser,* September 3, 1782; White and White, "Slave Clothing and African-American Culture," 160.

45. White and White, "Slave Clothing and African-American Culture," 160; Shane White, *Somewhat More Independent: The End of Slavery in New York City, 1770–1810* (Athens: University of Georgia Press, 1991), 195–96.

46. White and White, "Slave Clothing and African-American Culture," 160.

47. Ibid.; *South Carolina Gazette,* August 27, 1772.

48. *Charleston South Carolina Gazette and Country Journal,* August 24, 1773; White and White, "Slave Clothing and African-American Culture," 161.

49. White and White, "Slave Clothing and African-American Culture," 161; *South Carolina Gazette,* November 5, 1744; August 27, 1772; September 24, 1772; Philip D. Morgan, "Black Life in Eighteenth-Century Charleston," *Perspectives in American History,* new series Vol. 1 (1984): 187–232.

50. Philip Curtin, *The Atlantic Slave Trade: A Census* (Madison: University of Wisconsin Press, 1969), 138; "Estimated Population of the American Colonies: 1610 to 1780," in *Historical Statistics of the United States, Colonial Time to 1957* (Washington, D.C., 1960), ser. Z, 756; Jack Greene, *The Intellectual Construction of America* (Chapel Hill: University of North Carolina Press, 1993), 85.

51. Hilary Beckles, *Afro-Caribbean Women and Resistance to Slavery in Barbados* (London: Karnak House, 1988), 20.

52. Ibid., 5.

53. Ibid., 10.

54. William Dickson, *Mitigation of Slavery* (London, 1814), 439.

55. Virginia Gazette, April 5, 1770; Hagist, *Wives, Slaves, and Servant Girls,* 4; Philip Morgan, *Slave Counterpoint: Black Culture in the Eighteenth Century Chesapeake and Lowcountry* (Chapel Hill: University of North Carolina Press, 1998), 76, 486–87; www .slavevoyages.org, Voyage ID 25232; 36295; 3630, accessed April 12, 2019. Three slave trading vessels arrived in Charleston from 1765 to 1769. Margaret told her enslavers she was born in South Carolina.

56. Morgan, *Slave Counterpoint,* 487; Bernard Powers, *Black Charlestonians: A Social History, 1822–1885* (Fayetteville: University of Arkansas Press, 1994), 267.

57. *Virginia Gazette,* April 5, 1770; Hagist, *Wives, Slaves, and Servant Girls,* 4.

58. Erica Armstrong Dunbar, *A Fragile Freedom: African American Women and Emancipation in the Antebellum City* (New Haven, Conn.: Yale University Press, 2008), 12.

59. Dunbar, *Fragile Freedom,* 9.

60. Ibid., 12.

61. Ibid., 9.

62. "Gist, Mordecai," in J.G. Wilson and J. Fiske eds., *Appleton's Cyclopedia of American Biography* (New York: D. Appleton, 1891), 663; Gist Papers, 1772–1813, MS 390, Maryland Historical Society, Baltimore, Md. During the war, Gist corresponded frequently with

George Washington. See George Washington Papers, Series 4, General Correspondence 1697–1799, MSS 44693, Reel 041, Library of Congress, Washington, D.C.

63. Seth Rockman, *Scraping By: Wage Labor, Slavery, and Survival in Early Baltimore* (Baltimore: Johns Hopkins University Press, 2009), 18.

64. Shaun Armstead, Brenann Sutter et al., "'And I a Poor Slave Yet': The Precarity of Black Life in New Brunswick, 1766–1835," in Marisa J. Fuentes and Deborah Gray White eds., *Slavery and Dispossession in Rutgers History* (Rutgers, N.J. : Rutgers University Press, 2016), 107; Viola Franziska Müller, "Illegal but Tolerated: Slave Refugees in Richmond, Virginia, 1800–1860," in Damian Alan Pargas ed., *Fugitive Slaves and Spaces of Freedom in North America* (Gainesville: University Press of Florida, 2018), 137–67.

65. Erica Armstrong Dunbar, *Never Caught: The Washingtons' Relentless Pursuit of Their Runaway Slave Ona Judge* (New York: Atria, 2017), 44.

66. White, "A Question of Style," 28–30; Hagist, *Wives, Slaves, and Servant Girls*. White indentured servants who ran away are also identified with surnames.

67. Sowande M. Mustakeem, *Slavery at Sea: Terror, Sex, and Sickness during the Middle Passage* (Urbana: University of Illinois Press, 2016), 29.

68. *Maryland Gazette*, October 4, 1749; November 11, 1756.

69. Ibid., March 9, 1758, February 6, 1775, and August 12, 1773; Alan Kulikoff, "The Beginnings of the Afro-American Family in Maryland," in Aubrey C. Land, Lois Green Carr et al. eds., *Law, Society, and Politics in Early Maryland* (Baltimore: Johns Hopkins University Press, 1977), 190–91.

70. Kulikoff, "The Beginnings of the Afro-American Family in Maryland," 190.

71. *Virginia Gazette*, April 5, 1770.

72. Rockman, *Scraping By*, 14.

73. Sandra W. Perot, "The Dairymaid and the Prince: Race, Memory, and the Story of Benjamin Banneker's Grandmother," *Slavery and Abolition* Vol. 38 No. 3 (2017): 449–50.

74. Marisa Fuentes, "Power and Historical Figuring: Racheal Pringle Polgreen's Troubled Archives," *Gender and History* Vol. 22 No. 3 (November 2010): 568. For a groundbreaking work on sexuality and slavery see Daina Ramey Berry and Leslie Harris eds., *Sexuality and Slavery: Reclaiming Intimate Histories in the Americas* (Athens: University of Georgia Press, 2018) and Jessica Marie Johnson, *Wicked Flesh: Black Women, Intimacy, and the Atlantic World* (Philadelphia: University of Pennsylvania Press, 2020).

75. Fuentes, "Power and Historical Figuring," 568.

76. *Virginia Gazette*, April 5, 1770; Hagist, *Wives, Slaves, and Servant Girls*, 4.

77. Lathan Windley, *Runaway Slave Advertisements*, Vol. II (Greenwood, CT: 1983), 111–12; Fuentes, "Power and Historical Figuring," 579.

78. Christopher Phillips, *Freedom's Port: The African American Community of Baltimore, 1790–1860* (Urbana: University of Illinois Press, 1997), 11–14.

79. *Maryland Gazette*, May 13, 1773; Hagist, *Wives, Slaves, and Servant Girls*, 37.

80. Ibid.

81. Fuentes, "Power and Historical Figuring," 580.

82. Berry, *The Price for Their Pound of Flesh*, 6.

83. Graham Russell Gao Hodges, "Black Self-Emancipation, Gradual Emancipation, and the Underground Railroad in the Northern Colonies and States, 1763–1804," in Damian Alan Pargas ed., *Fugitive Slaves and Spaces of Freedom in North America* (Gainesville: University Press of Florida, 2018), 23.

84. Matthew Spooner, "Freedom, Reenslavement, and Movement in the Revolutionary South," in Whitney Stewart et al. eds., *Race and Nation in the Age of Emancipation* (Athens: University of Georgia Press, 2018), 16; *New Jersey Gazette*, October 28, 1778.

85. Emily West, *Enslaved Women in America: From Colonial Times to Emancipation* (Lanham, Md.: Rowman and Littlefield Press, 2015), 54. See also Vincent Carretta, *Phillis Wheatley: Biography of a Genius* (Athens: University of Georgia Press, 2011).

86. Manisha Sinha, *The Slave's Cause: A History of Abolitionism* (New Haven, Conn.: Yale University Press, 2016), 29–33. See also G.J. Barker-Benfield, *Phillis Wheatley Chooses Freedom: History Poetry and the Ideals of the American Revolution* (New York: New York University Press, 2018).

87. Hodges, "Black Self-Emancipation," 27.

88. *Maryland Gazette*, May 13, 1773; Hagist, *Wives, Slaves, and Servant Girls*, 37.

89. Dunbar, *Never Caught*, 78.

90. Ibid. See also Alfred W. Blumrosen and Ruth G. Blumrosen, *Slave Nation: How Slavery United the Colonies and Sparked the American Revolution* (Naperville, Ill.: Sourcebooks, Inc., 2005), 1–14, which argues that the Somerset Case caused Southerners to want independence from England.

91. Wiecek, *The Sources of Anti-Slavery Constitutionalism*, 40; *Virginia Gazette*, November 12, 1772.

92. Douglas Egerton, *Death or Liberty: African Americans and Revolutionary America* (New York: Oxford University Press, 2009), 50–52.

93. *Virginia Gazette*, June 30, 1774; *Virginia Gazette*, Sept. 30, 1773; Egerton, *Death or Liberty*, 50–52; Gerald Mullin, *Flight and Rebellion: Slave Resistance in Eighteenth Century Virginia* (New York: Oxford University Press, 1972), 131.

94. Gary B. Nash, *The Forgotten Fifth: African Americans in the Age of Revolution* (Cambridge: Harvard University Press, 2006), 17–18; Adams to Jeremy Belknap, March 21, 1795, Massachusetts Historical Society *Collections*, 5th ser., 3 (1877), 402.

95. Nash, *The Forgotten Fifth*, 18.

96. Ibid., 23; Woody Holton, *Forced Founders: Indians, Debtors, Slaves, and the Making of the Revolution in Virginia* (Chapel Hill: University of North Carolina Press, 1999), 141.

97. Nash, *The Forgotten Fifth*, 26.

98. Ibid., 26–27; Dunmore to Secretary of State Lord George Germain, June 26, 1776, in William Bell Clark ed., *Naval Documents of the American Revolution*, 10 vols. (Washington D.C.: Government Printing Office, 1964–1996), Vol. V, 756; Jefferson to John Randolph, November 29, 1775, in Julian P. Boyd, ed., *The Papers of Thomas Jefferson*, 34 vols. (Princeton: Princeton University Press, 1950–), Vol. I, 268–70.

99. Nash, *The Forgotten Fifth*, 27–28.

100. "Trial of Negroe Man Slave Named Lewis the Property of Oliver Bowen for the Murder of John Casper Hersman, Robbing Philip Ulsmer, John Lowerman of Ga. & Col. Borquin of

South Carolina, 1787," in Slave File, Telamon Cuyler Collection, Manuscript Room, Hargrett Library, University of Georgia; Betty Wood, "Some Aspects of Female Resistance to Chattel Slavery in Low Country Georgia, 1763–1815," *The Historical Journal* Vol. 30 No. 3 (September 1987), 612. For previous attempts by White Georgians to destroy maroon communities, see Allen D. Candler and Lucian L. Knight, eds., *Colonial Records of the State of Georgia*, 26 vols. (Atlanta, 1904–1916), Vol. XIV, 292–93.

101. *Virginia Gazette*, January 12, 1775; January 21, 1775; *Boston Evening Post*, August 1, 1774; *Georgia Gazette*, April 4, 1764; Betty Wood, "Some Aspects of Female Resistance," 617.

102. *Georgia Gazette*, October 8, 1789.

103. Herbert Aptheker, *The Negro in the American Revolution* (New York: International Publishers, 1940), 11; Benjamin Quarles, *The Negro in the American Revolution* (Chapel Hill: University of North Carolina Press, 1996), 41.

104. H. Niles, *Principles and Acts of the Revolution* (Baltimore, Md., 1882), 199; Quarles, *The Negro in the American Revolution*, 41–42.

3 "A WELL DRESSED WOMAN NAMED JENNY"

1. *Purdie's Virginia Gazette*, April 11, 1777; Don N. Hagist, *Wives, Slaves, and Servant Girls: Advertisements for Female Runaways in American Newspapers, 1770–1783* (Yardley, Pa.: Westholme Publishing, 2016), 109–10.

2. *Virginia Gazette*, November 13, 1778; www.freeafricanamericans.com/Stewart_Family .htm.

3. *Purdie's Virginia Gazette*, April 11, 1777; Hagist, *Wives, Slaves, and Servant Girls*, 109–10. A durant is a woolen fabric. For a discussion of the use of fire as natural light to guide enslaved people see Tyler Parry, "A Meditation on Natural Light and the Use of Fire in United States Slavery," *Black Perspectives*, January 13, 2020, www.aaihs.org/a-meditation-on-natural-light-and-the-use-of-fire-in-united-states-slavery/.

4. Marisa J. Fuentes, *Dispossessed Lives: Enslaved Women, Violence, and the Archive* (Philadelphia: University of Pennsylvania Press, 2016), 16–17.

5. Ibid.; Stephanie Camp, *Closer to Freedom: Enslaved Women and Everyday Resistance in the Plantation South* (Chapel Hill: University of North Carolina Press, 2004), xxix.

6. Fuentes, *Dispossessed Lives*, 17.

7. William Waller Hening ed., *The Statutes At Large: Being a Collection of All the Laws of Virginia from the First Session of the Legislature in the Year 1619*, 13 vols. (Philadelphia: Bartow, 1823), 132; Fuentes, *Dispossessed Lives*, 17.

8. Samuel Hopkins, *A Dialogue, concerning the Slavery of the Africans; Shewing It to Be the Duty and Interest of the American Colonies to Emancipate All Their African Slaves* (Norwich: Judah P. Spooner, 1776). The *Dialogue* was reprinted in a second edition, 1785, with the word "Colonies" appropriately changed to "States." William M. Wiecek, *The Sources of Anti-slavery Constitutionalism in America, 1760–1848* (Ithaca: Cornell University Press, 1977), 42–43; www.archives.gov/founding-docs/declaration/what-does-it-say.

9. John Allen, *An Oration on the Beauties of Liberty, or The Essential Rights of the Americans* (Boston: E. Russell, 1773), 15; Wiecek, *The Sources of Anti-slavery Constitutionalism*, 42.

10. The petition, dated 1777, is in Parish transcripts, New York Historical Society, Massachusetts, folder 202; See also others collected in Herbert Aptheker ed., *A Documentary History of the Negro People in the United States*, Vol. I (5th ed., New York: Citadel, 1968), 6–12; and in "Negro Petitions for Freedom," Massachusetts Historical Society *Collections*, 5th ser., III, 432–37; Wiecek, *The Sources of Anti-slavery Constitutionalism*, 42–44.

11. Herbert Aptheker, *The Negro in the American Revolution* (New York: International Publishers, 1940), 9.

12. Aptheker, *A Documentary History of the Negro People in the United States*, Vol. I, 5–12; Benjamin Quarles, *The Negro in the American Revolution* (Chapel Hill: University of North Carolina Press, 1996), 43–50. See also Christopher Cameron, *"To Plead Our Own Cause": African Americans in Massachusetts and the Making of the Anti-Slavery Movement* (Kent, Ohio: The Kent State University Press, 2014) for a discussion of Black agency in the early abolitionist movement.

13. Charles J. Hoadley ed., *The Public Records of the State of Connecticut*, Vol. II (Hartford, 1894), 427–28; Quarles, *The Negro in the American Revolution*, 44.

14. Aptheker, *A Documentary History of the Negro People in the United States*, Vol. I, 12–13.

15. Quarles, *The Negro in the American Revolution*, 44.

16. William Cooper Nell, *Colored Patriots of the American Revolution* (New York: Arno Press, 1968), 52; Quarles, *The Negro in the American Revolution*, 44. See also Catherine Adams and Elizabeth Pleck, *Love of Freedom: Black Women in Colonial and Revolutionary New England* (New York: Oxford University Press, 2010).

17. Daina Ramey Berry and Kali Nichole Gross, *A Black Women's History of the United States* (Boston: Beacon Press, 2020), 41; "Belinda Sutton and Her Petitions," Royall House and Slave Quarters, https://royallhouse.org/slavery/belinda-sutton-and-her-petitions/, accessed February 4, 2020. Belinda received 15 pounds and 12 shillings in 1783 and had to petition the Massachusetts legislature for back payment of the pension she was owed between 1785 and 1793.

18. Lorenzo Greene, *The Negro in Colonial New England* (New York: Atheneum Press, 1968), 74.

19. Ibid., 89.

20. *Connecticut Gazette and Weekly Advertiser*, October 4, 1776, January 17, 1777; *Connecticut Gazette and Weekly Intelligencer*, April 21, 1775, March 8, 1776; Hoadley ed., *Public Records of the State of Connecticut*, Vol. II (Hartford, 1894), 557.

21. Antonio T. Bly ed., *Escaping Bondage: A Documentary History of Runaway Slaves in Eighteenth-Century New England, 1700–1789* (Lanham, Md.: Lexington Books, 2012), 7.

22. *Public Records of the Colony of Connecticut, 1636–1776*, Vol. XIV (Hartford, 1890), 483–92; Lorenzo Greene, "The New England Negro as Seen in Advertisements for Runaway Slaves," *Journal of Negro History* Vol. 10 (April 1944): 128. See also Elaine Forman Crane, *A Dependent People: Newport, Rhode Island in the Revolutionary Era* (New York: Fordham University Press, 1985).

23. Greene, "The New England Negro as Seen in Advertisements," 132.

24. Ibid.

25. Robert Ewell Greene, *Black Courage: Documentation of Black Participation in the American Revolution, 1775–1783* (Washington, D.C.: National Society of the Daughters of the American Revolution, 1984), 1.

26. *Continental Journal and Weekly Advertiser*, August 28, September 12, 1782; Greene, "The New England Negro as Seen in Advertisements," 129; Greene, *The Negro in Colonial New England*, 110.

27. Quarles, *The Negro in the American Revolution*, 10–11; Judith Van Buskirk, *Standing in Their Own Light: African American Patriots in the American Revolution* (Norman: University of Oklahoma Press, 2017), 51–52; Nell, *Colored Patriots*, 21.

28. Van Buskirk, *Standing in Their Own Light*, 51.

29. David McCullough, *1776* (New York: Simon and Schuster, 2005), 96–105.

30. Donald R. Wright, *African Americans in the Colonial Era: From African Origins through the American Revolution* (Wheeling, Ill.: Harlan Davidson Press, 2000), 93; Greene, *The Negro in Colonial New England*, 82.

31. *New England Chronicle*, June 22–29, 1775; Bly, *Escaping Bondage*, 189.

32. Greene, *The Negro in Colonial New England*, 82–83; www.ancestry.com/genealogy/reco rds/william-gilliland-esquire_180253125, accessed June 5, 2019.

33. Greene, *The Negro in Colonial New England*, 82–83.

34. *Boston News-Letter*, June 14, 1770; Bly, *Escaping Bondage*, 173; *Connecticut Gazette and the Universal Intelligencer*, April 21, 1775; Benjamin Brawley, *A Social History of the American Negro* (New York: AMS Press, 1971), 53.

35. *New England Chronicle*, March 21, March 28, 1776; Bly, *Escaping Bondage*, 193–94.

36. U.S. Continental Congress, *In Congress, Saturday …* (Watertown, Mass., 1776) www .loc.gov/item/rbpe.03901000.

37. Edward Countryman, *The American Revolution* (New York: Hill and Wang, 2003), 103; Kevin Phillips, *1775: A Good Year for Revolution* (New York: Penguin Group, 2012), 450; "Dates in History: 1776," www.nps.gov/revwar/revolution_day_by_day/1776_main .html

38. Alan Taylor, *American Revolutions: A Continental History* (New York: W.W. Norton, 2016), 154.

39. *Connecticut Gazette*, February 23, April 12, June 7, 1776; *Continental Journal*, November 14, 1776; Greene, *The Negro in Colonial New England*, 146; Hagist, *Wives, Slaves, and Servant Girls*, 87, 104.

40. *New England Chronicle*, April 25, 1776; Greene, *The Negro in Colonial New England*, 146.

41. *Connecticut Courant and Weekly Intelligencer*, March 9, 1779.

42. *Continental Journal and Weekly Advertiser*, September 19, 1776.

43. *The Newport Mercury*, August 2, 1773; Bly, *Escaping Bondage*, 265.

44. *The Providence Gazette*, April 2, 1785; Bly, *Escaping Bondage*, 285.

45. *The Providence Gazette*, April 2, 1785; Bly, *Escaping Bondage*, 285.

46. Graham Russell Gao Hodges and Alan Edward Brown, *"Pretends to Be Free":Runaway Slave Advertisements from Colonial and Revolutionary New York and New Jersey* (New York: Fordham University Press, 2019), 213–14.

47. Ibid., xxxiii. See also Graham Russell Hodges, *Root and Branch: African Americans in New York and East Jersey, 1613–1863* (Chapel Hill: University of North Carolina Press, 1999).

48. Ibid.

49. Ibid., xxxiii–xxxiv.

50. Nash, *The Forgotten Fifth*, 30–31.

51. Billy G. Smith and Richard Wojtowicz, *Blacks Who Stole Themselves: Advertisements for Runaways in the Pennsylvania Gazette, 1728–1790* (Philadelphia: University of Pennsylvania Press, 1989), 135–36.

52. Ibid., 141.

53. Ibid.

54. Lathan Windley, *Runaway Slave Advertisements: A Documentary History from the 1730s to 1790*, Vol. I (Westport, Conn.: Greenwood Press, 1983); Gerald Mullin, *Flight and Rebellion: Slave Resistance in Eighteenth Century Virginia* (New York: Oxford University Press, 1972), 103; Fuentes, *Dispossessed Lives*, 122.

55. Quoted in Frederick Law Olmsted, *A Journey in the Seaboard Slave States, with Remarks on Their Economy* (New York: New American Library, 1856), 125; David Brion Davis, *The Problem of Slavery in the Age of Revolution, 1770–1823* (2nd ed., New York: Oxford University Press, 1999), 84–85.

56. Davis, *The Problem of Slavery*, 85; Gary B. Nash, *Race and Revolution* (Madison: University of Wisconsin Press, 1990), 11.

57. Ibid.; Julian P. Boyd et al. eds., *The Papers of Thomas Jefferson* (Princeton, N.J.: Princeton University Press, 1950–), Vol. II, 672–73.

58. Davis, *The Problem of Slavery*, 85.

59. Ibid.

60. Bernard Bailyn, *Ideological Origins of the American Revolution* (Cambridge, Mass.: Harvard University Press, 1967), 235–36; Nash, *Race and Revolution*, 7–8.

61. James Otis, *Rights of the British Colonists Asserted and Proved* (Columbia: University of Missouri Press, 1929), 29; Nash, *Race and Revolution*, 7–8.

62. Nash, *Race and Revolution*, 8.

63. Robert G. Parkinson, *The Common Cause: Creating Race and Nation in the American Revolution* (Chapel Hill: University of North Carolina Press, 2016), 10.

64. Ibid., 101.

65. Greene, *Black Courage*, 1. See also Sidney Kaplan, *The Black Presence in the Era of the American Revolution, 1770–1780* (Washington, D.C.: Smithsonian Institution Press, 1973).

66. Ibid., 2, 8, 43; Headquarters, *Army Service Forces Manual M5 Training and Leadership and the Negro Soldier* (Washington, D.C.: U.S. Government Printing Office, 1944), 77–78. Four Black men from South Carolina received pensions for their service in the Revolutionary War; Van Buskirk, *Standing in Their Own Light*, 25–26.

67. Greene, *Black Courage*, 8, 43.

68. Gerald Horne, *The Counter Revolution of 1776: Slave Resistance and the Origins of the United States of America* (New York: New York University Press, 2014), ix.

69. Nancy K. Loane, *Following the Drum: Women at the Valley Forge Encampment* (Lincoln, Neb.: Potomac Books, 2009), 106–08.

70. Ibid.

71. Ibid.

72. Margaret Thomas to Caleb Gibbs, April 4, 1778, Revolutionary War Accounts, Vouchers, and Receipted Accounts 1, 1776–1780, Image 235, Series 5: Financial Papers, Washington Papers, LOC; Washington to Biddle, July 28, 1784; Loane, *Following the Drum*, 108–09.

73. Purdie and Dixon's *Virginia Gazette*, February 10, 1774; Hagist, *Wives, Slaves, and Servant Girls*, 50; Van Buskirk, *Standing in Their Own Light*, 54.

74. Nash, *The Forgotten Fifth*, 27; Ray Raphael, *A People's History of the American Revolution: How Common People Shaped the Fight for Independence* (New York: The New Press, 2016), Chapter 6.

75. Dunmore to Secretary of State Lord George Germain, June 26, 1776, in William Bell Clark ed., *Naval Documents of the American Revolution*, 10 vols. (Washington, D.C.: Government Printing Office, 1964–1996), vol. V, 756. See also Woody Holton, *Forced Founders: Indians, Debtors, Slaves, and the Making of the American Revolution in Virginia* (Chapel Hill: University of North Carolina Press, 1999), 137.

76. Aptheker, *The Negro in the American Revolution*, 14–15.

77. Ibid.

78. Matthew Spooner, "Freedom, Reenslavement, and Movement in the Revolutionary South," in Whitney Stewart et al. eds., *Race and Nation in the Age of Emancipation* (Athens: University of Georgia Press, 2018), 18.

79. Aptheker, *The Negro in the American Revolution*, 14–15.

80. Ibid., 15–16.

81. Quarles, *The Negro in the American Revolution*, 31; Thad Tate, *The Negro in Eighteenth Century Williamsburg* (Charlottesville: University of Virginia Press, 1965), 218.

82. Mullin, *Flight and Rebellion*, 133; *Virginia Gazette* (Purdie), March 29, 1776; *Virginia Gazette* (Dixon and Hunter), April 13, 1776. Reports of boatloads of slaves fleeing to Dunmore's ships are included in *Virginia Gazette* (Pinckney), November 30, 1775; (Dixon and Hunter), December 2, 1775.

83. Mullin, *Flight and Rebellion*, 136; Sylvia Frey, "Between Slavery and Freedom: Virginia Blacks in the American Revolution," *The Journal of Southern History* Vol. 49 Issue 3 (August 1983): 349; John Selby, *The Revolution in Virginia, 1775–1783* (2nd ed., Charlottesville: University of Virginia Press, 2007); Jacqueline Jones, "Race, Sex, and Self-Evident Truths: The Status of Slave Women during the Era of the American Revolution," in Ronald Hoffman and Peter J. Albert eds., *Women in the Age of the American Revolution* (Charlottesville: University Press of Virginia, 1989), 328; List of Dunmore's Fleet, 1776, Maryland Council of Public Safety Journal and Correspondence, Vol. XII, Maryland State Archives: Annapolis, Md., 24–25; Phillips, *1775*, 490; Alan Taylor, *The Internal Enemy: Slavery and War in Virginia* (New York: W.W. Norton, 2014), 245–67.

84. Windley, *Runaway Slave Advertisements*, Vol. I; Mullin, *Flight and Rebellion*, 103; Fuentes, *Dispossessed Lives*, 29.

85. *Virginia Gazette* (Purdie), January 20, 1774; Windley, *Runaway Slave Advertisements*, Vol. I, 142–43; Mullin, *Flight and Rebellion*, 103, 187.

86. *Virginia Gazette* (Purdie), January 20, 1774; Windley, *Runaway Slave Advertisements*, Vol. I, 142–43; Mullin, *Flight and Rebellion*, 103, 187.

87. *Virginia Gazette* (Purdie), January 20, 1774; Windley, *Runaway Slave Advertisements*, Vol. I, 142–43; Mullin, *Flight and Rebellion*, 103, 187.

88. Andrew DelBanco, *The War Before the War: Fugitive Slaves and the Struggle for America's Soul from the Revolution to the Civil War* (New York: Penguin Press, 2018), 74.

89. Windley, *Runaway Slave Advertisements*, Vol. I; Mullin, *Flight and Rebellion*, 187.

90. Windley, *Runaway Slave Advertisements*, Vols. I–IV; Herbert Aptheker, "We Will Be Free: Advertisements for Runaways and the Reality of American Slavery," Occasional Paper No. 1, Ethnic Studies Program, University of Santa Clara, 1984, 11.

91. *Virginia Gazette* (Purdie), July 10, 1778; Windley, *Runaway Slave Advertisements*, Vol. I, 274; Frey, *Water from the Rock*, 149–50; Norman Fuss, "Prelude to Rebellion: Dunmore's Raid on the Williamsburg Magazine," *Journal of the American Revolution*, April 2, 2015, https://allthingsliberty.com/2015/04/prelude-to-rebellion-dunmores-raid-on-the-williamsburg-magazine-april-21-1775/, accessed June 28, 2019.

92. Mullin, *Flight and Rebellion*, 187.

93. *Virginia Gazette* (Hayes), June 22, 1782; Windley, *Runaway Slave Advertisements*, Vol. I, 340.

94. Ibid.

95. *Virginia Gazette* (Hayes), June 22, 1782; Mullin, *Flight and Rebellion*, 133–34.

96. Windley, *Runaway Slave Advertisements*, Vol. II, 67.

97. *State Gazette of South Carolina* (Timothy), February 11, 1788; Windley, *Runaway Slave Advertisements*, Vol. III, 406.

98. *Virginia Gazette* (Dixon and Hunter), April 8, 1775; Mullin, *Flight and Rebellion*, 104.

99. *Virginia Gazette* (Dixon and Hunter), April 8, 1775.

100. *Virginia Gazette* (Purdie), November 21, 1777.

101. Mullin, *Flight and Rebellion*, 105.

102. *Virginia Gazette* (Purdie), December 5, 1777; (Dixon and Hunter), September 4, 1777, February 12, 1779.

103. *Virginia Gazette* (Dixon and Hunter), December 26, 1777; Windley, *Runaway Slave Advertisements*, Vol. I, 191.

104. *Virginia Gazette* (Dixon and Nicolson), February 12, 1779; Windley, *Runaway Slave Advertisements*, Vol. I, 197.

105. *Virginia Gazette* (Dixon and Hunter), October 16, 1778; Windley, *Runaway Slave Advertisements*, Vol. I, 194.

106. Aptheker, "We Will Be Free," 9.

107. *Maryland Journal and Baltimore Advertiser*, February 25, 1777; Windley, *Runaway Slave Advertisements*, Vol. II, 194; Nash, *The Forgotten Fifth*, 30–31.

108. *Maryland Journal and Baltimore Advertiser*, January 24, 1778; Windley, *Runaway Slave Advertisements*, Vol. II, 202.

109. *Maryland Journal and Baltimore Advertiser*, January 24, 1778; Windley, *Runaway Slave Advertisements*, Vol. II, 202.

110. *Maryland Gazette*, Annapolis, September 3, 1779; Windley, *Runaway Slave Advertisements*, Vol. II, 123.

111. Aptheker, "We Will Be Free," 10.

112. Smith and Wojtowicz, *Blacks Who Stole Themselves*, 135.

113. Lathan Windley, *A Profile of Runaway Slaves in Virginia and South Carolina* (New York: Garland Publishing), 7.

114. Joan Gunderson, *To Be Useful to the World: Women in Revolutionary America, 1740–1790* (Chapel Hill: University of North Carolina Press, 2006), 41; Countryman, *The American Revolution*, 153; Maya Jasanoff, *Liberty's Exiles: American Loyalists in the Revolutionary World* (New York: Vintage Books, 2011), 44.

115. *Royal Georgia Gazette* (Savannah), September 7, 1780; Windley, *Runaway Slave Advertisements*, Vol. IV, 79.

116. Nash, *The Forgotten Fifth*, 31–32; Frey, *Water from the Rock*, 192.

117. Betty Wood, "High Notions of Liberty: Women of Color and the American Revolution in Lowcountry Georgia and South Carolina, 1765–1783," in Philip Morgan ed., *African American Life in the Georgia Lowcountry: The Atlantic World of the Gullah Geechee* (Athens: University of Georgia Press, 2010), 58; *South Carolina Gazette*, June 6–13, 1761; Inspection Roll of Negroes, Book 2, 17, 18, Nova Scotia Museum, Black Cultural Database.

118. *Royal Georgia Gazette* (Savannah), July 24, August 3, 1779; Windley, *Runaway Slave Advertisements*, Vol. IV, 74.

119. *Royal Georgia Gazette* (Savannah), July 24, August 3, 1779; Windley, *Runaway Slave Advertisements*, Vol. IV, 74; Windley, *A Profile of Runaway Slaves in Virginia and South Carolina*, 17.

120. *Royal Georgia Gazette* (Savannah), August 29, 1779; Windley, *Runaway Slave Advertisements*, Vol. IV, 75.

121. John S. Bassett, "Slavery and Servitude in the Colony of North Carolina," in H.B. Adams, ed., Johns Hopkins University Studies in Historical and Political Science, XIV (Baltimore: The Johns Hopkins Press, 1896), 32; Windley, *A Profile of Runaway Slaves in Virginia and South Carolina*, 20.

122. *Royal Georgia Gazette* (Savannah), August 29, 1772; Windley, *A Profile of Runaway Slaves in Virginia and South Carolina*, 20.

123. Windley, *Runaway Slave Advertisements*, Vol. IV, 5.

124. Ibid., 6.

125. Ibid., 81.

126. Ibid., 17.

127. Ibid., 81.

128. Ibid.

129. Wood, "High Notions of Liberty," 58; Johann von Ewald, *Diary of the American War: A Hessian Journal*, trans. and ed. Joseph P. Tustin (New Haven, Conn.: Yale University Press, 1979), 305.

130. *South Carolina Gazette*, December 10, 1779; Wood, "High Notions of Liberty," 58–59.

131. Wood, "High Notions of Liberty," 58–59; Inspection Roll of Negroes, Book 1, 47, Nova Scotia Museum, Black Cultural Database.

132. Wood, "High Notions of Liberty," 60; Inspection Roll of Negroes, Book 3, 3, Nova Scotia Museum, Black Cultural Database.

133. Wood, "High Notions of Liberty," 60.

134. Karen Cook Bell, *Claiming Freedom: Race, Kinship, and Land in Nineteenth Century Georgia* (Columbia: University of South Carolina Press, 2018), 2–3.

135. Ibid.

136. Herbert Aptheker, "We Will Be Free," 10.

137. Frey, *Water from the Rock*, 108.

138. Alan Gilbert, *Black Patriots and Loyalists: Fighting for Emancipation in the War for Independence* (Chicago: University of Chicago Press, 2012), 123.

139. Frey, *Water from the Rock*, 108.

140. R.W. Gibbes ed., *Documentary History of the American Revolution, 1764–1776*, Vol. III (New York: D. Appleton & Company, 1855), 131.

141. John Richard Alden, *The South in the Revolution* (Baton Rouge: Louisiana State University Press, 1957), 225.

142. Ibid., 226. Nonetheless, at least four Black men who received pensions served with Patriot forces in South Carolina. See Greene, *Black Courage*, 43; Van Buskirk, *Standing in Their Own Light*, 142–72; Gilbert, *Black Patriots and Loyalists*, 92.

143. Nash, *The Forgotten Fifth*, 32; Frey, *Water from the Rock*, 109.

144. William Snow to Mr. Rhoades, Sept. 1, 1781, Francis Marion Papers, Special Collections, New York Public Library, New York.

145. *Royal Georgia Gazette* (Savannah), January 4, 1781; Windley, *Runaway Slave Advertisements*, Vol. IV, 81–82. Although Kate, Scipio, Town Sue, and Will are not identified as having blood relations, fictive kin relations among Lowcountry slaves was common.

146. Windley, *Runaway Slave Advertisements*, Vol. IV, 82–83.

147. Windley, *A Profile of Runaway Slaves in Virginia and South Carolina*, 111, 115.

148. Ibid.

149. Windley, *Runaway Slave Advertisements*, Vol. III, 165–66. The husband of Alcie is not identified in the advertisement but is likely one of the five men listed in the advertisement.

150. Philip Morgan, *Slave Counterpoint: Black Culture in the Eighteenth Century Chesapeake and Lowcountry* (Chapel Hill: University of North Carolina Press, 1998), 542, n. 72.

151. Thomas Pinckney to Eliza L. Pinckney, May 17, 1779, 38-3-5, Pinckney Family Papers, South Carolina Historical Society; Frey, *Water from the Rock*, 115.

152. Thomas Pinckney to Eliza L. Pinckney, May 17, 1779, 38-3-5, Pinckney Family Papers, South Carolina Historical Society; Frey, *Water from the Rock*, 115.

153. James Harold Easterby ed., *Wadboo Barony: Its Fate as Told in Colleton Family Papers, 1773–1793* (Columbia: University of South Carolina Press, 1952), 4; Frey, *Water from the Rock*, 115.

154. *South Carolina and American General Gazette* (Charleston), April 9, 1779; Windley, *Runaway Slave Advertisements*, Vol. III, 554.

155. *South Carolina and American General Gazette* (Charleston), May 29, 1779; Windley, *Runaway Slave Advertisements*, Vol. III, 554.

156. *South Carolina and American General Gazette* (Charleston), July 30, 1779; Windley, *Runaway Slave Advertisements*, Vol. III, 556.

157. *South Carolina and American General Gazette* (Charleston), July 16, 1779; Windley, *Runaway Slave Advertisements*, Vol. III, 555.

158. *South Carolina and American General Gazette* (Charleston), July 30, 1779; Windley, *Runaway Slave Advertisements*, Vol. III, 557.

159. Frey, *Water from the Rock*, 119, 121–22.

160. Windley, *A Profile of Runaway Slaves in Virginia and South Carolina*, 128; Van Buskirk, *Standing in Their Own Light*, 233.

161. Frey, Water from the Rock, 109.

162. Ibid.

163. *South Carolina Gazette and General Advertiser* (Charleston), July 19, 1783; Windley, *Runaway Slave Advertisements*, Vol. III, 718.

164. Letter from Thomas Jefferson to Col. Thos. Newton, Feb. 3, 1781, Executive Letter Book, December 24, 1780–February 27, 1781, Virginia State Library, Richmond, Va.; Windley, *A Profile of Runaway Slaves in Virginia and South Carolina*, 128.

165. E.C. Burnett, *Letters of Members of the Continental Congress*, Vol. VI (Washington, D.C.: Carnegie Institution of Washington, 1933), 497; Windley, *A Profile of Runaway Slaves in Virginia and South Carolina*, 128.

166. Burnett, *Letters of Members of the Continental Congress*, Vol. VIII, 264; Windley, *A Profile of Runaway Slaves in Virginia and South Carolina*, 128.

167. Robert Taylor to Neil Jamieson, April 2, 1783, Neil Jamieson Papers, 1776–1783, Vol. XXI, Library of Congress, Washington, D.C.; Windley, *A Profile of Runaway Slaves in Virginia and South Carolina*, 128–29.

168. Carol Berkin, *Revolutionary Mothers: Women in the Struggle for American Independence* (New York: Alfred A. Knopf, 2005), 126; Mary Louise Clifford, *From Slavery to Freetown: Black Loyalists After the American Revolution* (Jefferson, N.C.: McFarland and Company, 1999), 50; Ellen Gibson Wilson, *The Loyal Blacks* (New York: G.P. Putnam's Sons, 1976), 95.

169. Frey, *Water from the Rock*, 130.

170. Ibid., 131.

171. Ibid., 132.

172. *South Carolina Gazette and General Advertiser* (Charleston), July 29, August 23, September 2–6, November 8 and 18, 1783.

173. Aptheker, "We Will Be Free," 9–10.

174. *Virginia Gazette or American Advertiser* (Hayes), September 14, 1782; Windley, *Runaway Slave Advertisements*, Vol. I, 342–43.

175. Nash, *The Forgotten Fifth*, 33.

176. Lucia Stanton, *Free Some Day: The African American Families of Monticello* (Charlottesville, Va.: Thomas Jefferson Foundation, 2000), 52, 56–57.

177. Ewald, *Diary of the American War*, 305; Nash, *The Forgotten Fifth*, 34; Frey, *Water from the Rock*, 167–68.

178. *Virginia Gazette or American Advertiser* (Hayes), July 13, 1782; Windley, *Runaway Slave Advertisements*, Vol. I, 339–40.

179. Mary Beth Norton, *Liberty's Daughters: The Revolutionary Experience of American Women, 1750–1800* (Ithaca: Cornell University Press, 1996), 209–10.

180. Jessica Millward, "'A Choice Parcel of Country Born': African Americans and the Transition to Freedom in Maryland, 1770–1840" (Ph.D. dissertation, UCLA, 2003), 63–64. See also Millward, *Finding Charity's Folk: Enslaved and Free Black Women in Maryland* (Athens: University of Georgia Press, 2015).

181. Ewald, *Diary of the American War*, 335–36; Nash, *The Forgotten Fifth*, 37–38; Gilbert, *Black Patriots and Loyalists*, 129.

182. James Kirby Martin, *Ordinary Courage: The Revolutionary War Adventures of Joseph Plumb Martin* (St. James, N.Y.: Brandywine Press, 1993), 141–42; Nash, *The Forgotten Fifth*, 38.

183. Martin, *Ordinary Courage*, 141–42; Nash, *The Forgotten Fifth*, 38.

184. Nash, *The Forgotten Fifth*, 39; Cassandra Pybus, *Epic Journeys of Freedom: Runaway Slaves of the American Revolution and Their Global Quest for Liberty* (Boston: Beacon Press, 2006), 21–37; Stanton, *Free Some Day*, 52–57.

185. *Virginia Gazette or American Advertiser* (Hayes), August 17, 1782; Windley, *Runaway Slave Advertisements*, Vol. I, 341.

186. *Royal Gazette*, July 27, 1782; Lilla M. Hawes, "Miscellaneous Papers of James Jackson, 1781–1798," *Georgia Historical Quarterly* Vol. 37 (1953): 78; Frey, *Water from the Rock*, 174; Nash, *The Forgotten Fifth*, 39–40.

187. Report of the Peace Agreement, 1782–1783, Maryland Council of Public Safety Journal and Correspondence, Vol. XLVIII, Maryland State Archives, Annapolis, Md., 512; Frey, *Water from the Rock*, 177–78; Nash, *The Forgotten Fifth*, 42.

188. Ralph Izzard, Letters Concerning the British Evacuation of Charleston, 1782, New York Public Library; Frey, *Water from the Rock*, 177; Nash, *The Forgotten Fifth*, 43.

189. Nash, *The Forgotten Fifth*, 42–43.

190. Douglas R. Egerton, *Death or Liberty: African Americans and Revolutionary America* (New York: Oxford University Press, 2009), 194.

191. Ibid.; Nash, *The Forgotten Fifth*, 43; Frey, *Water from the Rock*, 179–80.

192. Frey, *Water from the Rock*, 179.

193. Ibid., 179–81. For an examination of fugitivity in Florida during the nineteenth century see Larry Eugene Rivers, *Rebels and Runaways: Slave Resistance in Nineteenth Century Florida* (Urbana: University of Illinois Press, 2012).

194. Frey, *Water from the Rock*, 182.

195. Ibid.

196. Inspection Roll of Negro Emigrants, April 17–23, 1783, M332, reel 7, p. 5, Miscellaneous Papers of the Continental Congress, 1774–1789, National Archives, Washington, D.C.; Frey, *Water from the Rock*, 193. See also Pybus, *Epic Journeys of Freedom*; and Simon Schama, *Rough Crossings: Britain, the Slaves, and the American Revolution* (New York: Harper Collins, 2006).

197. Robin Winks, *The Blacks in Canada: A History* (New Haven, Conn.: Yale University Press, 1971), 29–30; Frey, *Water from the Rock*, 193.

198. Winks, *The Blacks in Canada*, 33; Frey, *Water from the Rock*, 193.

199. Winks, *The Blacks in Canada*, 24–26; Frey, *Water from the Rock*, 194; John N. Grant, "Black Immigration into Nova Scotia, 1776–1815," *Journal of Negro History* Vol. 58 (1973): 253–61.

200. Pybus, *Epic Journeys of Freedom*, 215; Jasanoff, *Liberty's Exiles*.

201. Berkin, *Revolutionary Mothers*, 128; Graham Russell Hodges ed., *The Black Loyalist Directory: African Americans in Exile After the American Revolution* (New York: Garland Publishing, 1996).

4   "A NEGRO WOMAN CALLED BETT"

1. *Pennsylvania Gazette*, July 18, 1781; Don N. Hagist, *Wives, Slaves, and Servant Girls: Advertisements for Female Runaways in American Newspapers, 1770–1783* (Yardley, Pa.: Westholme Publishing, 2016), 150; Stephanie Camp, *Closer to Freedom: Enslaved Women and Everyday Resistance in the Plantation South* (Chapel Hill: University of North Carolina Press, 2004), 51–53.

2. Michel-Rolph Trouillot, *Silencing the Past: Power and the Production of History* (Boston: Beacon Press, 1995), 22–23.

3. Camp, *Closer to Freedom*, 53.

4. Edward Raymond Turner, "Slavery in Colonial Pennsylvania," *The Pennsylvania Magazine of History and Biography* Vol. 35 No. 2 (1911): 148.

5. Gary B. Nash, "Slaves and Slaveowners in Colonial Philadelphia," in Gary B. Nash ed., *Race, Class, and Politics: Essays on American Colonial and Revolutionary Society* (Urbana: University of Illinois Press, 1986), 91–118.

6. Gary B. Nash and Jean R. Soderlund, *Freedom by Degrees: Emancipation in Pennsylvania and Its Aftermath* (New York: Oxford University Press, 1991), 12–13.

7. Donald R. Wright, *African Americans in the Colonial Era: From African Origins through the American Revolution* (Wheeling, Ill.: Harlan Davidson Press, 2000), 118–19, 122.

8. Marisa Fuentes, "Power and Historical Figuring: Rachael Pringle Polgreen's Troubled Archives," *Gender and History* Vol. 22 No. 3 (November 2010): 579.

9. Rebecca Scott, *Degrees of Freedom: Louisiana and Cuba after Slavery* (New York: Cambridge University Press, 2005); Richard S. Newman, "'Lucky to be born in Pennsylvania': Free Soil, Fugitive Slaves and the Making of Pennsylvania's Anti-Slavery Borderland," *Slavery and Abolition*, Vol. 32 No. 3 (September 2011):414.

10. Wright, *African Americans in the Colonial Era*, 169.

11. William M. Wiecek, *The Sources of Anti-slavery Constitutionalism in America, 1760–1848* (Ithaca: Cornell University Press, 1977), 50.

12. Ibid., 169–70; Arthur Zilversmit, *The First Emancipation: The Abolition of Slavery in the North* (Chicago: University of Chicago Press, 1967), 175–77. See also Howard Pashman, *Building a Revolutionary State: The Legal Transformation of New York, 1776–1783* (Chicago: University of Chicago Press, 2018).

13. Wiecek, *The Sources of Anti-Slavery Constitutionalism*, 50; Billy G. Smith and Richard Wojtowicz, *Blacks Who Stole Themselves: Advertisements for Runaways in the Pennsylvania Gazette, 1728–1790* (Philadelphia: University of Pennsylvania Press, 1989), 12–13.

14. Smith and Wojtowicz, *Blacks Who Stole Themselves*, 12–13.

15. Wright, *African Americans in the Colonial Era*, 170.

16. Newman, "Lucky to be born in Pennsylvania," 414–15.

17. Ibid., 417.

18. Ibid.

19. Ibid., 417–18.

20. Ibid., 418.

21. Ibid., 47; Mary Wilds, *Mumbet: The Life and Times of Elizabeth Freeman, The True Story of a Slave Who Won Her Freedom* (Greensboro: Avisson Press Inc., 1999), 53.

22. Ben Z. Rose, *Mother of Freedom: Mum Bett and the Roots of Abolitionism* (Waverley, Mass.: TreeLine Press, 2009), 4. In recognition of her freedom to name herself, I have chosen to use the name Elizabeth Freeman instead of Mum Bett.

23. Wilds, *Mumbet*, 14–15, 20.

24. Emile Piper and David Levinson, *One Minute a Free Woman: Elizabeth Freeman and the Struggle for Freedom* (Salisbury, Conn.: Upper Housatonic Valley National Heritage Area, 2010), 2, 7; Catherine Adams and Elizabeth Pleck, *Love of Freedom: Black Women in Colonial and Revolutionary New England* (New York: Oxford University Press, 2010), 133–54. See also Patrick Rael, *Eighty-Eight Years: The Long Death of Slavery in the United States, 1777–1865* (Athens: University of Georgia Press, 2015), 65–66 and Joanne Pope Melish, *Disowning Slavery: Gradual Emancipation and "Race" in New England, 1780–1860* (Ithaca: Cornell University Press, 2016).

25. Catherine Sedgwick, Essay on Mumbet, undated, Catherine Marie Sedgwick Papers, Massachusetts Historical Society, Boston; Rose, *Mother of Freedom*, 57–59; Piper and Levinson, *One Minute a Free Woman*, 65.

26. Piper and Levinson, *One Minute a Free Woman*, 65–66.

27. Ibid., 67.

28. Rose, *Mother of Freedom*, 65.

29. The Journal of the Convention for Framing a Constitution of Government for the State of Massachusetts Bay (Boston: n.p., 1832), 225; Piper and Levinson, *One Minute a Free Woman*, 67.

30. Piper and Levinson, *One Minute a Free Woman*, 67.

31. Arthur Zilversmit, "Quok Walker, Mum Bett, and the Abolition of Slavery in Massachusetts," *William and Mary Quarterly* Vol. 25 No. 4 (October 1968): 620; Wilds, *Mumbet*, 68.

32. Zilversmit, "Quok Walker, Mum Bett, and the Abolition of Slavery in Massachusetts," 621; Transcript of Case No. 1, Brom & Bett vs. J. Ashley, Esq., Book 4A, p. 55, Inferior Court of Common Pleas, Berkshire County, Great Barrington, MA, 1781, transcribed by Brady Barrows at Berkshire County Courthouse, 1998; www.mumbet.com: The website provides both images of the original document and a transcription.

33. Piper and Levinson, *One Minute a Free Woman*, 71–72.
34. Emily West, *Enslaved Women in America: From Colonial Times to Emancipation* (Lanham, Md.: Rowman and Littlefield, 2014), 58.
35. Ibid.
36. Wilds, *Mumbet*, 94.
37. Ibid., 82–83.
38. Emily Blanck, *Tyrannicide: Forging an American Law of Slavery in Revolutionary South Carolina and Massachusetts* (Athens: University of Georgia Press, 2014), 4.
39. Smith and Wojtowicz, *Blacks Who Stole Themselves*, 151.
40. Graham Russell Gao Hodges and Alan Edward Brown, *"Pretends to Be Free": Runaway Slave Advertisements from Colonial and Revolutionary New York and New Jersey* (New York: Fordham University Press, 2019), xvii–xix.
41. Wright, *African Americans in the Colonial Era*, 176.
42. Ibid.
43. Ibid., 190–91; Gary B. Nash, *Forging Freedom: The Formation of Philadelphia's Black Community, 1720–1840* (Cambridge, Mass.: Harvard University Press, 1988), 125–26.
44. Woody Holton, *Black Americans in the Revolutionary Era: A Brief History with Documents* (New York: Bedford/St. Martins, 2009), 17.
45. Wright, *African Americans in the Colonial Era*, 191; Nash, *Forging Freedom*, 127–28.
46. Nash, *Forging Freedom*, 109.
47. Ibid., 111, 127.
48. Wright, *African Americans in the Colonial Era*, 195.
49. Paul E. Herron, "Slavery and Freedom in American State Constitutional Development," *Journal of Policy History* Vol. 27 No. 2 (2015): 308–09; Paul Finkleman, *Slavery and the Founders: Race and Liberty in the Age of Jefferson* (New York: Routledge, 2015), 7–10; Matthew Mason, *Slavery and Politics in the Early Republic* (Chapel Hill: University of North Carolina Press, 2006), 32–33.
50. Allen C. Guelzo, "Slavery and the Constitution: A Defense," *National Review*, May 6, 2019, 35.
51. Wright, *African Americans in the Colonial Era*, 196.
52. Holton, *Black Americans in the Revolutionary Era*, 19.
53. Quoted in Guelzo, "Slavery and the Constitution," 35.
54. Erica Armstrong Dunbar, *Never Caught: The Washingtons' Relentless Pursuit of their Runaway Slave Ona Judge* (New York: Atria, 2017), 105; Blanck, *Tyrannicide*, 147–69.
55. Erica Armstrong Dunbar, *A Fragile Freedom: African American Women and Emancipation in the Antebellum City* (New Haven, Conn.: Yale University Press, 2008), 38.
56. Ibid., 39.
57. Ibid.; Indenture of Negro Woman Teeny to William McMurtrie, August 16, 1786, Pennsylvania Abolition Society, Manumission Book A, 1780–1793, reel 20.
58. Dunbar, *A Fragile Freedom*, 38; Indenture of Negro Woman Teeny to William McMurtrie, August 16, 1786, Pennsylvania Abolition Society, Manumission Book A, 1780–1793, reel 20.

59. *Virginia Independent Chronicle* (Davis), March 4, 1789; Lathan Windley, *Runaway Slave Advertisements: A Documentary History from the 1730s to 1790*, Vol. I (Westport, Conn.: Greenwood Press, 1983), 404; Herbert Aptheker, "We Will Be Free: Advertisements for Runaways and the Reality of American Slavery," Occasional Paper No. 1, Ethnic Studies Program, University of Santa Clara, 1984, 17.

60. *State Gazette of South Carolina* (Timothy), August 11, 1785; Windley, *Runaway Slave Advertisements*, Vol. III, 391; Aptheker, "We Will Be Free," 17.

61. *Royal Georgia Gazette* (Savannah), May 13, 1790; Windley, *Runaway Slave Advertisements*, Vol. IV, 177; Aptheker, "We Will Be Free," 17.

62. *Royal Georgia Gazette* (Savannah), May 13, 1790; Windley, *Runaway Slave Advertisements*, Vol. IV, 177; Aptheker, "We Will Be Free," 17.

63. *Savannah Gazette of the State of Georgia*, April 10, 1788; Windley, *Runaway Slave Advertisements*, Vol. IV, 155; Aptheker, "We Will Be Free," 17–18.

64. *State Gazette of South Carolina* (Timothy), April 5, 1790; Windley, *Runaway Slave Advertisements*, Vol. III, 410–11; Aptheker, "We Will Be Free," 19.

65. *Maryland Journal and Advertiser*, September 13, 1785; Windley, *Runaway Slave Advertisements*, Vol. II, 335; Aptheker, "We Will Be Free," 23.

66. *Savannah Gazette of the State of Georgia*, January 6, 1785; Windley, *Runaway Slave Advertisements*, Vol. IV, 121; Aptheker, "We Will Be Free," 23.

67. *Pennsylvania Gazette*, August 7, 1776; Hagist, *Wives, Slaves, and Servant Girls*, 97.

68. Ibid.

69. Renee K. Harrison, *Enslaved Women and the Art of Resistance in Antebellum America* (New York: Palgrave Macmillan, 2009), 169.

70. Edlie L. Wong, *Neither Fugitive Nor Free: Atlantic Slavery, Freedom Suits, and the Legal Culture of Travel* (New York: New York University Press, 2009), 114; William Still, *The Underground Railroad* (Philadelphia, Pa.: Porter and Coates, 1872), electronic copy: www.gutenberg.org/files/15263/15263-h/15263-h.htm#ChStill

71. Still, *The Underground Railroad*.

72. Wright, *African Americans in the Early Republic, 1789–1831* (Arlington Heights, Ill.: Harlan Davidson, Inc., 1993), 120.

73. Ibid., 119.

74. Alejandro de la Fuente and Ariela J. Gross, *Becoming Free, Becoming Black: Race, Freedom and the Law in Cuba, Virginia, and Louisiana* (New York: Cambridge University Press, 2020), 84–85.

75. Ibid. See also Loren Schweninger, *Appealing for Liberty: Freedom Suits in the South* (New York: Oxford University Press, 2018).

76. Cynthia A. Kierner, *Southern Women in Revolution, 1776–1800* (Columbia: University of South Carolina Press, 1998), 208.

77. Ibid.; Petition of Grace Davis, Race & Slavery Petitions Project, Petition Analysis Record 11279109, University of North Carolina, Greensboro, https://library.uncg.edu/slavery/petitions/index.aspx, accessed July 2, 2020.

78. Fuente and Gross, *Becoming Free, Becoming Black*, 85–86.

79. Ibid., 86–87.

80. Ibid., 87; Accomack Petition, June 3, 1782, Accession No. 36121, Box 1, Folder 10, Legislative Petitions of the General Assembly, 1776–1785, Library of Virginia.

81. Fuente and Gross, *Becoming Free, Becoming Black*, 90–91; Accomack County Deeds, vol. 6, 1783–1788, microfilm reel 14, #496, Library of Virginia.

82. Eva Sheppard Wolf, *Race and Liberty in the New Nation: Emancipation in Virginia from the Revolution to Nat Turner's Rebellion* (Baton Rouge: Louisiana State University Press, 2006), 63–64; Eady Cary alia Idy Cary vs. Stith E. Burton, Box 1, 007520827, Petersburg County District Court Judgements (Freedom Suits), Library of Virginia; Fuente and Gross, *Becoming Free, Becoming Black*, 92.

83. Miscellaneous Record Books LL to ZZ, South Carolina Department of Archives and History, Columbia; Philip D. Morgan, "Black Society in the Low Country, 1760–1810," in Ira Berlin and Ronald Hoffman eds., *Slavery and Freedom in the Age of the American Revolution* (Charlottesville: University of Virginia Press, 1983), 115–16.

84. Wiecek, *The Sources of Anti-Slavery Constitutionalism*, 92.

85. Ibid., 92–93.

86. Gary B. Nash, *Race and Revolution* (Madison: University of Wisconsin Press, 1990), 18.

87. Ibid., 18–19.

88. Wiecek, *The Sources of Anti-Slavery Constitutionalism*, 56–57; U.S. Bureau of the Census, *Negro Population in the United States, 1790–1915* (Washington, D.C.: GPO, 1918), 57.

89. Graham Russell Gao Hodges, "Black Self-Emancipation, Gradual Emancipation, and the Underground Railroad in the Northern Colonies and States, 1763–1804," in Damian Alan Pargas ed., *Fugitive Slaves and Spaces of Freedom in North America* (Gainesville: University Press of Florida, 2018), 29.

90. Dunbar, *Never Caught*, 110; Gary B. Nash, *The Forgotten Fifth: African Americans in the Age of Revolution* (Cambridge: Harvard University Press, 2006), 61–62.

91. *The Granite Freeman*, Concord, New Hampshire, May 22, 1845. Two interviews from *The Granite Freeman* and *The Liberator* on Ona Judge Staines can be read at www.ushistory.org /presidentshouse/slaves. See also Evelyn Gerson, "Ona Judge Staines: Escape from Washington," at www.seacoastnh.com/Blackhistory/ona.html.

92. Ibid.

93. Ibid.

94. Nash, *The Forgotten Fifth*, 62–63.

95. *The Granite Freeman*, Concord, New Hampshire, May 22, 1845.

96. Woody Holton, *Forced Founders: Indians, Debtors, Slaves and the Making of the American Revolution in Virginia* (Chapel Hill: University of North Carolina Press, 1999), 219.

97. Nash, *The Forgotten Fifth*, 62–63; Dunbar, *Never Caught*, 191–92. George Washington's nephew Bushrod Washington inherited Mount Vernon upon the death of Martha Washington. See Ana Lucia Araujo, *Slavery in the Age of Memory: Engaging the Past* (New York: Bloomsbury Press, 2020), 7.

98. Dunbar, *Never Caught*, xvii.

99. Ibid., 186.

100. Dunbar, *A Fragile Freedom*, 44; Deborah Norris Logan, Diary of Deborah Norris Logan, July 1822, vol. 5, Historical Society of Pennsylvania.

101. Dunbar, *A Fragile Freedom*, 43.

102. Dunbar, *A Fragile Freedom*, 43; *Philadelphia City Directory*, 1795, Historical Society of Pennsylvania.

103. John Hope Franklin and Loren Schweninger observed that "most runaways remained in the South, few were aided by abolitionists or anyone else." Likewise, Peter Kolchin has argued that slaves who fled stayed in the slaveholding states, "making their way to cities and merging with the free black population." Cities with relatively large free black populations served as magnets for runaway slaves in the surrounding plantation districts. William Link found that in Richmond, Virginia, a "permanent runaway population blended with local African Americans." Link's observation that these were permanent runaways is important, as many scholars have assumed that fugitives who stayed in the South were truants or temporary runaways. Franklin and Schweninger estimated that "tens of thousands of fugitives headed to the towns and cities of the South in search of freedom and work," but they assumed that only a small fraction stayed for extended periods of time. In their dismissal of the majority of Southern fugitive slaves as truants, Franklin and Schweninger stop short of in-depth analysis of the experiences of permanent freedom seekers in the Southern states. Likewise, based on her study on enslaved women, Stephanie Camp noted that women made up 19 to 41 percent of truants and argued that women in the South ran away only temporarily. Camp's assessment dismisses a large number of fugitive women who were able to make their escape permanent. See John Hope Franklin and Loren Schweninger, *Runaway Slaves: Rebels on the Plantation* (New York: Oxford University Press, 1999), 145–46; Peter Kolchin, *American Slavery, 1619–1877* (New York: Penguin Books, 1995), 158; William Link, *Roots of Secession: Slavery and Politics in Antebellum Virginia* (Chapel Hill: University of North Carolina Press, 2003), 106; Stephanie Camp, *Closer to Freedom*, 54.

104. Damian Pargas, "Seeking Freedom in the Midst of Slavery: Fugitive Slaves in the South," in Pargas, *Fugitive Slaves and Spaces of Freedom in North America*, 116–36; Viola Franziska Müller, "Illegal but Tolerated: Slave Refugees in Richmond, Virginia, 1800–1860," in Pargas, *Fugitive Slaves and Spaces of Freedom in North America*, 139.

105. Müller, "Illegal but Tolerated," 138.

106. Ibid., 140.

107. U.S. Bureau of the Census, *Negro Population of the United States, 1790–1915*.

108. Ibid.

109. Amrita Chakrabarti Myers, *Forging Freedom: Black Women and the Pursuit of Liberty in Antebellum Charleston* (Chapel Hill: University of North Carolina Press, 2011), 23.

110. *South Carolina Gazette and General Advertiser*, January 20, 1784; Windley, *Runaway Slave Advertisements*, Vol. 3, 727.

111. Philip D. Morgan, "Black Society in the Low Country, 1760–1810," in Ira Berlin and Ronald Hoffman eds., *Slavery and Freedom in the Age of the American Revolution* (Charlottesville: University of Virginia Press, 1983), 127.

112. Charleston Library Society, South Carolina Newspapers, 1732–1782 (microfilm), The Johns Hopkins University, Baltimore; Morgan, "Black Society in the Low Country," 102.

113. Amani Marshall, "'They Will Endeavor to Pass for Free': Enslaved Runaways' Performances of Freedom in Antebellum South Carolina," *Slavery & Abolition* Vol. 31 No. 2 (2010): 161–80.

114. U.S. Bureau of the Census, *Negro Population of the United States, 1790–1915*; Myers, *Forging Freedom*, 23.

115. Myers, *Forging Freedom*, 24.

116. Seth Rockman, *Scraping By: Wage Labor, Slavery, and Survival in Early Baltimore* (Baltimore: Johns Hopkins University Press, 2009), 124.

117. Ibid., 124–25.

118. Pargas, "Seeking Freedom," 123–24.

119. Ibid.

120. Charles L. Purdue and Thomas E. Barden, eds., *Weevils in the Wheat: Interviews with Virginia Ex-Slaves* (Charlottesville: University of Virginia Press, 1996), Mrs. Jennie Patterson, 220.

121. Pargas, "Seeking Freedom," 125.

122. *Royal Gazette*, March 15, 1783; Hagist, *Wives, Slaves, and Servant Girls*, 162.

123. Pargas, "Seeking Freedom," 125.

124. Ibid.

125. Pargas, "Seeking Freedom," 128.

126. Wright, *African Americans in the Early Republic*, 144–46.

127. Ira Berlin, *Slaves Without Masters: The Free Negro in the Antebellum South* (New York: The New Press, 2007), 95.

128. Nash, *The Forgotten Fifth*, 130; Wright, *African Americans in the Early Republic*, 146.

129. Wright, *African Americans in the Early Republic*, 146.

130. *South Carolina Gazette*, March 22, 1783; Hagist, *Wives, Slaves, and Servant Girls*, 162; Lorenzo Greene, *The Negro in Colonial New England* (New York: Atheneum Press, 1968), 147.

131. *New York Gazette*, June 29, 1783; Hagist, *Wives, Slaves, and Servant Girls*, 165–66.

132. *South Carolina Gazette and General Advertiser*, December 6–9, 1783; Windley, *Runaway Slave Advertisements*, Vol. III, 723.

133. *South Carolina Gazette and General Advertiser*, November 4–8, 1783; Windley, *Runaway Slave Advertisements*, Vol. III, 722.

134. *South Carolina Gazette and General Advertiser*, November 4–8, 1783; Windley, *Runaway Slave Advertisements*, Vol. III, 722.

135. Daina Ramey Berry, *The Price for Their Pound of Flesh: The Price of the Enslaved, from Womb to Grave, in the Building of a Nation* (Boston: Beacon Press, 2017), 96.

136. Allan Kulikoff, "Uprooted Peoples: Black Migrants in the Age of the American Revolution," in Berlin and Hoffman eds., *Slavery and Freedom in the Age of the American Revolution*, 167.

137. Ibid., 153.

138. Frederick Bancroft, *Slave Trading in the Old South* (Columbia: University of South Carolina Press, 1996), 19; Berry, *The Price for Their Pound of Flesh*, 32.

139. Wright, *African Americans in the Early Republic*, 31; Richard Sutch, "The Breeding of Slaves for Sale and the Westward Expansion of Slavery, 1850–1860" in Stanley L. Engerman and Eugene Genovese, eds., *Race and Slavery in the Western Hemisphere: Quantitative Studies* (Princeton, New Jersey: Princeton University Press, 1975), 195–96.

5 CONFRONTING THE POWER STRUCTURES

1. "Trial of Negroe Man Slave Named Lewis the Property of Oliver Bowen for the Murder of John Casper Hersman, Robbing Philip Ulsmer, John Lowerman of Ga. & Col. Borquin of South Carolina, 1787," in Slave File, Telamon Cuyler Collection, Manuscript Room, Hargrett Library, University of Georgia; Betty Wood, "Some Aspects of Female Resistance to Chattel Slavery in Low Country Georgia, 1763–1815," *The Historical Journal* Vol. 30 No. 3 (September 1987): 612. For previous attempts by White Georgians to destroy maroon communities, see Allen D. Candler and Lucian L. Knight eds., *Colonial Records of the State of Georgia*, 26 vols. (Atlanta, 1904–1916), Vol. XIV, 292–93; Timothy Lockley, *Maroon Communities in South Carolina: A Documentary Record* (Columbia: University of South Carolina Press, 2009), 40. See also the website Mapping Marronage, http://mapping-marronage.rll.lsa.umich.edu.

2. Neil Roberts, *Freedom as Marronage* (Chicago: University of Chicago Press, 2015), 13.

3. Lockley, *Maroon Communities in South Carolina*, ix.

4. Ibid.; Hugo Prosper Leaming, *Hidden Americans: Maroons of Virginia and the Carolinas* (New York: Garland Publishing, 1995), iii.

5. Marcus Nevius, *City of Refuge: Slavery and Petit Marronage in the Great Dismal Swamp, 1763–1856* (Athens: University of Georgia Press, 2020), 1–2; Karla Gottlieb, *The Mother of Us All: A History of Queen Nanny, Leader of the Windward Jamaican Maroons* (Trenton, N.J.: Africa World Press, 2000), 99; Mavis C. Campbell, *The Maroons of Jamaica, 1655–1796: A History of Resistance, Collaboration, and Betrayal* (Trenton, N.J.: Africa World Press, 1990), 41.

6. Richard Price ed., *Maroon Societies: Rebel Slave Communities in the Americas* (Garden City, N.Y.: Doubleday Anchor Press, 1973); Leaming, *Hidden Americans*, xiii. For a discussion of maroons in the Americas see Alvin O. Thompson, *Flight to Freedom: African Runaways and Maroons in the Americas* (Kingston, Jamaica: University of the West Indies Press, 2006).

7. Tom Maris-Wolf, "Between Slavery and Freedom: African Americans in the Great Dismal Swamp, 1763–1861" (Master's thesis, College of William and Mary, 2002), ix; Lockley, *Maroon Communities in South Carolina*, ix; Nevius, *City of Refuge*, 7.

8. Leaming, *Hidden Americans*, 222.

9. *William Byrd's Histories of the Dividing Line betwixt Virginia and North Carolina* (New York: Dover Publications, 1967), 56; Lockley, *Maroon Communities in South Carolina*, xvii.

10. Johann David Schoepf, *Travels in the Confederation, 1783–84* (Philadelphia: Wm. J. Campbell, 1911), 99–100.

11. John Ferdinand Smyth, *A Tour of the United States of America: Containing an Account of the Present Situation of That Country* (Dublin: G. Perrin, 1784), 65.

12. Ibid.

13. Leaming, *Hidden Americans*, 222.

14. Nevius, *City of Refuge*, 22–25; Leaming, *Hidden Americans*, 276.

15. Samuel Johnston to Thomas Barker, April 1763, Hayes Collection, #324, Southern Historical Collection, Wilson Library, University of North Carolina Chapel Hill; Articles of Agreement, Dismal Swamp Land Company, November 3, 1763, in W.W. Abbott and Dorothy Twohig eds., *The Papers of George Washington, Colonial Series*, Vol. VII: *January 1761–June 1767* (Charlottesville: University Press of Virginia, 1990), 271–73; Nevius, *City of Refuge*, 22–25.

16. Nevius, *City of Refuge*, 22–25.

17. Ibid., 26.

18. *Virginia Gazette*, June 23 and October 6, 1768, April 13, 1769; Daniel O. Sayers, *A Desolate Place for a Defiant People: The Archaeology of Maroons, Indigenous Americans, and Enslaved Laborers in the Great Dismal Swamp* (Gainesville: University Press of Florida, 2014), 88–89; Nevius, *City of Refuge*, 27; Maris-Wolf, "Between Slavery and Freedom," ix.

19. *William Byrd's Histories*, 27, 29.

20. Nevius, *City of Refuge*, 33; Sayers, *A Desolate Place*, 89.

21. Charles Royster, *The Fabulous History of the Great Dismal Swamp: A Story of George Washington's Times* (New York: Borzoi Books, 1999), 217.

22. Ibid., 147.

23. Ibid.; Maris-Wolf, "Between Slavery and Freedom," 51.

24. *Virginia Gazette* (Purdie & Dixon), February 18, 1773; *Virginia Gazette* (Purdie), July 10, 1778; Lathan Windley, *Runaway Slave Advertisements: A Documentary History from the 1730s to 1790*, Vol. I (Westport, Conn.: Greenwood Press, 1983), 130, 274; Sayers, *A Desolate Place*, 89; Smyth, *A Tour of the United States*, 65. For North Carolina runaway advertisements see Freddie L. Parker, *Running for Freedom: Slave Runaways in North Carolina, 1775–1840* (New York: Garland Publishing, 1993) and Freddie L. Parker, *Stealing a Little Freedom: Advertisements for Slave Runaways in North Carolina, 1791–1840* (New York: Garland Publishing, 1994).

25. Sylviane A. Diouf, *Slavery's Exiles: The Story of the American Maroons* (New York: New York University Press, 2014); Nevius, *City of Refuge*, 10.

26. Moses Grandy, *Narrative of the Life of Moses Grandy, Formerly a Slave in the United States of America* (Lenox, Mass.: Hard Press, 2013), 5.

27. Sayers, *A Desolate Place*, 89; Nevius, *City of Refuge*, 21.

28. Leaming, *Hidden Americans*, 278; William Byrd, *Description of Dismal Swamp and a Proposal to Drain the Swamp* (Metuchen, N.J.: Charles F. Heartman, Historical Series, 1922), 19.

29. Leaming, *Hidden Americans*, 278–79; Edmund Ruffin, "Observations Made During an Excursion to the Dismal Swamp," *The Farmers' Register* Vol. 4 (1837): 519.

30. Albert R. Ledoux, *Princess Anne: A Story of the Dismal Swamp and Other Sketches* (New York: The Looker-On Publishing Co., 1896), 41–42, 49; Leaming, *Hidden Americans*, 279. The other sketches in Ledoux's book are presented as fiction.

31. Sayers, *A Desolate Place*, 89; Nevius, *City of Refuge*, 21.

32. Elkanah Watson, *Men and Times of the Revolution: or, Memoirs of Elkanah Watson* (Elizabethtown, N.Y.: Crown Point Press, 1868), 36–37.

33. Maris-Wolf, "Between Slavery and Freedom," 58.

34. David Jameson to John Driver, December 5, 1783, letter copy, DSLC Records, Box 1, Folder 2, Duke University, Durham, North Carolina; Nevius, *City of Refuge*, 28.

35. John Driver Correspondence, August 26, 1780, Dismal Swamp Land Company (DSLC) Duke University, Durham, North Carolina.

36. Jacob Collee to David Jamison, July 31, 1781, DSLC; Royster, *The Fabulous History*, 272.

37. "Went from the Dismal," n.d., DSLC.

38. Royster, *The Fabulous History*, 230.

39. Jacob Collee Correspondence, December 12, 1782, DSLC.

40. Royster, *The Fabulous History*, 273.

41. December 1784 Correspondence, DSLC; Royster, *The Fabulous History*, 290.

42. Royster, *The Fabulous History*, 290, 319, 321, 379.

43. Jacob Collee to John Driver, January 25, 1787k, DSLC.

44. Bland Simpson, *The Great Dismal: A Carolinian's Swamp Memoir* (Chapel Hill: University of North Carolina Press, 1990), 47; Royster, *The Fabulous History*, 420; "1806 May, The Negroes to be Sold," 1763–1806 Memoranda, DSLC.

45. Herbert Aptheker, *American Negro Slave Revolts* (6th ed., New York: International Publishers, 1993), 211.

46. Ibid., 211–12.

47. Aptheker, *American Negro Slave Revolts*, 211; Leaming, *Hidden Americans*, 248.

48. Aptheker, *American Negro Slave Revolts*, 211–12.

49. Ibid., 215–18; Graham Russell Hodges, *Root and Branch: African Americans in New York and East Jersey, 1613–1863* (Chapel Hill: University of North Carolina Press, 1999), 174.

50. Hodges, *Root and Branch*, 177; Jean Fouchard, *The Haitian Maroons: Liberty or Death* (New York: E.W. Blyden Press, 1981), 13–181. See also Robert Alderson, "Charleston's Rumored Slave Revolt of 1793," in David P. Geggus ed., *The Impact of the Haitian Revolution in the Atlantic World* (Columbia: University of South Carolina Press, 2001).

51. Douglas R. Egerton, *Death or Liberty: African Americans and Revolutionary America* (New York: Oxford University Press, 2009), 270–73.

52. Ibid., 274.

53. Ibid.

54. Aptheker, *American Negro Slave Revolts*, 220–21; Egerton, *Death or Liberty*, 275. See also Douglas Egerton, "Gabriel's Conspiracy and the Election of 1800," *Journal of Southern History* Vol. 56 (May 1990): 191–214, and Egerton's, *Gabriel Rebellion: The Virginia Slave Conspiracies of 1800 and 1802* (Chapel Hill: University of North Carolina Press, 1993).

55. Aptheker, *American Negro Slave Revolts*, 220–23.

56. Ibid., 228–30; Leaming, *Hidden Americans*, 250.

57. Cynthia Vollbrecht Goode, "Engaging the Tools of Resistance: Enslaved Africans' Tactics of Collective and Individual Consumption in Food, Medicine, and Clothing in the Great Dismal Swamp" (Ph.D. diss., American University, 2018), 63.

58. Lockley, *Maroon Communities in South Carolina*, xviii; Marvin L. Michael Kay and Lorin Lee Cary, *Slavery in North Carolina, 1748–1775* (Chapel Hill: University of North Carolina Press, 1995), 99; Petition of Thomas Lucas, November 25, 1788, North Carolina General Assembly, Session records, North Carolina State Archives, Raleigh.

59. Aptheker, *American Negro Slave Revolts*, 217.

60. Aptheker, *American Negro Slave Revolts*, 217; Lockley, *Maroon Communities in South Carolina*, xviii; *Wilmington City Gazette*, July 18, 1795.

61. *Royal Georgia Gazette*, May 3, 1781; *Savannah Gazette of the State of Georgia*, May 12, 1785; Diouf, *Slavery's Exiles*, 188–89.

62. *Savannah Gazette of the State of Georgia*, May 17, 1787; Diouf, *Slavery's Exiles*, 339; *Charleston Morning Post*, October 26, 1786.

63. *Charleston Morning Post*, October 26, 1786.

64. Adele Stanton Edwards, *Journals of the Privy Council 1783–1789* (Columbia: University of South Carolina Press, 1971), 186, 204–05; Diouf, *Slavery's Exiles*, 191–92.

65. *Charleston Morning Post*, October 26, 1786; Edwards, *Journals of the Privy Council*, 186, 204–05; Diouf, *Slavery's Exiles*, 191–92. For examples of runaway camps near Charleston, see *Columbian Herald*, May 18, 1786, Charleston News; *City Gazette*, June 13, 1788, August 21, 1797.

66. Diouf, *Slavery's Exiles*, 192.

67. Gen. James Jackson to the Governor of South Carolina, 1787, *Joseph Vallence Bevan Papers*, Georgia Historical Society, 71, 86; Diouf, *Slavery's Exiles*, 193.

68. Diouf, *Slavery's Exiles*, 193.

69. "Proclamation," *State Gazette of South Carolina*, March 26, 1787; Thomas Pinckney to George Matthews, April 2, 1787, Thomas Pinckney Letter Book, 1787–1789, South Carolina Department of Archives and History; Diouf, *Slavery's Exiles*, 197.

70. *The State vs. Lewis a Negroe*, May 21, 1787, Telamon Cuyler Collection, MS 1170, Box 71, Folder 12, Hargrett Library, University of Georgia; William Bacon Stevens, *A History of Georgia*, 2 vols. (Savannah: E.H. Butler & Co., 1859), Vol. II, 376–78; Diouf, *Slavery's Exiles*, 202.

71. Stevens, *A History of Georgia*, Vol. II, 376–78; *Charleston Morning Post*, May 8, 1787; *Savannah Gazette of the State of Georgia*, May 17, 1787; Diouf, *Slavery's Exiles*, 202. It was not uncommon for authorities in South Carolina and Georgia to elicit the aid of Native Americans to capture fugitives. In exchange for their assistance, groups such as the Catawbas were promised provisions and other goods.

72. Jane Landers, *Atlantic Creoles in the Age of Revolutions* (Cambridge, Mass.: Harvard University Press, 2010), 98.

73. "Brought to the Workhouse," *Savannah Gazette of the State of Georgia*, May 31, 1787.

74. *The State vs. Lewis*; Diouf, *Slavery's Exiles*, 203.

75. *The State vs. Lewis*; Diouf, *Slavery's Exiles*, 204.

76. *The State vs. Lewis*; Diouf, *Slavery's Exiles*, 204.

77. Diouf, *Slavery's Exiles*, 205; *Columbian Herald*, May 28, 1787.

78. Sylviane Diouf, "Borderland Maroons," in Damian Alan Pargas ed., *Fugitive Slaves and Spaces of Freedom in North America* (Gainesville: University Press of Florida, 2018), 168,

186; "Records of the Superior Council of Louisiana," *Louisiana Historical Quarterly* Vol. 8 No. 3 (July 1925): 527–28. For a discussion of fugitivity in the Lower Mississippi Valley during the antebellum period see S. Charles Bolton, *Fugitivism: Escaping Slaves in the Lower Mississippi Valley, 1820–1860* (Fayetteville: The University of Arkansas Press, 2019).

79. Diouf, "Borderland Maroons," 186–87.

80. Ibid.

81. Ibid., 187; Glen R. Conrad, *The German Coast: Abstracts of the Civil Records of St. Charles and St. John the Baptist Parishes, 1804–1812* (Lafayette: University of Louisiana, Lafayette, 1981), 21.

82. Diouf, *Slavery's Exiles*, 158, 163.

83. Ibid.

84. Ibid.

85. Lockley, *Maroon Communities in South Carolina*, xix.

86. Gwendolyn Midlo Hall, *Africans in Colonial Louisiana: The Development of Afro-Creole Culture in the Eighteenth Century* (Baton Rouge: Louisiana State University Press, 1992), 218.

87. Ibid.

88. Ibid., 230, 232.

89. Ibid., 232; Diouf, *Slavery's Exiles*, 177.

90. Diouf, *Slavery's Exiles*, 182.

91. Diouf, "Borderland Maroons," 185.

92. "Singular Relation from the Petersburg Republican," *American Masonic Register and Ladies and Gentlemen's Magazine* Vol. 1 No. 3 (November 1820): 196; Diouf, "Borderland Maroons," 185–86.

93. Diouf, "Borderland Maroons," 183; "Singular Relation from the Petersburg Republican," 196.

94. *Georgia Gazette*, May 10, 1764; Windley, *Runaway Slave Advertisements*, Vol. IV, 6.

95. Nathaniel Millet, *The Maroons of Prospect Bluff and the Quest for Freedom in the Atlantic World* (Gainesville: University Press of Florida, 2015), 8–9, 156. For a discussion of runaways in nineteenth-century Florida see Larry Eugene Rivers, *Rebels and Runaways: Slave Resistance in Nineteenth Century Florida* (Urbana: University of Illinois Press, 2012).

96. Matthew Clavin, *The Battle of Negro Fort: The Rise and Fall of a Fugitive Slave Community* (New York: New York University Press, 2019), 63.

97. Ibid., 83.

98. Ibid.

99. Ibid.

100. Millet, *The Maroons of Prospect Bluff*, 7.

101. Herbert Aptheker, "Maroons within the Present Limits of the U.S.," *Journal of Negro History* Vol. 24 (April 1939): 171, 173–74; Matthew J. Clavin, *Aiming for Pensacola: Fugitive Slaves on the Atlantic and Southern Frontiers* (Cambridge: Harvard University Press, 2015), 57–58. For a discussion of Africans and their descendants in east Florida

see Jane Landers, *Black Society in Spanish Florida* (Urbana: University of Illinois Press, 1999).

102. Aptheker, "Maroons within the Present Limits of the U.S.," 171, 173–74.

CONCLUSION

1. Don N. Hagist, *Wives, Slaves, and Servant Girls: Advertisements for Female Runaways in American Newspapers, 1770–1783* (Yardley, Pa.: Westholme Publishing, 2016), 104; *Continental Journal* (Boston), November 14, 1776.

2. Hagist, *Wives, Slaves, and Servant Girls*, 104; Michael Gomez, *Exchanging Our Country Marks: The Transformation of African Identities in the Colonial and Antebellum South* (Chapel Hill: University of North Carolina Press, 1998), 126; Renee K. Harrison, *Enslaved Women and the Art of Resistance in Antebellum America* (New York: Palgrave Macmillan, 2009), 170.

3. James Mellon, *Bullwhip Days: The Slaves Remember, An Oral History* (New York: Grove Press, 2001), 302.

4. Alejandro De La Fuente and Ariela J. Gross, *Becoming Free, Becoming Black: Race, Freedom and the Law in Cuba, Virginia, and Louisiana* (New York: Cambridge University Press, 2020), 97.

5. Freddie L. Parker, *Stealing a Little Freedom: Advertisements for Slave Runaways in North Carolina, 1791–1840* (New York: Garland Publishing, 1994), 407.

6. Freddie L. Parker, *Running for Freedom: Slave Runaways in North Carolina, 1775–1840* (New York: Garland Publishing Inc., 1993), 71.

7. William Still, *The Underground Railroad* (Philadelphia: Porter and Coates, 1872), 242.

8. Race & Slavery Petitions Project, PAR 21685603, https://library.uncg.edu/slavery/petitions/index.aspx, accessed July 4, 2020; Sylviane Diouf, "Borderland Maroons," in Damian Alan Pargas ed., *Fugitive Slaves and Spaces of Freedom in North America* (Gainesville: University Press of Florida, 2018), 186.

9. Race & Slavery Petitions Project, PAR 21685603, https://library.uncg.edu/slavery/petitions/index.aspx, accessed July 4, 2020.

Bibliography

NEWSPAPERS

Augusta Chronicle
Boston Evening Post
Boston News-Letter
Charleston Mercury
Charleston Morning Post
Charleston Courier
Columbian Herald
Connecticut Courant and Weekly Intelligencer
Connecticut Gazette and Universal Intelligencer
Connecticut Gazette and Weekly Advertiser
Connecticut Gazette and Weekly Intelligencer
Continental Journal and Weekly Advertiser
Daily Advertiser
Georgia Gazette
Maryland Gazette
Maryland Journal and Baltimore Advertiser
New England Chronicle
New England Weekly Journal
New Jersey Gazette
New York Evening Post
New York Gazette
New York Journal
Pennsylvania Gazette
Royal Georgia Gazette (Savannah)
Savannah Gazette of the State of Georgia
South Carolina and American General Gazette (Charleston)
South Carolina Gazette
South Carolina Gazette and Country Journal
South Carolina Gazette and General Advertiser
State Gazette of South Carolina
The Newport Mercury
The Providence Gazette

Virginia Gazette
Virginia Gazette or American Advertiser
Virginia Independent Chronicle (Davis)
Wilmington City Gazette

MANUSCRIPTS

Catherine Marie Sedgwick Papers, Massachusetts Historical Society
Dismal Swamp Land Company Records (DSLC), Duke University
Ford Family Papers, South Caroliniana Library
Francis Marion Papers, New York Public Library, New York
Inspection Roll of Negroes, Nova Scotia Museum, Black Cultural Database
Joseph Vallence Bevan Papers, Georgia Historical Society
Miscellaneous Papers of the Continental Congress, 1774–1789, National Archives, Washington, D.C.
Natalie DeLage Sumter Diary, South Caroliniana Library
Neil Jamieson Papers, 1776–1783, Library of Congress
Pennsylvania Abolition Society, Manumission Book A, 1780–1793
Pinckney Family Papers, South Carolina Historical Society
Ralph Izzard, Letters Concerning the British Evacuation of Charleston, 1782, New York Public Library
Revolutionary War Pension and Bounty – Land Warrant Application Files, National Archives, Washington, D.C.
Telamon Cuyler Collection, Hargrett Library, University of Georgia
Thomas Pinckney Letter Book, 1787–1789, South Carolina Department of Archives and History
The George Washington Papers at the Library of Congress, 1741–1799, Library of Congress, Washington, D.C.

COURT RECORDS

Accomack County Deeds, vol. 6, 1783–1788, Library of Virginia
Miscellaneous Record Books, South Carolina Department of Archives and History
Petersburg County District Court Judgements (Freedom Suits), Library of Virginia
Rhode Island Supreme Court Judicial Records Center

PUBLISHED RECORDS

Abbott, W.W. and Dorothy Twohig eds. *The Papers of George Washington, Colonial Series.* Charlottesville: University Press of Virginia, 1990.
Boyd, Julian P. ed., *Papers of Thomas Jefferson*, 34 vols. Princeton, N.J.: Princeton University Press, 1950–.

Burnett, E.C. *Letters of Members of the Continental Congress*, Vol. VI. Washington, D. C.: Carnegie Institution of Washington, 1933.

Candler, Allen D. and Lucian L. Knight eds., *Colonial Records of the State of Georgia*, 26 vols. Atlanta, 1904–1916.

Clark, William Bell ed., *Naval Documents of the American Revolution*, 10 vols. Washington: Government Printing Office, 1964–1996.

Cooper, Thomas ed., *The Statutes at Large of South Carolina, 1682–1716*. Columbia: A.S. Johnson, 1837.

Hening, William Waller ed., *The Statutes At Large: Being a Collection of All the Laws of Virginia from the First Session of the Legislature in the Year 1619*, 3 vols. Philadelphia: Bartow, 1823.

Historical Statistics of the United States, Colonial Time to 1957. Washington, D.C., 1960.

Hoadley, Charles J. ed. *The Public Records of the State of Connecticut*, Vol. II. Hartford, 1894.

McCord, David J. ed. *The Statutes at Large of South Carolina*. Columbia: A.S. Johnson, 1840.

Public Records of the Colony of Connecticut, 1636–1776, Vol. XIV. Hartford, 1890.

Roberts, James. *The Narrative of James Roberts: A Soldier under Gen. Washington in the Revolutionary War, and under Jackson at the Battle of New Orleans, in the War of 1812 . . .*, Chicago: James Roberts, 1858.

Saunders, William L. ed., *The Colonial Records of North Carolina, 1734–1752*, 4 vols. Raleigh: Hale, 1886.

MISCELLANEOUS

An Act for the Better Ordering of Slaves, Records of the General Assembly, March 2–16, 1696, South Carolina Department of Archives and History.

List of Dunmore's Fleet, 1776, Maryland Council of Public Safety Journal and Correspondence, Vol. XII. Maryland State Archives: Annapolis, Md.

Report of the Peace Agreement, 1782–1783, Maryland Council of Public Safety Journal and Correspondence, Vol. XLVIII. Maryland State Archives, Annapolis, Md.

BOOKS AND ARTICLES

Adams, Catherine and Elizabeth Pleck. *Love of Freedom: Black Women in Colonial and Revolutionary New England*. New York: Oxford University Press, 2010.

Alden, John Richard. *The South in the Revolution*. Baton Rouge: Louisiana State University Press, 1957.

Alderson, Robert. "Charleston's Rumored Slave Revolt of 1793," in David P. Geggus ed. *The Impact of the Haitian Revolution in the Atlantic World*. Columbia: University of South Carolina Press, 2001.

Allen, John. *An Oration on the Beauties of Liberty, or The Essential Rights of the Americans*. Boston: E. Russell, 1773.

Aptheker, Herbert ed., *A Documentary History of the Negro People in the United States*, Vol. I. 5th ed. New York: The Citadel Press, 1968.

Aptheker, Herbert. *American Negro Slave Revolts.* 6th ed. New York: International Publishers, 1993.

Aptheker, Herbert. "Maroons within the Present Limits of the U.S.," *Journal of Negro History* Vol. 24 (April 1939).

Aptheker, Herbert. *The Negro in the American Revolution.* New York: International Publishers, 1940.

Aptheker, Herbert. "We Will Be Free: Advertisements for Runaways and the Reality of American Slavery." Occasional Paper No. 1, Ethnic Studies Program, University of Santa Clara, 1984.

Araujo, Ana Lucia. *Slavery in the Age of Memory: Engaging the Past.* New York: Bloomsbury Press, 2020.

Baptist, Edward. *The Half Has Never Been Told: Slavery and the Making of American Capitalism.* New York: Basic Books, 2014.

Barker-Benfield, G.J. *Phillis Wheatley Chooses Freedom: History Poetry and the Ideals of the American Revolution.* New York: New York University Press, 2018.

Bassett, John S. "Slavery and Servitude in the Colony of North Carolina," in H. B. Adams, ed., *Johns Hopkins University Studies in Historical and Political Science,* XIV. Baltimore, Md.: The Johns Hopkins Press, 1896.

Bausman, Lottie M. *The General Position of Lancaster County in Negro Slavery.* Lancaster County Historical Society, 1911.

Bailyn, Bernard. *Ideological Origins of the American Revolution.* Cambridge, Mass.: Harvard University Press, 1967.

Bancroft, Frederick. *Slave Trading in the Old South.* Columbia: University of South Carolina Press, 1996.

Beckles, Hilary. *Afro-Caribbean Women and Resistance to Slavery in Barbados.* London: Karnak House, 1988.

Bell, Karen Cook. *Claiming Freedom: Race, Kinship, and Land in Nineteenth Century Georgia.* Columbia: University of South Carolina Press, 2018.

Benezet, Anthony. *A Short Account of That Part of Africa Inhabited by the Negroes . . . ,* 2nd ed. Philadelphia: W. Dunlap, 1762.

Berkin, Carol. *Revolutionary Mothers: Women in the Struggle for American Independence.* New York: Alfred A. Knopf, 2005.

Berlin, Ira. *Generations of Captivity: A History of African American Slaves.* Cambridge, Mass.: Harvard University Press, 2003.

Berlin, Ira. *Many Thousands Gone: The First Two Centuries of Slavery in North America.* Cambridge, Mass.: Harvard University Press, 1998.

Berlin, Ira. *Slaves Without Masters: The Free Negro in the Antebellum South.* New York: The New Press, 2007.

Berlin, Ira and Ronald Hoffman, *Slavery and Freedom in the Age of the American Revolution.* Charlottesville: University of Virginia Press, 1983.

Berry, Daina Ramey. *The Price for Their Pound of Flesh: The Value of the Enslaved, from Womb to Grave, in the Building of A Nation.* Boston: Beacon Press, 2017.

Berry, Daina Ramey. *Swing the Sickle, For the Harvest is Ripe: Gender and Slavery in Antebellum Georgia.* Bloomington: University of Illinois Press, 2007.

Berry, Daina Ramey and Kali Nicole Gross. *A Black Women's History of the United States.* Boston: Beacon Press, 2020.

Berry, Daina Ramey and Leslie Harris, *Sexuality and Slavery: Reclaiming Intimate Histories in the Americas*. Athens: University of Georgia Press, 2018.

Blanck, Emily. *Tyrannicide: Forging an American Law of Slavery in Revolutionary South Carolina and Massachusetts*. Athens: University of Georgia Press, 2014.

Block, Sharon. *Colonial Complexions: Race and Bodies in Eighteenth Century America*. Philadelphia: University of Pennsylvania Press, 2018.

Blumrosen, Alfred W. and Ruth G. Blumrosen. *Slave Nation: How Slavery United the Colonies and Sparked the American Revolution*. Naperville, Ill.: Sourcebooks, Inc., 2005.

Bly, Antonio ed. *Escaping Bondage: A Documentary History of Runaway Slaves in Eighteenth-Century New England, 1700–1789*. Lanham, Md.: Lexington Books, 2012.

Bolster, Jeffrey W. *Black Jacks: African American Seamen in the Age of Sail*. Cambridge: Harvard University Press, 1997.

Bolton, S. Charles. *Fugitivism: Escaping Slaves in the Lower Mississippi Valley, 1820–1860*. Fayetteville: The University of Arkansas Press, 2019.

Brawley, Benjamin. *A Social History of the American Negro*. New York: AMS Press, 1971.

Brown, Kathleen M. *Good Wives, Nasty Wenches, and Anxious Patriarchs: Gender, Race, and Power in Colonial Virginia*. Chapel Hill: University of North Carolina Press, 1996.

Bush, Barbara. *Slave Women in Caribbean Society, 1650–1838*. Bloomington: Indiana University Press, 1990.

Buskirk, Judith Van. *Standing in Their Own Light: African American Patriots in the American Revolution*. Norman: University of Oklahoma Press, 2017.

Butterfield, L.H. ed. *Diary and Autobiography of John Adams*, 4 vols. Cambridge, Mass.: Harvard University Press, 1962.

Byrd, William. *Description of Dismal Swamp and a Proposal to Drain the Swamp*. Metuchen, N.J.: Charles F. Heartman, 1922.

Byrd, William. *William Byrd's Histories of the Dividing Line betwixt Virginia and North Carolina*. New York: Dover Publications, 1967.

Cameron, Christopher. *To Plead Our Own Cause: African Americans in Massachusetts and the Making of the Antislavery Movement*. Kent, Ohio: Kent State University Press, 2014.

Camp, Stephanie. *Closer to Freedom: Enslaved Women and Everyday Resistance in the Plantation South*. Chapel Hill: University of North Carolina Press, 2004.

Campbell, Mavis C. *The Maroons of Jamaica, 1655–1796: A History of Resistance, Collaboration, and Betrayal*. Trenton, N.J.: Africa World Press, 1990.

Cappon, Lester J. ed. *The Adams–Jefferson Letters: The Complete Correspondence between Thomas Jefferson and Abigail and John Adams*. Chapel Hill: University of North Carolina Press, 2012.

Carretta, Vincent. *Phillis Wheatley: Biography of a Genius*. Athens: University of Georgia Press, 2011.

Chaplin, Joyce E. "Slavery and the Principle of Humanity: A Modern Idea in the Early Lower South," *Journal of Social History* Vol. 24 (1990–91): 299–315.

Clavin, Matthew. *Aiming for Pensacola: Fugitive Slaves on the Atlantic and Southern Frontiers*. Cambridge: Harvard University Press, 2015.

Clavin, Matthew. *The Battle of Negro Fort: The Rise and Fall of a Fugitive Slave Community.* New York: New York University Press, 2019.

Clifford, Mary Louise. *From Slavery to Freetown: Black Loyalists After the American Revolution.* Jefferson, N.C.: McFarland and Company, 1999.

Coldham, Peter Wilson. *The Complete Book of Emigrants in Bondage, 1614–1775.* Baltimore, Md.: Genealogical Publishing Company, 2002.

Coleman, Charles Washington Jr., "The Southern Campaign, 1781, from Guilford Court House to the Siege of York Narrated by St. George Tucker in Letters to His Wife, Part II, The Peninsula Campaign," *Magazine of American History* 7 (September 1881).

Conrad, Glen R. *The German Coast: Abstracts of the Civil Records of St. Charles and St. John the Baptist Parishes, 1804–1812.* Lafayette: University of Louisiana, Lafayette, 1981.

Costa, Tom. "What Can We Learn from a Digital Database of Runaway Slave Advertisements," *International Social Science Review* Vol. 76 No. 1/2 (2001).

Countryman, Edward. *The American Revolution.* New York: Hill and Wang, 2003.

Countryman, Edward. *Enjoy the Same Liberty: Black Americans and the Revolutionary Era.* Lanham, Md.: Rowman & Littlefield, 2012.

Crane, Elaine Forman. *A Dependent People: Newport, Rhode Island in the Revolutionary Era.* New York: Fordham University Press, 1985.

Curtin, Philip. *The Atlantic Slave Trade: A Census.* Madison: University of Wisconsin Press, 1969.

Davis, David Brion. *The Problem of Slavery in the Age of Revolution, 1770–1823.* 2nd ed. New York: Oxford University Press, 1999.

DelBanco, Andrew. *The War Before the War: Fugitive Slaves and the Struggle for America's Soul from the Revolution to the Civil War.* New York: Penguin Press, 2018.

Dickson, William. *Mitigation of Slavery.* London, 1814.

Diouf, Sylviane A. *Slavery's Exiles: The Story of the American Maroons.* New York: New York University Press, 2014.

Duane, William and Thomas Balch trans. and eds. *The Journal of Claude Blanchard: Eyewitness Accounts of the American Revolution.* 1876; reprint ed. New York: The New York Times, 1969.

Dunbar, Erica Armstrong. *A Fragile Freedom: African American Women and Emancipation in the Antebellum City.* New Haven, Conn.: Yale University Press, 2008.

Dunbar, Erica Armstrong. *Never Caught: The Washingtons' Relentless Pursuit of their Runaway Slave Ona Judge.* New York: Atria, 2017.

Easterby, James Harold ed. *Wadboo Barony: Its Fate as Told in Colleton Family Papers, 1773–1793.* Columbia: University of South Carolina Press, 1952.

Edwards, Adele Stanton. *Journals of the Privy Council 1783–1789.* Columbia: University of South Carolina Press, 1971.

Egerton, Douglas. *Death or Liberty: African Americans and Revolutionary America.* New York: Oxford University Press, 2009.

Egerton, Douglas. "Gabriel's Conspiracy and the Election of 1800," *Journal of Southern History* Vol. 56 (May 1990): 191–214.

Egerton, Douglas. *Gabriel Rebellion: The Virginia Slave Conspiracies of 1800 and 1802.* Chapel Hill: University of North Carolina Press, 1993.

Ellis, Franklin and Samuel Evans. *History of Lancaster County Pennsylvania with Biographical Sketches of Many of its Pioneers and Prominent Men.* Philadelphia: Everts and Peck, 1883.

Ewald, Johann von. *Diary of the American War: A Hessian Journal*, trans. and ed. Joseph P. Tustin. New Haven, Conn.: Yale University Press, 1979.

Fett, Sharla. *Working Cures: Healing, Health, and Power on Southern Slave Plantations.* Chapel Hill: University of North Carolina Press, 2002.

Finkleman, Paul. *Slavery and the Founders: Race and Liberty in the Age of Jefferson.* New York: Routledge, 2015.

Fleischner, Jennifer. *Mastering Slavery: Memory, Family, and Identity in Women's Slave Narratives.* New York: New York University Press, 1996.

Fogelman, Aaron S. "From Slaves, Convicts, and Servants to Free Passengers: The Transformation of Immigration in the Era of the American Revolution," *Journal of American History* Vol. 85 (June 1998): 43–76.

Foster, Thomas. *Rethinking Rufus: Sexual Violations of Enslaved Men.* Athens: University of Georgia Press, 2019.

Fouchard, Jean. *The Haitian Maroons: Liberty or Death.* New York: E.W. Blyden Press, 1981.

Franklin, John Hope and Loren Schweninger, *Runaway Slaves: Rebels on the Plantation.* New York: Oxford University Press, 1999.

Frey, Sylvia. "Between Slavery and Freedom: Virginia Blacks in the American Revolution," *The Journal of Southern History* Vol. 49 Issue 3 (August 1983): 375–98.

Frey, Sylvia. *Water from the Rock: Black Resistance in a Revolutionary Age.* Princeton, N.J.: Princeton University Press, 1991.

Fuente, Alejandro de la and Ariela J. Gross, *Becoming Free, Becoming Black: Race, Freedom and the Law in Cuba, Virginia, and Louisiana.* New York: Cambridge University Press, 2020.

Fuentes, Marisa J. *Dispossessed Lives: Enslaved Women, Violence, and the Archive.* Philadelphia: University of Pennsylvania Press, 2016.

Fuentes, Marisa. "Power and Historical Figuring: Rachael Pringle Polgreen's Troubled Archives," *Gender and History* Vol. 22 No. 3 (November 2010).

Fuentes, Marisa J. and Deborah Gray White eds. *Slavery and Dispossession in Rutgers History.* Rutgers, N.J. : Rutgers University Press, 2016.

Fuss, Norman. "Prelude to Rebellion: Dunmore's Raid on the Williamsburg Magazine," *Journal of the American Revolution*, April 2, 2015.

Gautier, Arlette. "Les Esclaves femmes aux Antilles françaises, 1635–1848," *Reflexions Historiques* Vol. 10 No. 3 (Fall 1983): 409–35.

Georgia Writers Project. *Drums and Shadows: Survival Stories among the Georgia Coastal Negroes.* Athens, Ga., reprint, 1986.

Gibbes, R.W. ed. *Documentary History of the American Revolution, 1764–1776*, Vol. III. New York: D. Appleton & Company, 1855.

Gilbert, Alan. *Black Patriots and Loyalists: Fighting for Emancipation in the War for Independence.* Chicago: University of Chicago Press, 2012.

Gomez, Michael. *Exchanging Our Country Marks: The Transformation of African Identities in the Colonial and Antebellum South.* Chapel Hill: University of North Carolina Press, 1998.

Goodell, Abner Cheney Jr. "The Trial and Execution, for Petit Treason, of Mark and Phillis Slaves of Captain John Codman, Who Murdered their Master at Charlestown, Mass., in 1755; for which the Man was Hanged and Gibbeted, and the Woman was Burned to Death, Including, also, Some Account of Other Punishments by Burning in Massachusetts," *Proceeding of the Massachusetts Historical Society* (1882): 122–49.

Gottlieb, Karla. *The Mother of Us All: A History of Queen Nanny, Leader of the Windward Jamaican Maroons.* Trenton, N.J.: Africa World Press, 2000.

Grandy, Moses. *Narrative of the Life of Moses Grandy, Formerly a Slave in the United States of America.* Lenox, Mass.: Hard Press, 2013.

Grant, John N. "Black Immigration into Nova Scotia, 1776–1815," *Journal of Negro History* Vol. 58 (1973): 253–61.

Greene, Jack. *The Intellectual Construction of America.* Chapel Hill: University of North Carolina Press, 1993.

Greene, Lorenzo. *The Negro in Colonial New England.* New York: Atheneum Press, 1968.

Greene, Lorenzo. "The New England Negro as Seen in Advertisements for Runaway Slaves," *Journal of Negro History* Vol. 10 (April 1944): 125–46.

Greene, Robert Ewell. *Black Courage: Documentation of Black Participation in the American Revolution, 1775–1783.* Washington, D.C.: National Society of the Daughters of the American Revolution, 1984.

Guelzo, Allen C. "Slavery and the Constitution: A Defense," *National Review,* May 6, 2019.

Gunderson, Joan R. *To Be Useful to the World: Women in Revolutionary America, 1740–1790.* Chapel Hill: University of North Carolina Press, 2006.

Hagist, Don N. *Wives, Slaves, and Servant Girls: Advertisements for Female Runaways in American Newspapers, 1770–1783.* Yardley, Pa.: Westholme Publishing, 2016.

Hahn, Stephen. *A Nation Under Our Feet: The Political Struggles of Rural Blacks from Slavery to the Great Migration.* Cambridge, Mass.: Harvard University Press, 2003.

Hall, Gwendolyn Midlo. *Africans in Colonial Louisiana: The Development of Afro-Creole Culture in the Eighteenth Century.* Baton Rouge: Louisiana State University Press, 1992.

Hardesty, Jared Ross. *Unfreedom: Slavery and Dependence in Eighteenth Century Boston.* New York: New York University Press, 2016.

Harrison, Renee K. *Enslaved Women and the Art of Resistance in Antebellum America.* New York: Palgrave Macmillan, 2009.

Hawes, Lilla M. "Miscellaneous Papers of James Jackson, 1781–1798," *Georgia Historical Quarterly* Vol. 37 (1953): 54–80.

Heerman, M. Scott. *The Alchemy of Slavery: Human Bondage and Emancipation in the Illinois Country, 1730–1865.* Philadelphia: University of Pennsylvania Press, 2018.

Herron, Paul E. "Slavery and Freedom in American State Constitutional Development," *Journal of Policy History* Vol. 27 No. 2 (2015): 308–09.

Heuman, Gad ed. *Out of the House of Bondage: Runaways, Resistance, and Marronage in Africa and the New World.* London: Frank Cass and Company, 1986.

Higginbotham, A. Leon. *In the Matter of Color: Race and the American Legal Process, The Colonial Period.* New York: Oxford University Press, 1978.

Hodges, Graham Russell ed. *The Black Loyalist Directory: African Americans in Exile After the American Revolution.* New York: Garland Publishing, 1996.

Hodges, Graham Russell. *Root and Branch: African Americans in New York and East Jersey, 1613–1863.* Chapel Hill: University of North Carolina Press, 1999.

Hodges, Graham Russell Gao and Alan Edward Brown. *"Pretends to Be Free": Runaway Slave Advertisements from Colonial and Revolutionary New York and New Jersey.* New York: Fordham University Press, 2019.

Hoffer, Peter C. *Cry Liberty: The Great Stono Rebellion of 1739.* New York: New York University Press, 2010.

Hoffman, Ronald and Peter J. Albert eds. *Women in the Age of the American Revolution.* Charlottesville: University Press of Virginia, 1989.

Holton, Woody. *Black Americans in the Revolutionary Era: A Brief History with Documents.* New York: Bedford/St. Martins, 2009.

Holton, Woody. *Forced Founders: Indians, Debtors, Slaves and the Making of the American Revolution in Virginia.* Chapel Hill: University of North Carolina Press, 1999.

Hopkins, Samuel. *A Dialogue, concerning the Slavery of the Africans; Shewing It to Be the Duty and Interest of the American Colonies to Emancipate All Their African Slaves.* Norwich: Judah P. Spooner, 1776.

Horne, Gerald. *The Counter Revolution of 1776: Slave Resistance and the Origins of the United States of America.* New York: New York University Press, 2014.

Innes, Stephen ed. *Work and Labor in Early America.* Chapel Hill: University of North Carolina Press, 1988.

Jackson, John Andrew. *The Experience of a Slave in South Carolina.* Chapel Hill: University of North Carolina Press, 2011.

Jackson, Zakiyyah Iman. *Becoming Human: Matter and Meaning in an Anti-Black World.* New York: New York University Press, 2020.

James, C.L.R. "The Atlantic Slave Trade and Slavery," in John R. Williams and Charles Harris eds., *Amistad I.* New York: Random House, 1971.

Jasanoff, Maya. *Liberty's Exiles: American Loyalists in the Revolutionary World.* New York: Vintage Books, 2011.

Johnson, Jessica Marie. *Wicked Flesh: Black Women, Intimacy, and the Atlantic World.* Philadelphia: University of Pennsylvania Press, 2020.

Johnson, Walter. "On Agency," *The Journal of Social History* (Fall 2003): 113–24.

Jones, Jacqueline. *Labor of Love, Labor of Sorrow: Black Women, Work, and the Family from Slavery to the Present.* New York: Basic Books, 2010.

Jones, Martha S. *Birthright Citizens: A History of Race and Rights in Antebellum America.* New York: Cambridge University Press, 2018.

Jones-Rogers, Stephanie. *They Were Her Property: White Women as Slave Owners in the American South.* New Haven, Conn.: Yale University Press, 2020.

Jordan, Winthrop. *White Over Black: American Attitudes Toward the Negro, 1550–1812.* Chapel Hill: University of North Carolina Press, 2012.

Joyner, Charles. *Down by the Riverside: A South Carolina Slave Community.* Urbana: University of Illinois Press, 1984.

Kaplan, Sidney. *The Black Presence in the Era of the American Revolution, 1770–1780.* Washington, D.C.: Smithsonian Institution Press, 1973.

Kay, Marvin L. Michael and Lorin Lee Cary, *Slavery in North Carolina, 1748–1775*. Chapel Hill: University of North Carolina Press, 1995.

Kennedy, Cynthia M. *Braided Relations, Entwined Lives: The Women of Charleston's Urban Slave Society*. Bloomington: Indiana University Press, 2005.

Kierner, Cynthia A. *Southern Women in Revolution, 1776–1800*. Columbia: University of South Carolina Press, 1998.

King, Wilma. "Suffer with Them Till Death: Slave Women and Their Children in Nineteenth Century America," in David Barry Gasper and Darlene Clark Hine eds. *More Than Chattel: Black Women and Slavery in the Americas*. Bloomington, Ind.: Indiana University Press, 1996.

Kolchin, Peter. *American Slavery, 1619–1877*. New York: Penguin Books, 1995.

Kyles, Perry. "Resistance and Collaboration: Political Strategies Within the Afro-Carolinian Slave Community, 1700–1750," *Journal of African American History* Vol. 93 No. 4 (Fall 2008): 497–508.

Land, Aubrey C., Lois Green Carr et al., eds. *Law, Society, and Politics in Early Maryland*. Baltimore: Johns Hopkins University Press, 1977.

Landers, Jane. *Atlantic Creoles in the Age of Revolutions*. Cambridge, Mass.: Harvard University Press, 2010.

Landers, Jane. *Black Society in Spanish Florida*. Urbana: University of Illinois Press, 1999.

Leaming, Hugo Prosper. *Hidden Americans: Maroons of Virginia and the Carolinas*. New York: Garland Publishing, 1995.

Ledoux, Albert R. *Princess Anne: A Story of the Dismal Swamp and Other Sketches*. New York: The Looker-On Publishing Co., 1896.

Link, William A. *Roots of Secession: Slavery and Politics in Antebellum Virginia*. Chapel Hill: University of North Carolina Press, 2003.

Loane, Nancy K. *Following the Drum: Women at the Valley Forge Encampment*. Lincoln, Neb.: Potomac Books, 2009.

Lockley, Timothy. *Maroon Communities in South Carolina: A Documentary Record*. Columbia: University of South Carolina Press, 2009.

McCullough, David. *1776*. New York: Simon and Schuster, 2005.

Mason, Matthew. *Slavery and Politics in the Early Republic*. Chapel Hill: University of North Carolina Press, 2006.

Marshall, Amani. "'They Will Endeavor to Pass for Free': Enslaved Runaways' Performances of Freedom in Antebellum South Carolina," *Slavery & Abolition* Vol. 31 No. 2 (2010): 161–80.

Martin, James Kirby. *Ordinary Courage: The Revolutionary War Adventures of Joseph Plumb Martin*. St. James, N.Y.: Brandywine Press, 1993.

Meaders, Daniel. "South Carolina Fugitives as Viewed Through Colonial Newspapers with Emphasis on Runaway Notices, 1732–1801," *Journal of Negro History* Vol. 60 No. 2 (1975): 288–317.

Melish, Joanne Pope. *Disowning Slavery: Gradual Emancipation and "Race" in New England, 1780–1860*. Ithaca: Cornell University Press, 2016.

Mellon, James. *Bullwhip Days: The Slaves Remember, An Oral History*. New York: Grove Press, 2001.

Millet, Nathaniel. *The Maroons of Prospect Bluff and the Quest for Freedom in the Atlantic World*. Gainesville: University Press of Florida, 2015.

Millward, Jessica. *Finding Charity's Folk: Enslaved and Free Black Women in Maryland.* Athens: University of Georgia Press, 2015.

Morgan, Gwenda and Peter Rushton, "Running Away and Returning Home: the Fate of English Convicts in the American Colonies," *Crime, History, and Societies* Vol. 7 No. 2 (2003): 61–80.

Morgan, Jennifer. *Laboring Women: Reproduction and Gender in New World Slavery.* Philadelphia: University of Pennsylvania Press, 2004.

Morgan, Philip ed. *African American Life in the Georgia Lowcountry: The Atlantic World of the Gullah Geechee.* Athens: University of Georgia Press, 2010.

Morgan, Philip. "Black Life in Eighteenth-Century Charleston," *Perspectives in American History,* new series Vol. 1 (1984): 187–232.

Morgan, Philip. *Slave Counterpoint: Black Culture in the Eighteenth Century Chesapeake and Lowcountry.* Chapel Hill: University of North Carolina Press, 1998.

Mullin, Gerald. *Flight and Rebellion: Slave Resistance in Eighteenth Century Virginia.* New York: Oxford University Press, 1972.

Mustakeem, Sowande M. *Slavery at Sea: Terror, Sex, and Sickness during the Middle Passage.* Urbana: University of Illinois Press, 2016.

Myers, Amrita Chakrabarti. *Forging Freedom: Black Women and the Pursuit of Liberty in Antebellum Charleston.* Chapel Hill: University of North Carolina Press, 2011.

Nash, Gary B. *Forging Freedom: The Formation of Philadelphia's Black Community, 1720–1840.* Cambridge, Mass.: Harvard University Press, 1988.

Nash, Gary B. *The Forgotten Fifth: African Americans in the Age of Revolution.* Cambridge, Mass.: Harvard University Press, 2006.

Nash, Gary B. *Race and Revolution.* Madison: University of Wisconsin Press, 1990.

Nash, Gary B. ed. *Race, Class, and Politics: Essays on American Colonial and Revolutionary Society.* Urbana: University of Illinois Press, 1986.

Nash, Gary B. and Jean R. Soderlund, *Freedom by Degrees: Emancipation in Pennsylvania and Its Aftermath.* New York: Oxford University Press, 1991.

Nell, William Cooper. *Colored Patriots of the American Revolution.* New York: Arno Press, 1968.

Nevius, Marcus. *City of Refuge: Slavery and Petit Marronage in the Great Dismal Swamp, 1763–1856.* Athens: University of Georgia Press, 2020.

Newell, Ellen. *Brethren by Nature: New England Indians, Colonists, and the Origins of American Slavery.* Ithaca: Cornell University Press, 2015.

Newman, Richard S. "'Lucky to be born in Pennsylvania': Free Soil, Fugitive Slaves and the Making of Pennsylvania's Anti-Slavery Borderland," *Slavery and Abolition* Vol. 32 No. 3 (September 2011): 413–30.

Niles, H. *Principles and Acts of the Revolution.* Baltimore, Md., 1882.

Noble, John. "The Case of Maria in the Court of Assistants in 1681," *Publications of the Colonial Society of Massachusetts* 6 (1904): 323–26.

Norton, Mary Beth. *Liberty's Daughters: The Revolutionary Experience of American Women, 1750–1800.* Ithaca: Cornell University Press, 1996.

Olmsted, Frederick Law. *A Journey in the Seaboard Slave States, with Remarks on Their Economy.* New York: New American Library, 1856.

Olson, Edwin. "Some Aspects of Slave Life in New York," *Journal of Negro History* Vol. 26: 66–77.

Otis, James. *Rights of the British Colonists Asserted and Proved.* Columbia: University of Missouri Press, 1929.

Paine, Thomas. *Writing of Thomas Paine: A Collection of Pamphlets from America's Most Radical Founding Father.* St. Petersburg, Fla.: Red and Black Publishers, 2010.

Pargas, Damian Alan ed. *Fugitive Slaves and Spaces of Freedom in North America.* Gainesville: University Press of Florida, 2018.

Pargas, Damian Alan. *The Quarters and the Fields: Slave Families in the Non-Cotton South.* Gainesville: University Press of Florida, 2010.

Parker, Freddie L. *Running for Freedom: Slave Runaways in North Carolina, 1775–1840.* New York: Garland Publishing, 1993.

Parker, Freddie L. *Stealing a Little Freedom: Advertisements for Slave Runaways in North Carolina, 1791–1840.* New York: Garland Publishing, 1994.

Parkinson, Robert G. *The Common Cause: Creating Race and Nation in the American Revolution.* Chapel Hill: University of North Carolina Press, 2016.

Pashman, Howard. *Building a Revolutionary State: The Legal Transformation of New York, 1776–1783.* Chicago: University of Chicago Press, 2018.

Perot, Sandra W. "The Dairymaid and the Prince: Race, Memory, and the Story of Benjamin Banneker's Grandmother," *Slavery and Abolition* Vol. 38 No. 3 (2017): 449–50.

Phillips, Christopher. *Freedom's Port: The African American Community of Baltimore, 1790–1860.* Urbana: University of Illinois Press, 1997.

Phillips, Kevin. *1775: A Good Year for Revolution.* New York: Penguin Group, 2012.

Pierson, William D. *Black Yankees: The Development of the Afro-American Subculture of New England.* Amherst: University of Massachusetts Press, 1988.

Piper, Emile and David Levinson, *One Minute a Free Woman: Elizabeth Freeman and the Struggle for Freedom.* Salisbury, Conn.: Upper Housatonic Valley National Heritage Area, 2010.

Powers, Bernard. *Black Charlestonians: A Social History, 1822–1885.* Fayetteville: University of Arkansas Press, 1994.

Price, Richard ed. *Maroon Societies: Rebel Slave Communities in the Americas.* Garden City, N.Y.: Doubleday Anchor Press, 1973.

Purdue, Charles L. and Thomas E. Barden eds. *Weevils in the Wheat: Interviews with Virginia Ex-Slaves.* Charlottesville: University of Virginia Press, 1996.

Pybus, Cassandra. *Epic Journeys of Freedom: Runaway Slaves of the American Revolution and Their Global Quest for Liberty.* Boston: Beacon Press, 2006.

Quarles, Benjamin. *The Negro in the American Revolution.* Chapel Hill: University of North Carolina Press, 1996.

Quintana, Ryan A. *Making a Slave State: Political Development in Early South Carolina.* Chapel Hill: University of North Carolina Press, 2018.

Rael, Patrick. *Eighty-Eight Years: The Long Death of Slavery in the United States, 1777–1865.* Athens: University of Georgia Press, 2015.

Randolph, Edmund. *History of Virginia,* ed. Arthur H. Shaffer. Charlottesville: University Press of Virginia, 1970.

Raphael, Ray. *A People's History of the American Revolution: How Common People Shaped the Fight for Independence.* New York: The New Press, 2016.

Rawick, George. *The American Slave,* Vol. IV. Westport, Conn.: Greenwood Publishing, 1972.

Rediker, Marcus et al. eds. *Runaways: Workers, Mobility, and Capitalism, 1600–1850.* Oakland: University of California Press, 2019.

Richardson, David ed. *Abolition and Its Aftermath: The Historical Context, 1790–1916.* London: Frank Cass Publishers, 1985.

Rivers, Larry Eugene. *Rebels and Runaways: Slave Resistance in Nineteenth Century Florida.* Urbana: University of Illinois Press, 2012.

Robbins, Karen. "Power Among the Powerless: Domestic Resistance By Free and Slave Women in the McHenry Family of the New Republic," *Journal of the Early Republic* Vol. 23 No. 1 (Spring 2003): 47–69.

Roberts, Neil. *Freedom as Marronage.* Chicago: University of Chicago Press, 2015.

Rockman, Seth. *Scraping By: Wage Labor, Slavery, and Survival in Early Baltimore.* Baltimore: Johns Hopkins University Press, 2009.

Rose, Ben Z. *Mother of Freedom: Mum Bett and the Roots of Abolitionism.* Waverley, Mass.: TreeLine Press, 2009.

Royster, Charles. *The Fabulous History of the Great Dismal Swamp: A Story of George Washington's Times.* New York: Borzoi Books, 1999.

Ruffin, Edmund. "Observations Made During an Excursion to the Dismal Swamp," *The Farmers' Register* Vol. 4 (1837): 513–21.

Sayers, Daniel O. *A Desolate Place for a Defiant People: The Archaeology of Maroons, Indigenous Americans, and Enslaved Laborers in the Great Dismal Swamp.* Gainesville: University Press of Florida, 2014.

Schama, Simon. *Rough Crossings: Britain, the Slaves, and the American Revolution.* New York: Harper Collins, 2007.

Scharf, John Thomas. *History of Maryland,* Vol. I. Baltimore: John B. Piet, 1879.

Schermerhorn, Calvin. *Unrequited Toil: A History of United States Slavery.* New York: Cambridge University Press, 2018.

Schoepf, Johann David. *Travels in the Confederation, 1783–84.* Philadelphia: Wm. J. Campbell, 1911.

Schwalm, Leslie Ann. *A Hard Fight for We: Women's Transition from Slavery to Freedom in South Carolina.* Urbana: University of Illinois Press, 1997.

Schweninger, Loren. *Appealing for Liberty: Freedom Suits in the South.* New York: Oxford University Press, 2018.

Scott, Julius. *The Common Wind: Afro-American Currents in the Age of the Haitian Revolution.* New York: Verso Books, 2018.

Scott, Rebecca. *Degrees of Freedom: Louisiana and Cuba after Slavery.* New York: Cambridge University Press, 2005.

Selby, John. *The Revolution in Virginia, 1775–1783.* 2nd ed. Charlottesville: University of Virginia Press, 2007.

Simpson, Bland. *The Great Dismal: A Carolinian's Swamp Memoir.* Chapel Hill: University of North Carolina Press, 1990.

Sinha, Manisha. *The Slave's Cause: A History of Abolitionism.* New Haven, Conn.: Yale University Press, 2016.

Smith, Billy G. and Richard Wojtowicz. *Blacks Who Stole Themselves: Advertisements for Runaways in the Pennsylvania Gazette, 1728–1790.* Philadelphia: University of Pennsylvania Press, 1989.

Smith, Mark M. "Remembering Mary, Shaping Revolt: Reconsidering the Stono Rebellion," *Journal of Southern History* Vol. 67 No. 3 (August 2001): 513–34.

Smyth, John Ferdinand. *A Tour of the United States of America: Containing an Account of the Present Situation of That Country.* Dublin: G. Perrin, 1784.

Spooner, Matthew. "Freedom, Reenslavement, and Movement in the Revolutionary South," in Whitney Stewart et al. eds. *Race and Nation in the Age of Emancipation.* Athens: University of Georgia Press, 2018.

Stanton, Lucia. *Free Some Day: The African American Families of Monticello.* Charlottesville, Va.: Thomas Jefferson Foundation, 2000.

Stevens, William Bacon. *A History of Georgia*, 2 vols. Savannah, Ga.: E.H. Butler & Co., 1859.

Stevenson, Brenda. *Life in Black and White: Family and Community in the Slave South.* New York: Oxford University Press, 1996.

Still, William. *The Underground Railroad.* Philadelphia, Pa.: Porter and Coates, 1872.

Sutch, Richard. "The Breeding of Slaves for Sale and the Westward Expansion of Slavery, 1850–1860," in Stanley L. Engerman and Eugene Genovese eds. *Race and Slavery in the Western Hemisphere: Quantitative Studies.* Princeton, N.J.: Princeton University Press, 1975.

Sweet, John Wood. *Bodies Politic: Negotiating Race in the American North, 1730–1830.* Baltimore: Johns Hopkins University Press, 2003.

Tate, Thad. *The Negro in Eighteenth Century Williamsburg.* Charlottesville: University of Virginia Press, 1965.

Taylor, Alan. *American Revolutions: A Continental History.* New York: W.W. Norton, 2016.

Taylor, Alan. *The Internal Enemy: Slavery and War in Virginia.* New York: W.W. Norton, 2014.

Thompson, Alvin O. *Flight to Freedom: African Runaways and Maroons in the Americas.* Kingston, Jamaica: University of the West Indies Press, 2006.

Thornton, John K. "African Dimensions of the Stono Rebellion," *American Historical Review* Vol. 96 No. 4 (October 1991): 1101–13.

Tomich, Dale W. *Slavery in the Circuit of Sugar: Martinique and the World Economy, 1830–1848.* Baltimore: Johns Hopkins University Press, 1990.

Trouillot, Michel-Rolph. *Silencing the Past: Power and the Production of History.* Boston: Beacon Press, 1995.

Turner, Edward Raymond. "Slavery in Colonial Pennsylvania," *The Pennsylvania Magazine of History and Biography* Vol. 35 No. 2 (1911): 129–42.

Urwin, Gregory J.W. "When Freedom Wore a Red coat: How Lord Cornwallis' 1781 Campaign Threatened the Revolution in Virginia", *Army History*, No. 68 (Summer 2008): 7–23.

U.S. Bureau of the Census. *Negro Population in the United States, 1790–1915.* Washington, D.C.: GPO, 1918.

Watson, Elkanah. *Men and Times of the Revolution: or, Memoirs of Elkanah Watson.* Elizabethtown, N.Y.: Crown Point Press, 1868.

Warren, Wendy. *New England Bound: Slavery and Colonization in Early America.* New York: Liveright, 2016.

Weiner, Marli. *Mistresses and Slaves: Plantation Women in South Carolina, 1830–1880.* Urbana: University of Illinois Press, 1998.

West, Emily. *Enslaved Women in America: From Colonial Times to Emancipation.* Lanham, Md.: Rowman and Littlefield, 2014.

White, Deborah Gray. *Ar'n't I a Woman? Female Slaves in the Plantation South.* New York: W.W. Norton, 1999.

White, Shane. "A Question of Style: Blacks in and around New York City in the Late Eighteenth Century," *Journal of American Folklore* Vol. 102 No. 403 (January–March 1989): 23–44.

White, Shane. *Somewhat More Independent: The End of Slavery in New York City, 1770–1810.* Athens: University of Georgia Press, 1991.

White, Shane and Graham White, "Slave Clothing and African-American Culture in the Eighteenth and Nineteenth Centuries," *Past and Present* No. 148 (August 1995): 149–86.

Wiecek, William W. *The Sources of Anti-Slavery Constitutionalism in America, 1760–1848.* Ithaca: Cornell University Press, 1977.

Wiecek, William W. "The Statutory Law of Slavery and Race in the Thirteen Mainland Colonies of British America," *William and Mary Quarterly* Vol. 34 No. 2 (April 1977): 258–80.

Wilds, Mary. *Mumbet: The Life and Times of Elizabeth Freeman, The True Story of a Slave Who Won Her Freedom.* Greensboro: Avisson Press Inc., 1999.

Wilson, David K. *The Southern Strategy: Britain's Conquest of South Carolina and Georgia, 1775–1780.* Columbia: University of South Carolina Press, 2005.

Wilson, Ellen Gibson. *The Loyal Blacks.* New York: G.P. Putnam's Sons, 1976.

Windley, Lathan. *A Profile of Runaway Slaves in Virginia and South Carolina.* New York: Garland Publishing, 1995.

Windley, Lathan. *Runaway Slave Advertisements: A Documentary History from the 1730s to 1790.* Westport, Conn.: Greenwood Press, 1983.

Winks, Robin. *The Blacks in Canada: A History.* New Haven, Conn.: Yale University Press, 1971.

Wolf, Eva Sheppard. *Race and Liberty in the New Nation: Emancipation in Virginia from the Revolution to Nat Turner's Rebellion.* Baton Rouge: Louisiana State University Press, 2006.

Wong, Edlie L. *Neither Fugitive Nor Free: Atlantic Slavery, Freedom Suits, and the Legal Culture of Travel.* New York: New York University Press, 2009.

Wood, Betty. *Gender, Race and Rank in a Revolutionary Age: The Georgia Lowcountry, 1750–1820.* Athens: University of Georgia Press, 2000.

Wood, Betty. *Slavery in Colonial Georgia, 1619–1776.* Lanham, Md.: Rowman & Littlefield, 2005.

Wood, Betty. "Some Aspects of Female Resistance to Chattel Slavery in Low Country Georgia, 1763–1815," *The Historical Journal* Vol. 30 No. 3 (September 1987): 603–22.

Wood, Betty. *Women's Work, Men's Work: The Informal Slave Economies of Lowcountry Georgia.* Athens: University of Georgia Press, 1995.

Wood, Peter. *Black Majority: Negroes in Colonial South Carolina.* New York: Alfred A. Knopf, 1974.

Wright, Donald R. *African Americans in the Colonial Era: From African Origins through the American Revolution.* Wheeling, Ill.: Harlan Davidson Press, 2000.

Wright, Donald. *African Americans in the Early Republic, 1789–1831.* Arlington Heights, Ill.: Harlan Davidson, Inc., 1993.

Zilversmit, Arthur. *The First Emancipation: The Abolition of Slavery in the North.* Chicago: University of Chicago Press, 1967.

Zilversmit, Arthur. "Quok Walker, Mum Bett, and the Abolition of Slavery in Massachusetts," *William and Mary Quarterly* Vol. 25 No. 4 (October 1968): 614–24.

Zuckerman, Michael and Patrick Spero eds. *The American Revolution Reborn: New Perspectives for the Twenty-First Century.* Philadelphia: University of Pennsylvania Press, 2016.

THESES AND DISSERTATIONS

Goode, Cynthia Vollbrecht. "Engaging the Tools of Resistance: Enslaved Africans' Tactics of Collective and Individual Consumption in Food, Medicine, and Clothing in the Great Dismal Swamp." Ph.D. dissertation. American University, 2018.

Maris-Wolf, Tom. "Between Slavery and Freedom: African Americans in the Great Dismal Swamp, 1763–1861." Master's thesis, College of William and Mary, 2002.

Marshall, Amani N. "Enslaved Women Runaways in South Carolina, 1820–1864." Ph.D. dissertation. Indiana University, 2007.

Millward, Jessica. "'A Choice Parcel of Country Born': African Americans and the Transition to Freedom in Maryland, 1770–1840." Ph.D. dissertation. UCLA, 2003.

Thomas, Felicia Y. "Entangled with the Yoke of Bondage: Black Women in Massachusetts, 1700–1783." Ph.D. dissertation. Rutgers University, 2014.

WEBSITES

"Belinda Sutton and Her Petitions," Royall House & Slave Quarters, https://royallhouse.org/slavery/belinda-sutton-and-her-petitions/

"Dates in History: 1776," www.nps.gov/revwar/revolution_day_by_day/1776_main.html

Stewart Family, www.freeafricanamericans.com/Stewart_Family.htm.

Mapping Marronage, http://mapping-marronage.rll.lsa.umich.edu

Mumbet Records, www.mumbet.com

Ona Judge Staines, www.seacoastnh.com/Blackhistory/ona.html.

The Granite Freeman and *The Liberator*, www.ushistory.org/presidentshouse/slaves

Race & Slavery Petitions Project, https://library.uncg.edu/slavery/petitions/index.aspx

Transatlantic Slave Trade Database, www.slavevoyages.org

James Roberts, https://docsouth.unc.edu/neh/roberts/roberts.html

U.S. Continental Congress, *In Congress, Saturday* . . . (Watertown, Massachusetts, 1776), www.loc.gov/item/rbpe.03901000

William Still, The Underground Railroad, www.gutenberg.org/files/15263/15263-h/15263-h.htm#ChStill

Index